IMPROVING QUALITY OF EDUCATIONAL RESEARCH

QUEST OF SCHOOL PRACTITIONERS AND RESEARCHERS

Volume 1

Rashmi Diwan

ATLANTIC

PUBLISHERS & DISTRIBUTORS (P) LTD

Published by

ATLANTIC

PUBLISHERS & DISTRIBUTORS (P) LTD

7/22, Ansari Road, Darya Ganj, New Delhi-110002
Phones : +91-11-40775252, 40775214, 23273880, 23275880
Fax : +91-11-23285873
Web : www.atlanticbooks.com
E-mail : orders@atlanticbooks.com

Printed & bound in India by Atlantic Print Services

DEDICATED TO

My father
Late Shri K.K. Gupta,
Former Registrar, University of Jammu
who has been the prime vitality behind
all my ventures

Foreword

One witnesses a crisis of relevant research carried out in a systematic manner with a view to make improvements in our educational institutions. On the one hand, where an enormous effort on the part of researchers as students at the higher level has gone into the production of research on school education, on the other, there is a dearth of organised researches carried out by practitioners as learners at the school level. Unfortunately, the research outputs, that are supposed to be instrumental in bringing improvements in the entire education system, are confined to fetching of degrees for students of higher learning institutions which are finally left in the library stacks unused, unattended and unrecognized. One may find that sometimes they are a rich source of information for finding solutions to the most ardent problems facing education at all levels. The need for dissemination of such productions is increasingly being realized now. In this direction, it will be more worthwhile and meaningful if beginning is made by documentation of the existing research outputs available in university libraries. This will certainly create a rich resource for the use of researchers interested in taking up further research work for the benefit of our educational institutions. This exercise is expected to create a constructive climate for meaningful and practical research efforts by our researchers either as scholars or practitioners. At the same time, there is every need for engendering research interest among practitioners at the school levels to help them to come out with most practical solutions to challenges which they face in their day-to-day functioning. Generation and sustenance of research climate is an urgently felt need if honest efforts to make amendments in the entire educational system are to be brought in. In order to achieve this target, a three-way channel needs to be created: (i) documentation of abstracts of conducted researches, (ii) identifying gaps and weaknesses in researches for facilitating further research that is relevant to present-day practices and needs and (iii) encouraging research among practitioners and helping them to conduct research projects in a systematic manner.

The book comprising two volumes has arrived at the most opportune time when it is increasingly being realised the world over that we need to build a strong empirical base and support for making the pillars of our educational institutions strong and sturdy to face the emerging challenges from more conscious society and globalization in addition to the explosion of knowledge and technology. The volumes are expected to cater to the needs of the young researchers on one hand, and seasoned and experienced practitioners on the other, by offering useful directions to them about how to go about a meaningful and relevant research in a systematic manner so that our educational system improves.

B.P. Khandelwal
Director
National Institute of Educational Planning and Administration

Preface

The research output emanates as a consequential feedback in the spectrum of education intending more toward transforming, redesigning and modifying our educational system. This notion has emerged out of the realisation that our educational institutions honestly need to do something substantial so that it keeps in tune with the changing needs and demands of people to which it is catering. When the whole social, economic, political, technological, ideological scenario is in transition, how can educational system afford to retain the same age-old traditions?

There is an underlying feeling that it is high time for our educational institutions to replace conventional modalities with approximate demanding situations encouraging inputs from existing researches into the educational practices. Schools as highly professional institutions are being perceived as those institutions that systematically work to develop their capacity to become responsive to the developments taking place all over and, therefore, develop their ability to continuously adapt and transfigure as per the demands and expectations. Schools cannot afford to continue to function in the similar manner as these have been doing in the past. They have to become more vigilant and receptive to the requirements posed by the changing times. Now the question arises: Are the schools really coming up to those standards? Honestly speaking, the majority of them in Indian conditions fail to provide the minimum of meaningful inputs to its clientele. Now another question rolls out: What can be done? The most pertinent answer at this juncture seems to be reflections on educational scene and for this one can depend upon the most authentic instrument and that is what have researches on school education to say? Whether research conducted on school education is relevant or not? Whether it has something substantial to share and contribute for bringing improvements in the educational system? Who can best carry it out? How are these to be disseminated for bringing more fruitful results? Can researches be made free from bureaucratic pressures and present a realistic picture? The volumes, while capturing the crux of queries posed, examine the possibility of making use of available research for improving the system and research by practitioners as paramount significance for locking schools in the cycle of continuous improvement and progress. This can happen only when schools strive continually to search and research the answers to the problems facing it. It requires interventions of relevant research carried out in a systematic manner by those who are exposed to the practical problems faced in real school situations. Hegarty (1998), Director of the National Foundation for Educational Research (NFER), as reported in Middlewood, Coleman and Lumby (1999), defines "good" research as "research that is relevant to the intelligence needs of teachers, trainers, administrators and policy makers — research above all that leads to the best possible education for our children and our communities."

The turn of the century has brought a message that research needs to be accorded a place of prime importance in educational institutions. It is envisaged that further impetus will be drawn when research within institutions will be carried out by those who form an integral part of the system, with the co-operative efforts of actual practitioners, that is, the heads of institutions and teaching personnel as group members. Seen in this perspective, the volumes, while dealing with the issue of research, flash two messages for improvement of quality of education: (1) Transcribe empirical findings of researchers and academicians at university and professional development institutions into actual practices as per its management and teaching-learning situations. (2) Carry out small meaningful researches at institutional level for bringing practical and workable solutions to certain problems anomalous to particular problems. This concept of practice-based research has been recognized as a feasible vehicle for facilitating the process of self-transforming institutions. We all know that researchers and practitioners have been living isolated lives although the objectives of both the groups have been to improve the educational institutions for which they stand.

The volumes draw attention of our academia that research by researchers and students at the university level and practitioners at the school level, who actually have to manage the show, do provide meaningful inputs to make the school elevate from the present position. Resentment from teachers could be a fundamental barrier in the beginning. When they constantly realize the importance of carrying out small and meaningful research projects, they will be seen enjoying the fruits of empirical evidence at the later stage when they apply them in their classroom interactions. It also happens often that the teaching faculty feels the need for carrying out projects but do not know how to go about it. The volumes sensitise the school practitioners to the importance of this vital input as well as give direction to facilitate our practitioners to carry out such exercises with proper plan of action and monitoring at every stage as one proceeds further. With the overall message for improving quality of schools through a good quality research, the primary layout of the volumes aims at: (1) documenting available research output on school education, (2) familiarising the teachers and school academia with the available researches on school education, (3) helping them to make best use of relevant ones for bringing improvement within the school systems and (4) encouraging and guiding practitioners to take up systematic research based on the specific problems to come out with practical solutions. Hargreaves (1998) points out that it is 'naive' to think this alone improves practice. He proposed that teachers, not only becomes 'co-producers' of research, but when they also become creators of research knowledge, the research act in itself is a fundamental form of professional development of teachers. An attempt has been made in the volumes to set the stage for induction and mentoring of teachers more on professional practice-based research results.

I wish to express my deep gratitude to the institution I belong to. The institution has always been providing motivation, enthusiasm and zeal to work on diverse educational issues of interest. This gratitude extends to my seniors at the institute who have provided impetus, strength and freedom of thought to be expressed in writing to reach a larger segment of this society. I gratefully acknowledge reverence for my seniors who have always been providing a great inspiration, who are with the institution at present and those who have left NIEPA (still hold in my heart), Prof. Moonis Raza, Prof. Satya Bhushan, Prof. Kuldip Mathur (Former Directors of NIEPA), Prof. B.P. Khandelwal (Present Director, NIEPA for unstinting nurture), Prof. M. Mukhopadhyay (Joint Director, NIEPA, always supporting), Prof. R. Govinda (Head of my Unit, School & Non-Formal Education Unit, the prime mover) and Dr. (Mrs.) Sudesh Mukhopadhyay (my senior in the same unit, the encouraging spirit). Thanks are due to my own family members in particular to my children who happened to share the major brunt because I neglected them for most of the time. It is due to their endless patience and silent support that I was able to complete this task while sitting late and sometime the entire nights on computer.

The large-scale library work would not have been possible if library of NIEPA had not been accessible on which I have extensively been depending upon? I owe my gratitude to this rich resource and I consider myself fortunate to have Ms. Nirmal Malhotra and all her staff who always help with a smile. My thanks are also due to the libraries of Departments of Education in the Universities and other institutes of Delhi *i.e.*, JNU, Delhi University, Jamia Millia Islamia, the ICSSR Library the IIT Library, the NCERT Library and faculty for helping me to collect research materials.

My thanks are also due to Dr. K.R. Gupta Managing Director, Atlantic Publishers and Distributors, for the keen interest he has taken in the publication of these volumes.

Rashmi Diwan

Contents

1

Introduction

School education is seen in a new perspective with new vision and mission in recent years. Just few decades ago, it was more of a rhetoric exchange of teaching-learning processes followed more as a ritual. Education has been a highly sensitive issue throughout, but now it is expected to cater to diverse social groups who exhibit different expectations from schools and the education imparted therein. To be more specific, the expectations have changed towards all processes and operations within a school system, which includes curriculum, teachers, examinations and management. In this perspective, the time has approached when quality of education has to be in consonance to the demanding school-society situations.

Quality of School Education

Our current education system was designed to meet the needs of the British rule. In the contemporary times the school system is becoming obsolete and there is a mismatch between the desired and actual practices. Now it is envisaged that schools must help students learn different kinds of skills for the future; they must be able to think independently in an era when knowing how to access information is more important than memorizing it. Productive citizens in tomorrow's world will need to be able to think creatively, solve problems efficiently, communicate effectively with colleagues across the globe, and provide leadership in diverse settings. Today's students must be able to master the basic "3 Rs" and move quickly beyond them to apply the acquired knowledge to real-world experiences. This calls for the necessity that schools and communities undertake new approaches to teaching and learning. The education system must invest in training its staff, most importantly, teachers and provide more incentives and greater flexibility to support improvements and innovations in classrooms settings.

When we look into the quality of education provided by our schools, the picture depicted becomes quite dismal. Our students have not been showing performance of high standards. It has become imperative at this stage that the level of students' academic performance be raised today in order to equip them for future challenges that they are going to encounter tomorrow. Raising the level of *student performance* requires a definite course of action on the part of all personnel functioning at different levels right from decision makers to practitioners — all those working within a system who are entrusted with the task of providing best possible support to our students.

The International Commission for 21st Century has also expressed the dire need for reforming education by making it a process that is open to all. This Commission of UNESCO in a report entitled "Learning: The Treasure Within" (1996) reported, "though there has been tremendous expansion of education, we are still far away from the goal of excellence as it is still not accessible to all." One may apprehend that the goals of educational excellence can be achieved when all concerned work together to make it happen. Our students are talented and full of potential; our teachers and administrators are capable, hardworking professionals; our parents want the best for their children; our legislators and educational leaders are willing to work side-by-side with the education community. Still there are many barriers to overcome. Too many children come to school each day not prepared to learn. Some teachers do not believe that all students can learn. Some parents do not feel welcome in schools. Professional development opportunities for teachers are inadequate. Parents and teachers share many concerns about the classroom environment. Some schools lack the basic learning inputs that also include books and other basic facilities. Teachers do not have sufficient time to plan and collaborate together. And the current school year does not provide the time and flexibility that some children need to develop their core skills and competencies to the maximum. This is the prime time when a transition in educational system is required where school communities are empowered to choose their own roads to excellence, roads that will enable all students to develop the knowledge and skills needed to become successful and productive citizens in this rapidly changing world.

To enable school communities to meet today's challenges, our education system must be restructured. It certainly requires sincere efforts to produce evidence that support the view that improvement in today's school education has become an essential component. Colluding research into school practices for bringing improvement within the system has become imperative in order to derive solutions to practical problems that inhibit quality parameter from coming into the way of desired school education. This message can flow from two agents, the *Practitioners* functioning at the grass-roots and the *Researchers* who attempt to come out with possible solutions to the most pressing problems and challenges being faced by our educational personnel.

Challenges in School Education

Reflecting back, right from the age of Gurukuls to British and post British epoch, one witnesses a change in the educational setting. Similarly, the second half of 19th century onwards has been in the throes of considerable turmoil. There has been disturbance that appears to be accompanying the shift from primitive to scientific and post scientific era in school practices. The preceding periods have seen a major shift in the overall situations. Intervention of corporate and business eon into the arena of school education are fueling the present ferment. Similarly, cultural and educational exchange programmes and open education markets have paved several avenues of thousands of students who yearn for deriving best in education. On the one hand, there are positive signals for this kind of environment but there have also been devastating attacks on the schools arising from the challenges from conscious society of today.

Changes in society have influenced school culture to a large extent. School education is greatly affected by the culture and ethos embedded in the strata of society a child comes from. The external milieu has gradually changed the mind set ideological, and philosophical orientations of its people. Our educational personnel find difficulty in coping with the demands gradually arising from the changing society as they are not equipped to provide the required or demanded. A different kind of climate emerges when schools are expected to perform certain functions beyond teaching and learning requirements. Such locales call for neoteric roles of schools as well as their leaders. And the net result is transfer of mistakes and failures from one set of educational officials to another and *vice versa.* What is happening today? The Department of Education passes on the flaws to school and school in turn to the government departments. Similarly within the schools, the heads are accused of showing insincerity towards their profession while expectations towards teachers are different but they live with their own grievances. The educators, educationists, academicians, have failed in developing coherent remedies to these pressing problems. We have demoralised teachers as compared to previous eras, we have a different set of clienteles coming to schools with diverse cultural backgrounds, we have a separate set of expectations of conscious society towards schools which is quite different from the past. Furthermore, it has also been proved that filling a school with unrelated programmes, however promising they might be do not improve the school as a whole. Finally, one comes to a conclusion that the nature of problems in schools, although inherited from another era, is to certain extent of our own making — our own creations that have been inherited from our cultural heritage. They reflect the failure of practice in too many places. Today's educational problems cannot be answered by citing the shortcomings of previous era. The results thus so far are dismal.

It is now slowly being realized that if schools are expected to extend their area of operation and processes, it is worthwhile that it takes support of researchers and practitioners to come out with certain suggestions based on empirical evidence and inferences. The empirical studies it is believed would present realistic picture of schools while becoming instrumental in offering practical suggestions that could also be experimented, which could be particular to specific problems encountered by a particular set of separate management schools. When one apprehends the present situation, one really wonders whether schools are honestly catering to teaching-learning requirements of the present times. Are they really preparing our children to face the challenges of coming eras? One could embark on research studies for finding solutions to the most fervent problems arising from the emerging school scenario.

The management of school education has always been a centralized phenomenon where certain decisions about educational system are taken at apex level. In accordance to the plan, the key functionaries comprising of academia, educational planners, administrators are assigned the task of formulating policies followed by Programme of Action thereof. The directive then flows from them to State and district levels. The school personnel are then expected to implement policies that may or may not be applicable or suited to the situation a school is placed in. The teachers at the grass-root level are mandated to adapt certain practices for which they may not be equipped even. The decisions for schools are taken by those who may not be aware of the practical difficulties in implementation and for whom the decisions are taken are not even involved or have any say in the process.

The challenges that secondary and senior secondary schools of today are facing are quite different from what was experienced even a decade ago. The problems faced today are early childhood education, multi-language and multi-cultural student population, emphasis upon rights of students, new generation of teachers, teacher power through associations and unions, community in an adversary role, rise and fall of financial support, pragmatic accountability demands, educational technology, personal computers, videos, demand for removal of social injustice in education and otherwise, student unrest and drug abuse. More conscious society of the needs of its children, psychological disturbances and feelings of insecurity among adolescents, behavioural problems among them especially at this stage, children of working parents, nuclear families, changes in the social structure, generation gap etc. have added to the problems of schools as it becomes the place where children find convenient to give vent to their oppressed feelings. They have to be tackled in a different manner. The schools are not in a position to take any drastic action against children since they have not been granted those powers nor are equipped to manage such critical situations or incidences that are more pronounced at secondary and senior secondary stages of education. These challenges call for restructuring of management of educational processes. The traditional practices would no longer survive in this sort of situation where a highly centralized management structure reigns. This certainly calls for the need to empower schools to take decisions as per their priorities and requirements instilling a high sense of ownership, belongingness and trust among them. It has come to realize that until people who are actually assigned the task of implementing changes within the school system are involved in decision-making, no improvement can take place. School practitioners themselves could initiate this move when they are equipped with empirical evidence to show that a particular decision taken for their schools is on the right direction or it is a wrong move. Shared decision-making can come only when practitioners have something substantial to offer that stands on strong research foundation.

Significance of Research in School Education

There has been a realisation that a shift towards relevant research needs to be emphasized. A major concern is being showed by our academia about what and how consistent relevant research be conducted in our educational institutions that facilitates in their improvement and progress. This issue has become more debatable within the research and training institutions where newer ways are being found to provide meaningful inputs to our practitioners who ultimately are expected to implement policy decisions. It has come to realize that the prominence of development and progress in schools becomes more substantial only when it stands on the strong foundation of research. The schools of today witness diversities so far teacher commitment; student learning environment at home or accountability of school heads towards their job is concerned. In this framework, school improvement holds no significance until visualized from the point of view of what research says. Everyone concerned with school education seems to be highly concerned about its enhancement. The underlying rationale is that research makes an important contribution to organisational improvement. The time has arrived when change within schools fail to produce desired results unless meaningful inputs from research is sought. Research into schools and its education certainly facilitates the effort of making substantial improvements within schools. Till recently, research reports, dissertations and even thesis remained confined to the shelves of the library and was conducted only to fulfil certain requirements or criteria for admissions to higher studies or promotions. But the time has arrived when these research output and results need wider dissemination and sharing in order to draw more meaningful directions emerging from the results of even a small piece of research that could be used for improving all kinds of schools under different management. In order to understand the nature of research conducted at the university and institutional levels and for perceiving possibilities of applying its findings to the actual practices, a study specifically confining to Delhi was taken up. A detailed analysis including gaps and weaknesses in present studies for application in actual school practices for extended exercises is presented in the preceding sections.

Creating Research-oriented Climate

Visualizing 21st century in the futuristic perspective, one may comprehend that research in educational venture is going to be a formidable task. This certainly requires a transition in the roles and responsibilities of existing set up, ushering in greater degree of autonomy to school personnel to take up research problems. Carrying out in-depth study of specific problems facing a particular school could be attributed as constructive contribution towards school excellence. One does not have to launch special additional programmes for this task, rather make modifications and adjustments, searching for alternatives within the existing structures to make it more practical to the changing demands of our main target group and that is the adolescents at the secondary stage of education. This can be made to happen only with practitioners' will to make it a part of the system. How research benefits could be introduced to the educational personnel in the schooling context is a matter of concern. It certainly depends upon how can a well-planned seriously chalked out programme be made implementable.

The beginning point is changing the mind-frame of people, which could be generated through diverting the attention of all concerned towards how effective research inputs are in making improvement in school education. They need to recognize that when they draw heavily from researches conducted by other research scholars and from their own research pieces on schools and education imparted therein, it is hoped that they will feel enlightened. It is at this stage that they will come to know where they stand and how to go about it in the future.

The plan can be followed with a definite course of action:

- Research feedback helps in getting rid of all such unpleasant practices that discourage students and teachers from doing their best. It is hoped that such efforts are essential to ensure that all children are prepared to focus on learning, not only when they enter school but as they grow and develop throughout their schooling years. It is their springboard to the future. Such initiatives call for reorganization of the complete schooling set up by granting freedom to teachers to develop their own accountability mechanisms and designing their own teaching-learning methodologies for bringing improved student performance. It is here where Research becomes a platform and an instrument for bringing improvements within school system. It is this freedom that needs to be allowed to them from their higher-ups.

- Sensitizing our practitioners about researches conducted at university level or by prime educational, training or research institutions is a vital issue. There is a need to reinforce a climate where research applications into actual practice are encouraged. At the same time readiness and preparedness can come through well-designed orientation/training programmes and workshops that facilitate the teaching faculty to know about the researches conducted on schools so that they could apply findings on actual practices and also in carrying out their functions with a strong empirical support. Now the question about proper guidance for carrying out a research project in a systematic manner arises. Again one will have to rely upon capacity building exercises. This complete activity requires building strong school-university partnerships with active interventions of educational decision-making authorities at the state, district and block levels. It certainly demands setting a stage for exchanging ideas, intensive discussions, and preparation exercises for making research an indispensable component of school education.
- There is a need to reallocate funds to invest in professional development activities for school heads and teachers to sharpen their research skills.
- Involvement of parents in research activities to ensure their contributions in their children's education.
- Find ways for providing more time for research activities in both the cases, when it is to be carried out by school personnel and when in-depth examination of conducted researches need to be consolidated to bring improvement in the school and education imparted therein.

STUDIES ON SCHOOL QUALITY AND RESEARCH PARAMETRES: THE BEGINNING FROM METROPOLITAN DELHI

The Educational Scenario in Delhi: An Overview

Delhi being an urban metropolitan city is also experiencing a number of similar situations arising from the teeming population in millions. The expectations and needs of each segment of society towards school education is different. At one end we have urban Delhi and on the other rural Delhi. Within urban Delhi, we find literate and illiterate inhabitants. The overall literacy rate in urban Delhi has been estimated to about 76.18% wherein 82.39% constitute males and 68.54% constitute females (Selected Educational Statistics, 1996-97). Literate population expects school education to be of high quality and standards, illiterate population either sends their children to school for gaining rudimentary 3 R's or do not send them to school at all. The literate population wish to educate their children in schools with good facilities depending upon their income while like to offer best school education to their children. Such segment would be willing to send their children to best of schools with best facilities. They certainly send their children to unaided schools proudly stated as public schools where exorbitant fees might be charged but offer quality education to its clientele. The other segment among literate sends their children to unaided private schools that may be recognized or unrecognized or to the aided schools. The third section of society, the illiterates, send children to government or local bodies schools where basic or no facilities may be provided to school going children. One finds a wide disparity in the expectations towards school education among different strata residing in different parts of Delhi. The elite in the posh colonies of Delhi demand for more sophisticated academic inputs entirely different from those residing in the authorized and unauthorized colonies of Delhi. Similarly school education also faces the challenge of educating those residing in J.J. clusters who do not want to educate themselves or even attend the school. School education in Delhi is a major challenge that in fact has to be tailored to meet the needs and expectations of diverse social groups with vast variations in living standards and conditions.

The Need

In order to bring changes and improvement in the quality of school system, all the attention and efforts of the government, educational planners and administrators, educationists, academicians and other concerned officers have been diverted towards meeting this goal. Visualizing the importance of emerging challenges being faced by school education, two studies on Delhi schools were taken up. One pertaining to the quality of school education imparted and the second study reports research studies carried out by research scholars and trainees at different research and training institutes and three universities based at Delhi. To be more specific, these have been collected from three universities of Delhi that is, Delhi University, Jawaharlal Nehru University, Jamia Millia Islamia, and other research and training institutes based in Delhi like I.C.S.S.R., D.I.E.T.s, S.C.E.R.T., N.C.E.R.T. and N.I.E.P.A. and also from Research surveys. It was with this background that these exercises were carried out with certain specific objectives in mind.

Objectives

The book is based on a comprehensive study on assessment of the quality of Education imparted in Delhi schools and what empirical studies have to contribute to the schools of Delhi. This study stretched over a period of almost three years was conducted with the following specific objectives:

- Examine the quality of school education imparted in Delhi with particular reference to the following:
  - (i) The School Head: training, qualification, selection, strong points of heads of better functioning schools, achievement of school objectives, discipline and school result, steps for improving internal school efficiency.
  - (ii) The Teachers: training both pre-service and in service, Behavioural and teaching quality, pressures on teachers.
  - (iii) School Processes: medium of instruction, subjects taught, facilities, teacher-pupil ratio, communication process within a school, involvement of personnel in the instructional improvement, decision-making

process, staff meetings, decentralization of school activities.

(iv) The Students: social class of students, pass percentage and achievement.

- Identify factors that impede school quality.
- Collect, review and document studies on school education in Delhi to facilitate researchers and educationists for its easy access at one place since no such exercise has been done so far.
- To identify lapses, gaps and weaknesses in researches in the light of actual school practices, operations and processes with a view to offer suggestions for carrying out further researches to improve school quality.

With separate management schools catering to clientele with diverse background, one can speculate that Delhi schools are facing a number of challenging situations arising from urbanization. Looking into the complexities of present-day problems encountered in urban school education, it was realized that a survey particularly in Delhi seems to be highly essential for tailoring education for children at various levels of education. It was, therefore, thought that a study could be beneficial with the objective of examining quality component of our schools along with research studies carried out in Delhi on different and diverse problems, issues, aspects etc., etc. facing school education. The prime objective of this exercise is to encourage research by school practitioners themselves or using research inputs of studies carried out by research scholars in different educational institutions. It is envisaged that when such exercises are extended further with more in-depth examination of research efforts, either by those who actually manage the show, that is our school personnel or those who can contribute a meaningful input in school education, it is assumed that these will certainly affect some changes in present school situations.

Limitations of Conducted Research Studies

The studies are confined to the capital of India, that is, Delhi. The study on quality of education in Delhi schools is restricted to twenty primary schools of Delhi, that is, the municipal corporation schools and primary sections of Sarvodaya schools under Directorate of Education, Delhi. The collection of research studies in the other study includes those studies whose reports/ dissertations/thesis were available in the respective libraries. This also excludes the studies undertaken by universities of other states on Delhi school education. Some of the reported studies, very few in numbers, do not however give a complete information. This is mainly due to the fact that the portion was found to be missing in the thesis/dissertation. Despite the problems faced the collection of about 400 research studies till the year 1991 were sufficient to address the issues of school education.

Although the magnitude of problems studied is limited and that too restricted to a particular district or area, but still these studies are of great significance to school education. It provides a platform for examining a wider spectrum of researches on school education with major focus on the needs of conscious masses directing it towards greater improvement. The review of researches on Delhi schools is the preliminary step towards making education more meaningful. This kind of survey has never been conducted earlier. It is envisaged that the reflections on various issues, problems, aspects etc., and followed by an analytical review will hopefully prove to be highly beneficial for formulating future plans, programmes and proposals for bringing improvement in the school system.

About the Book

The studies collected on Delhi schools were around 400 in number, out of which more than 200 studies were selected for analysis as these had consistent relevance to school education. The second chapter of the book is a simple compendium of abstracts of researches on school education. For the studies, which have relevance to school education to some extent, annotated bibliography has been prepared. This collection of about 260 abstracts and annotated studies were categorized and classified under different headings. These studies take in cognizance the quality parameter also in its description. The subsequent Chapters 3 and 4 in the book however captures the central idea of what research trends depict and how the research trends are deviating from facts and figures and what approach could be considered to be feasible at this juncture and what possibly could be the beginning point. The irony is that the studies although may be lacking in giving proper directions and may also seem to be imperfect and misleading, but its contributions cannot be ignored. Still it has certain messages that need to be taken into Consideration while framing school programmes. Only then some quality inputs, may be small but meaningful can be instilled in our schools. Another side of the story is that the attention of practitioners for that matter have never been drawn towards making use of the available research studies and encouraged to utilize the findings and suggestions of such studies to bring improvement in school education. In contrast, such attempts could have been made to provide a platform from which a direction could be set towards systematic research for improved school education. Chapter 5 suggests the ways by which research climate be created for making practitioner research work with a message that research by school practitioners seems to be the most practical alternative mode that is meaningful, worthwhile and instrumental in bringing improvement in the school system. The final chapter 6 introduces and explains the researchers and practitioners about how systematically research should be planned and carried out. It guides them with a definite course of research cycle in different developmental phases that are personally manageable. This leads to the message that a symbiotic approach, convergence of few but meaningful inputs from researcher and practitioners into actual school practices seem to be a workable solution for the present times. It is hoped that such attempts could be feasible in finding answers to the ardent questions on our degenerating standards.

Seen in this perspective, the investigation on quality of education along with researches in school education although confines itself to metropolitan city of Delhi but this information covers school practices followed in the entire country. The magnitude of areas covered in this investigation would give a comprehensive idea of existing nature of school education in Delhi, but at the same time is also not different from educational scenario emerging in majority of mega and urban cities of India.

2

What do Researches on Schools Say?

Reports on schooling in metropolitan cities, and Delhi not an exception is characterized by a list of failures in school education:

- falling standards of student achievement
- the failure of urban schools
- teacher incompetence
- 'out of control' student behaviour
- inadequate teacher training in basic skills of instruction in teaching
- subjects
- Irrelevant research in school education.

Everyone is well aware of the fact that school education is facing crises in different spheres. The study conducted on quality of education (Diwan, 1996, pp. 68-71) also contends that it has drastically been affected by a number of factors that need to be amended or modified. These factors are:

- Shortage of teachers in schools
- Policy of Teacher Transfer even in the mid of academic session
- Admissions all year round
- Disturbing elements in the adjoining areas where schools are located like factory areas, public parking places, bad pocket areas etc.
- Unattractive school environment and lack of infrastructure and physical facilities

- Limited arrangement of co-curricular activities in schools
- Lesser or no provision for value education
- Lesser interest or attention shown by parents in educating or helping their children in their studies
- Lesser zeal and enthusiasm among teachers to offer attractive and innovative teaching methods
- Non availability of books or teaching aids and other basic inputs
- Irregularity of teachers in taking classes
- Defective Non-Detention policy
- Appointment of inexperienced and untrained teachers in private unaided and aided schools that includes recognized schools as well
- Bureaucratic attitude of higher authorities in a centralised set up.

In order to understand what could be the possible ways to suggest alternatives and solutions to this deteriorating situation, an effort was made to examine and understand what research studies carried out on different issues of school education had to say. Unfortunately a dearth of substantive research studies on different issues especially in this area was felt. Although the research conducted on Delhi schools is quite comprehensive and voluminous where one finds a plethora of problems searched and researched at different times, but still lot needs to be done in order to supplement and complement the reported crises in the field.

It is due to this reason that a number of studies on school education in Delhi which have direct bearing on quality of schooling in Delhi have been reported in this section. In order to have a crystallized review of such studies, it was thought that classification under broader themes would give a more realistic picture:

(1) Tests and Examinations

(2) Evaluation and Performance

(3) Curriculum and Instructional Material

(4) Instructional Methodology

(5) Teacher and Teaching Issues
(6) Pupil Characteristics
(7) School Management
(8) Management of School Education
(9) Funds and Finances
(10) Quality Issues
(11) Education of Special Groups
(12) Gender Issues

The abstracts of research studies classified under each of these themes are detailed in the pages that follow:

TESTS AND EXAMINATION

A Study of Perceptions of Teachers and Students About Multiple Set System Recently Introduced in Delhi Schools in Class Xth

M.Ed., JMI, DEVENDAR KUMAR, 1993

The study was mainly carried out to investigate the perception of government and private schools secondary class passed and failed students about multiple set system and to study the perception of government and private school teachers about multiple set system. The sample comprised of total eight schools, 4 government and private 9 students of XI who passed last year, 5 students of each school who failed, and 5 teachers from each school.

The major findings highlighted: (1) The perceptions of passed students irrespective of schools were found positive about multiple set system. (2) The perception of failed students irrespective of schools were found negative about multiple set system. (3) The perception of teachers was found positive irrespective of their schools about multiple set system. (4) The perception of teachers was found positive irrespective their schools about multiple set system. (5) There was homogeneity found in perception about multiple set system in government schools passed students, private schools failed students and private schools' teachers as compared to their corresponding group. (6) There was significant difference in perception of government schools passed and private schools passed student. (7) There was no difference among failed government and private school students in terms of their perception.

(8) There was no significant difference in perception about MSS among the teachers of private schools and government schools. (9) The open ended items showed that the difficulty level of question was most criticized aspect of this system otherwise there is general acceptance of the multiple set system those who are not in favour show mild negative perception.

Study the Impact of Selection type and Construction type of items on Test Scores

M.Ed., C.I.E., D.U., NASIM AHMED, 1981

The main purpose of the study is to compare the effect of selection type of items on test scores of students. Since most of the tests used in classrooms are teacher made, the most important thing for the teachers is to know the efficacy of different items for better evaluation in Mathematics.

The study was conducted on the students of class VIII in one school, Government Co-Educational Secondary School, New Friends Colony. Two groups of 30 students each were selected and divided into two groups and administered Test I and Test II on rotational basis.

The major findings highlight: (1) Difference between the mean score on Test I and II for Group A is significant. Difference between the mean score on Test I and II for Group B significant. (3) Difference between the mean score on Test III and IV for Group A is significant. (4) Difference between the mean score on Test III and IV for Group B is significant. (5) Difference between the mean score on Test I and II for Group A & B combined is significant. (6) Difference between the mean score on Test III and IV for Group A & B combined is significant. (7) Difference between means of scores on test containing selection type of items and on test containing construction type of items was found to be significant.

EVALUATION PRACTICES IN PRIMARY SCHOOLS

Paper Presented in the 1996 International Seminar on School Effectiveness and Classroom Processes at Primary Stage

MAMTA AGARWAL & SARLA RAJPUT

With the objective of finding out all about the evaluation practices in framing schools in the 1994-95 academic session, the study was taken up.

The schools were taken from both urban and rural areas. Though most of the schools were from urban areas, 6 schools were from rural Delhi. 20 schools were co-educational, 4 were boys schools and only 1 school was exclusively for girls. The instruments used to study the evaluation practices. School questionnaire, Evaluation questionnaire, Investigator's diary and Question Papers of class III and the Report Cards.

The findings of the study showed: (1) All schools had a well-designed system of evaluation consisting of various class tests and examinations throughout the year at least in scholastic areas. (2) As to the question how frequently the tests/examinations are held and what weightages are given to different tests, it was seen that most of the schools have a scheme of testing consisting of quarterly, half-yearly and final examination supported by informal classroom test which the schools keep having at regular intervals. (3) The weightages given to different tests and examinations are more or less same in all the schools managed by state government and local bodies. Only Kendriya Vidyalayas give 20 per cent weightage to unit tests and 20 per cent to project work and assignments. All public schools adopt their own system of evaluation. In some schools like Mirambika School only project work is done. In another school only regular unit tests are given whereas in others like Springdales school children are evaluated on their day to day work. In some public schools there are half-yearly and annual examinations only with the class tests. (4) For doing continuous evaluation, by and large written tests are adopted by schools. In some subjects like environmental studies and languages oral testing is done but it has very little weightage as compared to written tests. Private and public schools give more attention to assignments, project work and oral work than the state run schools. Observation technique is also used for evaluating non-scholastic areas but it is not done systematically. (5) Most of the question papers were not balanced. In a question paper weightages should be allotted appropriately for various objectives like knowledge, understanding, application and skill. It was seen that in most of the schools the objective of knowledge was given 50 to 75 per cent weightage. Understanding and application got very little weightage. This shows that the question paper of our primary schools are not designed to test higher mental abilities. From this it can be assumed that the teachers do not have an idea of developing a good question paper. It was also seen that most of the school test only the student's textual knowledge and fall short of testing higher mental abilities. Only private public schools give attention to the testing of higher mental abilities. (6) As far as the types of questions are concerned, it was seen that most of the questions were of short answer and very short answer variety. This is understandable also because at primary level the children are small and it is difficult for them to write large answers. The objective type questions were total lacking in the question papers perhaps because the teachers are not trained in developing such questions. (7) In order to know whether the schools used the evaluation results for diagnosing the weaknesses of children in different areas and whether they tried to remedy those weakness. It was revealed that diagnosis and remediation is not well organized in schools. Some little diagnoses in informal way goes on as a routine matter in all the schools and some measures of remediation are also taken in routine. Most of the remediation is inbuilt with teaching. Only very few schools give separate time during assembly, games period or music period etc. to the weak children. Only in DTEA school regular remedial work is done after the school hours and St. Columbus organized formal remedial classes with a separate teacher appointed for the purpose. Another measure taken up by schools for remediation is peer group or child to child teaching where the brighter children of the same class or sometimes senior children help the weaker ones. Some schools just inform the parents about the weakness and expect them to help their children. (8) Regarding whether the non-scholastic areas of pupil growth are also evaluated and what particular aspects are evaluated, it was found that the evaluation of pupil's social personal qualities, his interests and values is not systematic. Most of the schools in Delhi do try to report some social, personal qualities but neither proper tools are used for evaluating these qualities, nor any records are kept of even of informal observations. At the time of filling up the report card the teacher grades the pupils on various traits on the basis of her impressions. In Government and MCD school the only quality evaluated is cleanliness. As far as the interests of children are concerned most of the school have activities like art, craft, music, dance, sports etc. In some schools the interest of children are graded and some give remarks about them. Many schools specially MCD schools and some Government aided schools do not report the interests at all. Regarding the evaluation of values it was found that schools in Delhi do try to inculcate socially accepted values in the children but they do not evaluate them at all. The schools do evaluate the children continuously as suggested by the frequency of formal and informal tests in various classes but it is not done comprehensively. It is only in a few schools that comprehensive evaluation is done *i.e.* along with scholastic areas non-scholastic areas are also covered. However, it was seen that it was not as systematically done as it should have been. (9) The managements of schools do not provide detailed guidelines for evaluation to their schools. Whatever guidelines are given are related to only the scholastic areas. The teachers do not have any training in the concept of evaluation and its importance in teaching learning process. (10) The MCD school presented the most dismal picture as educational institutions. It is perhaps because they were understaffed, had large number of children and had very poor physical facilities. Even sitting arrangement was not found to be proper. On the contrary the public schools had very congenial atmosphere with proper physical facilities and qualified and well aware staff. Even the unrecognized private schools seemed to be better off than MCD schools in this respect.

Predictive Efficiency of an Inductive-Deductive Reasoning test, An Intelligence test and Middle School Examination Marks to Predict Academic Success in Math's in IX Class

M.Ed., JMI, RADHEY SHAYAM AGGARWAL, 1974

The study envisaged to find out the predictive efficiency of an Inductive-Deductive reasoning test (developed by investigator) and an intelligence test (Raven's Progressive Matrices Test) to predict academic success of middle school examination (class VIII) in mathematics. It was found that middle school examination marks in maths gave best prediction with the midterm marks. Reasoning and intelligence test scores did not predict as good with the criterion as middle school examination marks in mathematics. As far as combination of the predictor is concerned it was found that the middle school marks combined with the reasoning test scores gave better predictors than the middle schools examinations alone.

Prognostic Value of Higher Secondary Examination of Delhi

Ph.D., C.I.E., D.U., S. DUTT, 1954

The main purpose of the present study was to investigate the predictive value of higher secondary examinations of Delhi and to suggest certain modifications so as to make these examinations better predictors of college success. The second aim was to ascertain how far the promise held out at the time of higher secondary examinations was fulfilled by subsequent performance at the degree level.

Names and roll numbers of the successful candidates at higher secondary examinations who immediately proceeded for degree course and completed the examinations after a regular study for three years were collected after a careful scrutiny of the relevant records in the concerned offices. The subjects of this study were 1642 students who passed higher secondary examinations from 1944 to 1949 and 986 students who having passed the qualifying examination in the said period, studied for three years in the colleges and appeared for degree examinations. The two groups were distinctly maintained for the analysis of the results. Subject marks were recorded in order to make a comparative study of the performance at higher secondary as well as at degree levels. In addition to these ranks, the class ranks, chronological age of the students, etc., were secured. A ten-item questionnaire was issued to all the teachers to rate their students on a five-point scale. The items covered the mental capacity, industriousness, capacity to assume responsibility and independent work, knowledge of English language, skills in taking down notes, and method of preparing for examinations, etc. Two hundred and four questionnaires, duly filled were received back. For the purpose of analysis, techniques of linear regression, bivariate or multivariate, according to the number of variables involved in the process of prediction were employed.

The conclusions drawn indicated: (1) The choice and selection of optional subject at the university by these students obtaining less than 45 per cent in the aggregate or in individual subjects in the university entrance examination should be made with great caution and they should be advised to offer more or less allied subjects and those subjects that were taken at school. Such students require special tutoring and guidance. (2) Though the university has laid down certain limits for admission, yet each case must be decided on its own merit. (3) The scores in English can be used as an additional selective factor along with the score of the subject which is to be offered in the case of mathematics, Hindi and Sanskrit. (4) For selection to the honours degree courses in science, the university entrance examination scores in science subjects are of primary importance. (5) Though the present study underestimates the value of the modern Indian language scores in predicting scores in other subjects in degree examinations, yet it can be profitably employed at the time of selection of students for honours degree courses in Hindi and Sanskrit. (6) The chronological age can also be used as a useful adjunct to other predictive measures and the minimum university entrance requirement may be regarded as seventeen years. (7) Though the school marks are not regarded to be useful in predicting the levels of success at the degree examination, yet the average school marks of three years should be regarded as one of the principal criteria for admission to the university, specially of the borderline candidates. (8) The collective teachers' estimates from the school would also be of great value for the purpose of such prediction. (9) The scrutiny of the scores of the candidates who passed higher secondary examination with distinction, their choice of subjects, results in the degree examination, etc., indicated the great need for guidance service at school and college levels.

Study of Failures in Home Examination in Some Schools in Delhi

NCERT, New Delhi, 1964

A study on the incidence of failure in the school examination was conducted in 1962 by the Central Examination Unit of the

Directorate of Extension Programmes for Secondary Education in twenty higher secondary schools of all categories in Delhi.

The results indicated the following trends: (i) percentage of failures was higher in classes IX and X than in lower classes; (ii) percentage of failures in class VIII was the least; and (iii) the total percentage of failure from class VI to X was 23.1. Analysis of failures in individual subjects showed that in all classes except in class VI, the number of failures registered was the maximum in three subjects, whereas very few failed in six or seven subjects. Up to class VIII, English and mathematics took the heaviest toll, and they accounted for a very high proportion of failures in all classes. Backwardness in certain subjects became more and more pronounced as the pupils progressed from class to class through grace promotions. Otherwise, the wastage which was high would have been higher still.

Construction and Standardization of an Achievement test in Indian History *Ph.D., C.I.E., D.U.,* S. SARAF, 1964

The aim of the study was to construct and standardize a test of achievement in Indian history for class XI of schools in Delhi. The tryout sample consisted of 400 students from twenty-two schools in Delhi, who had taken Indian history as one of the electives. The final test consisted of 128 items after item-analysis of the final tryout test. It was administered to 924 students of forty-five schools. The split-half, to 924 students of forty-five schools. The split-half, the K-R formula, analysis of variance and Guttman methods of testing reliability were used to calculate reliability coefficients. The reliability coefficients which ranged between .79 and .85, were fairly comparable with standardized achievement and intelligence tests prepared in India. The validity coefficients calculated with various criteria, *viz.,* board marks, teacher ratings, etc., varied between .28 and .68. Percentile norms and standard score norms were also worked out. The test results showed that the achievements of boys and girls in Indian history were significantly different. This was also revealed by the results of the Delhi Board of Higher Secondary Education.

Prognostic Value of Board's Examination

NCERT, M.B. BUCH, 1963

The major aims of the investigation were to know the extent to which the success at the university level is predicted at the S.S.C.E. examination, the extent of failures and dropouts and what happened to the borderline cases of S.S.C.E. admitted to the university course.

The study was confined to those students who passed their C.E. in the year 1958 and joined the university. The faculty wise split of the students selected for the sample was commerce 254, arts 177 and science 501. The examination scores at S.S.C.E. level were treated as predictors, whereas achievement scores at the university examination stage were treated as criteria measures.

It was found that the correlation between composite scores at S.S.C.E. and the preuniversity examination was .49; between S.S.C.E. composite scores and first year degree examination was 59, between composite scores at S.S.C.E. and second year degree examination was .53, and between S.S.C.E. composite scores and degree examination was .59.

Construction and Standardization of an Achievement Test in Hindi For Class VIII

C.I.E., New Delhi, 1962

This investigation aimed at standardizing an achievement test in Hindi for grade VIII students of Delhi.

Keeping in view (i) the objectives of teaching Hindi at grade VIII level and (ii) the appropriate level of difficulty of language as well as the complexity of the material which the students were expected to deal with, it was decided to go through textbooks, children's exercise books and other books and magazines. Based upon these source-materials the achievement test in Hindi was designed and it included six subjects, *viz.,* reading comprehension, word meanings, meanings of proverbs, sentence structures, diction (the use of most appropriate word), and spellings. Item analysis with the help of difficulty index and discriminating index was carried out and thus the final form consisted of 100 items of the six types of subjects.

The sample of the study consisted of students of Delhi schools. For reliability study, the sample consisted of 84 girls and 106 boys; and for validity study, the sample consisted of 123 students of grade VII, 128 students of grade VIII and 82 students of grade IX. In case of the study for establishing norms, sample was drawn from all parts of Delhi and it consisted of 1,932 boys and 1,538 girls. The systematic randomized design was used to draw the sample. It was found that the CIE Achievement Test in Hindi had test-retest reliability coefficient of .89 (N=88), split- half coefficients calculated by Spearman-Brown formula were .93 for girls (N=84) and .95 for boys (N=106). Two criteria were used for the purposes of validation, *viz.*, (a) the rise in average score from grade VII to grade IX on this test and (b) correlation of the scores on this test with the scores on the teacher made achievement test in Hindi.

It was found that there was a sharp increase in the mean scores from lower to upper grades. The concurrent validity coefficient against teacher made test was .69. Percentile norms for boys and girls were also established.

A Comparative Psychosocial Study of Students Using and not Using Unfair Means During Annual Examinations in Government Senior Secondary Schools

M.Ed., JMI, ADHIKARI, 1984

The main objectives of the study were to compare school adjustment of students using fair and unfair means and to study the family environment of such students. Two government boys senior secondary schools were taken up as sample for the study. The school adjustment inventory by N.M. Bhagia, the family environment scale by Rudolf H. Moos and Bernice S. Moos were used in the study. The findings of the study revealed that there is average degree of school adjustment among the students involved and not involved in using unfair means. Both groups do not differ in their school adjustment. There is a lower degree of expressiveness of active recreational orientation and conflict with the group using unfair means. There is lower degree of family environment with respect to conflict, active recreational orientation and control within the group not involved in using unfair means. There is lowest degree of conflict within the group not using unfair means.

Development and Validation of Scale to Assess the Attitude Towards Science for Secondary School Students

M.Ed., C.I.E., D.U., A.S. RAUTELA, 1995

The study envisaged to develop a scale to assess the attitude of secondary school students towards science. It was confined to one Senior Secondary School, in which 250 boys and 150 girls studying in class IX and X were selected for developing the scale. The developed scale was administered on these students. Item analysis etc. was done on the basis of response of these students. Reliability and validity of the scale was computed. The attitude scale toward science can effectively be used to improve science teaching, learning and instruction, on industrial, educational, health and political organizations.

Development of Vocabulary Test in Chemistry for Class IX Students

M.Ed., JMI, NISHA CHATTERJEE, 1995

The objectives of the study were to develop a chemistry vocabulary test for students of class IX and to determine the reliability and validity of the test, study the level of class IX students with respect to chemistry vocabulary and to compare chemistry vocabulary of class IX boys and girls. The sample for the study was confined to 110 students from three Senior Secondary Schools, consisting of 60 boys and 50 girls. The findings of the study revealed that the level of class IX students with respect to CVT is above average. The level of half of the student with respect to CVT is above average. Maximum number of students scored above average. The reliability of the test is high, validity of the test is moderate. There is no significant difference between the performance of boys and girls with respect to chemistry vocabulary test. The distribution of score is close to the normal distribution.

An Analysis of the Context of History Textbook Prescribed in Union Territory of Delhi for Classes VI, VII, VIII in the Light of National Integration

M.Ed., JMI, BLAKTI SINGH, 1985-86

The main aim of the study was to analyze the Indian history textbook prescribed for middle classes in Delhi and to find out how far the subject matter included in the textbook is likely to promote the concept of National Integration among students. The findings showed that they were not likely to promote the concept of National Integration.

Evaluation of Physics Textbooks (Part-I) Prescribed for Middle Classes in Schools of Delhi

M.Ed., JMI, KUSUM CHOPRA, 1971-72

The study mainly emphasized on analyzing the content of the textbook for some of its aspects *viz.,* subject matter, illustrations and exercises in the light of the objectives of new science curriculum and objectives of new science curriculum and of teaching physics. The study was conducted to appraise the book for its worth in the light of the objectives of the new science curriculum and the principles of textbook preparation recommended by the UNESCO experts. Qualitative and quantitative analysis was carried out. The teachers rated the book qualitatively as 'good' but it was only slightly above "average".

A Critical Study of the Ideational Content in Hindi Textbook of Class VI in Delhi

M.Ed., JMI, GEETA VERMA, 1970

The study mainly concentrated on the kinds of (ideals) values, attitudes and concepts reflected in the textbook, the extent to which ideational content of the book is desirable by its reflection, gradation and presentation in the context of the aims and objectives of education in Indian Society. It was found that the book did provide good and enough material for its ideational context.

Development of an Evaluation tool on Process Based Learning in science

M.Ed., C.I.E., D.U., RAJNI JOSHI, 1989

The objectives of the study were to identify various science processes, develop test items on each science process and develop a comprehensive tool for testing various processes.

The tool to assess the understanding of science processes by students of eighth grade was developed which consisted of 70 multiple choice questions meant to test eight science processes.

The major findings of the study revealed that (1) it is possible to pencil-paper tests to assess the science processes. (2) The understanding of processes measuring and quantifying was found to be developed significantly than other science processes. (3) The understanding of processes experimenting and hypothesis formation was found to be significantly lower than other processes.

A Study of Various Areas of Adjustment Among Test-Anxious and non-Test-Anxious Students

M.Ed., C.I.E., D.U., VEENA VERMA, 1986

The objectives of the present investigation was to study the relationships if any, (1) between the test-anxious and the non-test-anxious public school boys group in various areas of adjustment. (2) in the test-anxious and the non-test-anxious government schoolboys group in various areas of adjustment. (3) in test-anxious and non test-anxious public schoolgirls in various areas of adjustment. (4) in test-anxious and non-text-anxious government, schoolgirls in various areas of adjustment. (5) between public school boys and girls on test-anxiety variable. (6) between government school boys and girls on test-anxiety. (7) between low S.E.S. boys and middle S.E.S. boys on test-anxiety. (8) between low S.E.S. and upper middle S.E.S. boys on test-anxiety. (9) between low S.E.S. and high S.E.S and boys on text-anxiety. (10) between middle S.E.S. and upper middle S.E.S. boys on test-anxiety. (11) between middle S.E.S. and high S.E.S. boys on test-anxiety. (12) between upper middle S.E.S. and high S.E.S. boys on test-anxiety.

(13) between low S.E.S. girls and middle S.E.S. girls on test-anxiety. (14) between low S.E.S. and upper middle S.E.S. girls on text-anxiety. (15) between low S.E.S. and high S.E.S. girls on test-anxiety. (16) between middle S.E.S. and upper middle S.E.S. girls on test-anxiety. (17) between middle S.E.S. and high S.E.S. girls on test-anxiety. (18) between upper middle S.E.S. and high S.E.S. girls on test- anxiety.

500 students (boys and girls) from Government and Public schools of Delhi were selected as sample for study. The tools used were: Dutt-Gupta Personality Inventory, Test-anxiety scale by Malika, socio-economic status scale by Urmil Nagpal. The major findings of the study were: (1) There is significant difference in test-anxious and non-test-anxious public schoolboys in various areas of adjustment. (2) There is significant difference in test-anxious and non-test-anxious government school boys in various areas of adjustment. (3) There is significant difference in test-anxious and non-test-anxious public schoolgirls in various areas of adjustment. (4) There is no significant difference in test-anxious and non test-anxious government schoolgirls in various areas of adjustment. (5) There is significant difference in public school boys and girls on test-anxiety. (6) There is no significant difference between Govt. school boys and girls on test-anxiety. (7) There is significant difference between low S.E.S. boys and middle S.E.S. boys on test-anxiety. (8) There is significant difference between low S.E.S. boys and upper middle S.E.S. boys on test-anxiety. (9) There is significant difference between low S.E.S. and high S.E.S. boys on test-anxiety. (10) There is significant difference between middle S.E.S. and upper middle S.E.S. boys on test-anxiety. (11) There is no significant difference between middle S.E.S. and high S.E.S. boys on test-anxiety. (12) There is no significant difference between upper middle S.E.S. and high S.E.S. boys on test-anxiety. (13) There is no significant difference between low S.E.S. girls and middle S.E.S. girls on test-anxiety. (14) There is no significant difference between low S.E.S. girls and upper middle S.E.S. girls on test-anxiety. (15) There is no significant difference between low S.E.S. and high S.E.S. girls on test-anxiety. (16) There is no significant difference between

middle S.E.S. and upper middle S.E.S. girls on test-anxiety. (17) There is no significant difference between middle S.E.S. and high S.E.S. girls on test-anxiety. (18) There is no significant difference between upper middle S.E.S. and high S.E.S. girls on test-anxiety.

An Investigation into the Extent of Deficiency of Class X Students in Hindi Language as Revealed Through CBSE's Secondary Examinations Answer Books

M.Ed., C.I.E., D.U., RAJNI JOSHI, 1986

The study was conducted by keeping the following objectives in view: (1) to identify and study the errors of class X students in respect of Hindi language. (2) to collect and classify these errors with a view to provide classroom teacher an insight into the nature, magnitude of these errors and (3) to suggest if possible a remedial programme with regard to these errors.

The sample of this study consisted of a set of 100 answer books selected at random from among the answer books of candidates who appeared in Hindi (Core) examination in March 1985.

The major findings show: (1) Ignorance of correct symbol of a particular sound leads to script error. (2) Ignorance about the rules of grammar leads to serious mistakes in writing including syntax. (3) Not all the errors in Hindi writing can be attributed to the filter language influence. (4) Quite a number of script error seem to be more due to the lack of perfect match between the sound, pronunciation and writing of Hindi words. The other causes of scripts errors are: (5) The absence of suitable textbooks and Teacher guides. Lack of specialized guidance to the teachers for teaching Hindi as the second language. Lack of specially qualified or trained teachers. Absence of reference books and specific material. No special work is done by the teachers. Uninterested teachers. Lack of motivation from teachers to students. Lack of suitable methodology of language teaching. Ungraded books. Lack of clarity regarding: Hindi language and literature, and aim of teaching Hindi (Whether teaching as first language or second language), influence and interference of teacher, his/her pronunciation, the filter language and linguistics.

❑❑❑

EVALUATION AND PERFORMANCE

A Comparative Study of MCD and NDMC School Students Reading Ability of the Stage Where they are Appearing for Class V Examinations

M.Ed., C.I.E., D.U., MRIDULA SHARMA, 1995

The objectives of the study were: (1) To study the levels of achievement in reading ability of MCD and NDMC school students in their first language; (2) To study these levels of achievement in comparative terms.

Four MCD and four NDMC schools from urban Delhi were selected. A passage from prescribed book of geography for class VI was selected to test the reading ability through comprehension.

The major finding of the study showed that both the groups of children attained almost an equal degree of reading ability. The mean scores on 'interpretation skill and written expression' (skill No. 2) are quite poor as compared to the mean scores for the other two reading skills. The students belonging to both the groups have developed only a limited ability to interpret. The meaningful reading does not stress pupil's understanding and clear comprehension of different types of presentations only, but also his ability to select, interpret and apply facts or ideas according to his purpose of reading. Therefore, this ability seems to be lacking equally in the NDMC as well as MCD schools. On the whole there does not appear to be much difference between the 'reading ability' in the first language of the students studying in NDMC and MCD schools.

A Comparative Study of Urban and Rural Students of XI Class of Delhi Administration Regarding their Attitude Towards Science (Chemistry) and their Achievement

M.Ed., C.I.E., D.U., 1983

The study had the objectives of finding out the attitude of XI class pupils towards science (chemistry), how this attitude relates to achievement in the subject and a comparison between rural and urban students.

100 Class XI students were selected from five Government Senior Secondary schools. Girls from rural area of Delhi could

not be involved since they did not opt for science in these areas. An achievement test was developed by the investigator to administer on the students from rural and urban Delhi.

The major findings of the study revealed the following: (1) So far chemistry is concerned, the difference is non-significant between the rural and urban students of XI Class of Delhi Administration. (2) As far as comparison between rural and urban students are concerned a significant difference does exist in the achievement in chemistry.

EVALUATION PRACTICES IN PRIMARY SCHOOLS

MAMTA AGARWAL & SARLA RAJPUT

Paper Presented at the 1996 the International Seminar on School effectiveness and Classroom process at Primary Stage, NCERT

With the objective of finding out all about the evaluation practices in framing schools in the 1994-95 academic session, the study was taken up.

The schools were taken from both urban and rural areas. Though most of the schools were from urban areas, 6 schools were from rural Delhi. 20 schools were co-educational, 4 were boys schools and only 1 school was exclusively for girls. The instruments used to study the evaluation practices. School questionnaire, Evaluation questionnaire, Investigator's diary and Question Papers of class III and the Report Cards.

The findings of the study showed: (1) All schools had a well-designed system of evaluation consisting of various class tests and examinations throughout the year at least in scholastic areas. (2) As to the question how frequently the tests/examinations are held and what weightages are given to different tests, it was seen that most of the schools have a scheme of testing consisting of quarterly, half-yearly and final examination supported by informal classroom test which the schools keep having at regular intervals. (3) The weightages given to different tests and examinations are more or less same in all the schools managed by state government and local bodies. Only Kendriya Vidyalayas give 20 per cent weightage to unit tests and 20 per cent to project work and assignments. All public schools adopt their own system of evaluation. In some schools like Mirambika School only project work is done. In another school only regular unit tests are given whereas in others like Springdales School children are evaluated on their day to day work. In some public schools there are half-yearly and annual examinations only with the class tests. (4) For doing continuous evaluation, by and large written tests are adopted by schools. In some subjects like environmental studies and languages oral testing is done but it has very little weightage as compared to written tests. Private and public schools give more attention to assignments, project work and oral work than the state run schools. Observation technique is also used for evaluating non-scholastic areas but it is not done systematically. (5) Most of the question papers were not balanced. In a question paper weightage should be allotted appropriately for various objectives like knowledge, understanding, application and skill. It was seen that in most of the schools the objective of knowledge was given 50 to 75 per cent weightage. Understanding and application got very little weightage. This shows that the question paper of our primary schools is not designed to test higher mental abilities. From this it can be assumed that the teachers do not have an idea of developing a good question paper. It was also seen that most of the school test only the student's textual knowledge and fall short of testing higher mental abilities. Only private public schools give attention to the testing of higher mental abilities. (6) As far as the types of questions are concerned, it was seen that most of the questions were of short answer and very short answer variety. This is understandable also because at primary level the children are small and it is difficult for them to write large answers. The objective type questions were total lacking in the question papers perhaps because the teachers are not trained in developing such questions. (7) In order to know whether the schools used the evaluation results for diagnosing the weaknesses of children in different areas and whether they tried to remedy those weakness. It was revealed that diagnosis and remediation is not well organized in schools. Some little diagnoses in informal way goes on as a routine matter in all the schools and some measures of remediation are also taken in routine. Most of the remediation is inbuilt with teaching.

Only very few schools give separate time during assembly, games period or music period etc. to the weak children. Only in DTEA school remedial work is done regularly after school hours and St. Columbus organized formal remedial classes with a separate teacher appointed for the purpose. Another measure taken up by schools for remediation is peer group or child to child teaching where the brighter children of the same class or sometimes senior children help the weaker ones. Some schools just inform the parents about the weakness and expect them to help their children. (8) Regarding whether the non-scholastic areas of pupil growth are also evaluated and what particular aspects are evaluated, it was found that the evaluation of pupil's social personal qualities, his interests and values is not systematic. Most of the schools in Delhi do try to report some social personal qualities but neither proper tools are used for evaluating these qualities, nor any records are kept of even of informal observations. At the time of filling up the report card the teacher grades the pupils on various traits on the basis of her impressions. In Government and MCD school the only quality evaluated is cleanliness. As far as the interests of children are concerned most of the school have activities like art, craft, music, dance, sports etc. In some schools the interest of children are graded and some give remarks about them. Many schools specially MCD schools and some Government aided schools do not report the interests at all. Regarding the evaluation of values it was found that schools in Delhi do try to inculcate socially accepted values in the children but they do not evaluate them at all. The schools do evaluate the children continuously as suggested by the frequency of formal and informal tests in various classes but it is not done comprehensively. It is only in a few schools that comprehensive evaluation is done *i.e.* along with scholastic areas non-scholastic areas are also covered. However, it was seen that it was not as systematically done as it should have been. (9) The managements of schools do not provide detailed guidelines for evaluation to their schools. Whatever guidelines are given are related to only the scholastic areas. The teachers do not have any training in the concept of evaluation and its importance in teaching learning process. (10) The MCD school presented the most dismal picture as educational institutions. It is perhaps because they were understaffed, had large number of children and had very poor physical facilities. Even sitting arrangement was not found to be proper. On the contrary the public schools had very congenial atmosphere with proper physical facilities and qualified and well aware staff. Even the unrecognized private schools seemed to be better off than MCD schools in this respect.

A Study of Predictive Efficiency of Objective type Examination, Short-Answer type Examination and type Examination to Predict Academic Success in Science Subjects in IX Class

M.Ed., JMI, R.L. CHHABRA, 1973

The objectives of the study were to find out the predictive efficiency of objective type test of general mental ability (including verbal ability, language usage, numerical ability and general information) short answer type of examination in Hindi, science and mathematics and essay type examination (middle school exam) to predict the academic success in science subjects. It was found that short answer examination were more significant than objective type and essay type. The short answer type examination was the best predicator variable and also that, it would be an effective tool for predicting academic success in science subjects.

To Develop a Mechanism for Conducting Organizational Evaluation and Diagnosis in Government Senior Secondary and Secondary Schools of Delhi

Project Report, DEPA, NTEPA, PRATAP SINGH, 1985

The present study was conducted specifically to evolve a mechanism for conducting organizational evaluation and diagnosis of education institutions.

The sample for present study was drawn from Govt. schools only. The sampling was done at three stages, namely: Case nominations by E.O's & Dy. E.O's, teacher Respondent of the cases nominated and sampled out and principal respondent of the cases nominated and sampled out. The instrument for study was Institutional Profile Questionnaire (I.P.Q.).

Analysis of data, discussion on profile charts of individual schools and group mean chart of both sets of schools suggests us to raise a question as to what makes a difference in opinions with regard to the two set of schools. The major findings drawn from the study were: (1) In good running schools, the teachers have good relations with principal, they rate principal as leader, the resources are better, they are more satisfied with the jobs, they make more outside contacts, the instruction methodology is better rated, the examination conducted in a better way. Students are well disciplined. The school organizes more co-curricular activities and teachers are better qualified. All the above traits are supplementary to another. So in a good school there exists a congenial environment. In a poorly run school these traits are less quantitatively obviously because the teacher-principal relationship is not better. The principal does not take many initiatives. The resources are scarce or if there exist any nobody makes use of these. In such an unhealthy environment naturally the staff is less satisfied. Students are not much disciplined. The co-curricular activities are lesser organized or never take place. Teachers are less qualified or they seem to be less qualified because they do not want to put their maximum efforts.

Tuition as a Factor in Mathematics Achievement at the Secondary Stage

M.Ed., C.I.E., D.U., MALEY CHAKRABORTY, 1996

The objectives of the study were: to study the nature of mathematics tuition, to evaluate students' perception and experiences about mathematics tuition, to obtain parental feedback and teachers views on the nature and effectiveness of mathematics tuition, to study the relationship between mathematics tuition and mathematics achievement.

The study was conducted in two phases. Phase I consisted of investigating the nature of mathematics tuition with a total sample of 276 students from a public school. All students of classes IX and X were constituted the sample for this phase. In phase II, 50 students from among those identified in phase I, who were taking tuition were selected at random, for more in-depth probing, mathematics teachers dealing with the secondary and senior secondary level mathematics teaching in that school.

The tools used in study comprised of a self-constructed questionnaire for students, a detailed questionnaire to study in- depth views of 50 students (taking tuition) selected at random, a questionnaire for parents of the fifty students identified as the sample of phase II, a questionnaire to seek the view of teachers and average mathematics achievement scores of students' entire years performance in Mathematics.

The major findings of the study highlight: (1) Taking mathematics tuition is quite common among students of secondary level. (2) Percentage of students taking tuition increases substantially from class IX to class X. (3) In class X most students start taking mathematics tuition 6-8 months before the board examination. (4) More students take group tuitions than individual tuition. (5) The most preferred size of the group is 4-6 in number of students. (6) Most students seem to invest 3-5 hours of their time per week for mathematics tuition. (7) Students from business family seem to be taking tuition the most followed by service and professional. (8) Anxiety in mathematics, lack of practice and making silly mistakes are the reasons stated by students for not doing well in mathematics. (9) Decreasing performance and parents' decision account for the main reasons why students start taking tuition in mathematics. (10) To get good marks is almost the universal expectation from mathematics tuition. (11) A substantial percentage of students said that their performance has improved after taking mathematics tuition. (12) Getting personal attention as the number of students in tuition group is less as compared to the classroom is cited as the main advantage of taking mathematics tuition. (13) More practice, weekly tests and regular checking of work are the suggestions given by students for improving mathematics teaching in school. (14) Gaining confidence is one of the main benefits reported by students from mathematics tuition. (15) To get regular practice, an essential component of doing well in mathematics, which they won't do without a tutor is a very common reason for taking mathematics tuition. (16) Teachers feel that the rate charged by the tutors is not too high considering the time devoted by them per week. (17) Poor knowledge of mathematical concepts taught in previous classes is given as the main reason by teachers for students taking mathematics tuition. (18) Reasons given by teachers for tuitions being taken by high achievers as well, include student's desire for improvement in mathematics marks and mathematical ability. (19) According to teachers if student concentrated more in class, the need for taking mathematics tuition would decrease. (20) Teachers are of the opinion that mathematics tuition and mathematics achievement are not significantly related. (21) Parents send their children for mathematics tuition to enable them to score more marks. (22) Competence of the tutor is what parents look for in the tutor they engage. (23) Basics of child not being clear and lack of individual attention are the reasons given by the parents for developing mathematics phobia among their children. (24) More practice and individual attention are expected by parents, from school, to develop a positive attitude towards mathematics among students. (25) Many students use help/ guidebooks even if they are taking tuition. (26) Taking mathematics tuition is primarily the student's own decision rather than his parents or teachers'. (27) Tuition as a factor on mathematics achievement appears to be significant (t-ratio significant, $p<.01$).

A Study of the Contribution of Project Work at the +2 Level in Biology to the Development of Certain Inductive Aspects of Scientific Thinking

M.Ed., C.I.E., D.U., 1983

The objective of the study was to assess the ability of science students of senior secondary classes.

The sample comprising of 94 students were taken from class XII biology group of four public schools in Delhi. All schools selected followed the All India Senior Certificate Examination System. The study is an *ex post facto* study where experimental and controlled groups were formed on the basis of marks obtained in the test of scientific thinking.

The major findings of the study were as follows: (1) Investigatory projects done at the +2 level in biology are not contributing significantly towards the development of scientific thinking in the students of schools under study. (2) The existing methods of conducting and doing project work are not up to the mark. This influences the poor performance of students in the test. (3) The conditions in the school classroom, library, laboratory is not congenial for effective planning and execution of projects. Students and teachers are not satisfied about the conditions under which they have to work and feel strongly that the evaluation is also not proper.

Effectiveness of Programmed Lessons as a Remedial tool for low Achievers in Learning Some Geometrical Concepts (VIth Class)

M.Ed., C.I.E., D.U., 1983

The study was taken up to investigate into the effectiveness of programmed lessons as a remedial tool for low achievers in learning some geometrical concepts among Class VI. The study was confined to one government school. The students who achieved below 30% in pretest were taken up as low-achiever. Initially 40 students were selected. Later based on their average percentage in the pretest of Geometry, they were matched score-wise to form Group A and Group B. Group I was taught through programmed instruction and Group II was taught through the routiniwise classroom instruction.

The major findings show: (1) Teaching and learning through programmed instruction can definitely help students and teachers. Students receiving programmed lessons as a help, remove their deficiency in learning of the unit under investigation. (2) Most of the students were not able to do questions of completion of diagrams. So it can be said that drawing skill cannot be improved by programmed lessons.

A Study of Achievement in Mathematics of XIth Class Students in Relation to their Entering Behaviour

M.Ed., C.I.E., D.U., DAMYANTI BATRA, 1983

The study proceeded with the objective of making an attempt to find out how do the alternative Course A and Course B at secondary level influence the achievement in mathematics at +2 level.

In order to carry on the study, three Government Girls Senior Secondary Schools were selected and administered the following tools: (1) Kuppuswamy's Rating scale to study social-economic status. (2) Raven's Progressive matrices test.

The major finding as revealed by the study was that the students having course A in mathematics at secondary level would achieve higher in mathematics at +2 levels as found to be significant at 05 level.

Effectiveness of Peer Interactive Learning in Improving Scholastic Achievement and Retention

M.Ed., C.I.E., D.U., MAUSUMI MANJIT, 1996

The study proceeded with the objective of finding out how the co-operative learning in a classroom learning works. The study reached a major conclusion that Peer Interactive Learning is significantly effective in improving scholastic achievement, retention and incorporating positive transformation in the group dynamics of the class.

The study also indicated that a pupil should never be branded as average or below average because this status is not permanent. Certain situational factors place a student at certain level at a particular time period. When the situational factors change, the performance and achievement of the pupil also change. The study established that managing one's own learning and assuming responsibilities goes a long way in helping the students become not only task oriented, but also disciplined.

The study established that not only older students are able to manage their tasks by themselves, young learners of pre-adolescent stage can also learn from experience and need not be spoon fed every time.

The success of cooperative learning approach in small group settings depends upon the vision of the teacher and her preparedness for playing the necessary roles as the academic leader, a facilitating agent and a sympathetic human being to whom children look up for guidance as well as help.

Children readily accept peer feedback on their own effort and also the peer support provided for improving their learning skills and performance.

Children who are adjudged as below average ability learners are not of below average ability on all aspects of academic performance and for all time. They can improve their performance sooner than expected and catch up with others adjudged at higher ability levels under favourable situations: Cooperative learning approach based on small group setting provides a very favourable environment for improving academic performance to these children. Psychological acceptance by peers is an essential condition for improving academic achievement for the so-called below average ability learners.

Factors Involved in the Learning of Maths at VIIIth Grade Level

M.Ed., C.I.E., D.U., 1983

The purpose of the study was to find out criteria for selection in terms of tests of necessary abilities to predict success in the future achievement in Maths. This exercise was taken up to help teachers to select students according to their abilities and percentage of failures.

The sample for the study consisted of 200 students selected randomly in class VIII from Delhi Public School, Mathura Road. Test Administration Psychological test was administered on the selected sample. On the basis of the obtained results, the test was developed.

An Investigation into the Psychological Abilities Involved in Learning Modern Mathematics at the Secondary Level

M.Ed., C.I.E., D.U., UJJAL SINGH, 1980

The present study tried to achieve the objectives of studying the correlation between abstract reasoning and achievement in Modern Mathematics. To study the correlation between Numerical ability and achievement in Modern Mathematics and to study the correlation between space relations and achievement in Modem Mathematics.

The findings arrived at highlight: (1) Abstract Reasoning and achievement in Modern Mathematics are highly correlated to the extent of +.769 which was found significant. (2) Numerical ability correlates significantly with achievement in Modern Mathematics to the extent of .335 which was found significant.

(3) Spatial ability was not found significantly correlated with the achievement in Modern Maths. (4) Partial correlation of co-efficients r 12.34 under r 13.24 were found significant while r 14.23 was found not significant. (5) Multiple correlation co-efficient from a multiple regression Equation in variables of abstract reasoning. Numerical ability and space relations correlates .812 with scores obtained in Modern Mathematics. (6) abstract reasoning and numerical ability play significant role in determining success in modern Mathematics.

Development of Remedial Course in Mathematics for Rising the Standard of Low-achievers of Grade VI

M.Ed., C.I.E., D.U., AJEET SINGH MALIK, 1995

The main objectives of the study were to find out the reasons of deficiencies in the achievement of the course content in the grade VI, to develop a remedial course for the low-achievers in mathematics at the level of grade VI, to find out the ways and means of communicating the content of remedial course to low- achievers and lastly to study the effect of the material course communicated to the low-achievers.

The main cause of deficiencies in the achievement of the course-content in the grade VI, is the poor command over computational skills, which are learnt at primary level. The analysis of errors made by the students showed that 54% students did wrong operation; they multiplied instead of dividing a fraction by another fraction. 54% students were deficient in computational skills. Majority of students were lacking in computational skills. Majority off students were lacking in comprehension of the process of division. 34% students faced difficulty in reducing fractions to lowest terms. 68% students faced cancellation difficulties.

The remedial course improves the performance of the low-achievers, by remedying the defects. The difference between the means of pre-test and post post-test scores, is significant at 0.1 level, which further shows that the group had made significant improvement in mathematics.

An Investigation into the Pattern of Relationship Between Pupils Space Concept Maturity and their Achievement of Geometrical Concepts

Ph.D., JMI, NAIYERR ALAM, 1986

The study was concerned with innovations is the geometry curriculum. It specifically investigated the pattern of relationship between pupil's maturity of space concepts and concept achievement in geometry so that strategies in curriculum development could be worked out to secure harmony between the geometry curriculum with the stage of cognitive maturation of boys from six Hindi-medium government boys' schools in South Delhi. In the results it was reported that both general space concept maturation and maturation of mental imagery emerged as significant determiners of achievement of geometrical concepts. Similarly the results also show that general space concept maturation and maturation of mental imagery are both viable determiners of scholastic achievement in geometry.

Cognitive Achievement in Algebra of Sixth Class Students Comparing Structural and Traditional Programmes

M.Ed., JMI, SHASHI MAKKAR, 1995

The main objective of the study was to investigate whether cognitive achievement amongst students of sixth standard will be better with structured programme or with instructions as in the traditional programme. The sample was drawn from one government senior secondary school and two equivalent groups, controlled and the experimental group. The tools comprised of Age and Past Academic Achievements, the Numerical Ability Test for measuring numerical ability, Coloured Progressive Matrices Test for measuring Intelligence.

The major finding highlighted that the Structured programme method of instruction was better and more effective in terms of achievement in handling all the four operations involving algebraic polymials in the fields of algebra as compared to traditional methods.

An Investigation into Effectiveness of Graphic Organizers on Cognitive Achievement in Biology of Ninth Grade Students of Kendriya Vidyalayas of Badarpur in Delhi

M.Ed., JMI, MADAN MOHAN JOSHI, 1991

The objective of the study was to investigate whether cognitive achievement amongst students of 9th grade will be better when they undergo instruction with graphic organizers or with verbal organizers. Three equivalent group of students were formed, one was taught through graphic organizer and the other one through traditional programme and the third one verbal organizer programme.

The findings of the study revealed that the graphic organizer programme method of instruction was better and more effective in terms of cognitive achievement in Biology than the verbal organizer programme method of instruction and traditional programme method of instruction.

A Study of Achievement in Mathematics of XIth Class Students in Relation to their Entering Behaviour

M.Ed., C.I.E., D.U., 1983

The study will attempt to find answer to how do the alternative courses in Maths namely course A and B at secondary level influence the achievement in mathematics at +2 level?

The sample consisted of 3 Government Girls Senior Secondary Schools of Delhi. Tools used were Kuppuswami's Rating scale for studying social-economic status; Raven's Progressive Matrices test; for studying achievement level, marks were considered.

The major findings of the study revealed that in general, (1) the achievement in mathematics of Senior Secondary Students with background of Course A in mathematics at Secondary level is higher than the achievement in mathematics of Senior Secondary students with background of course B in mathematics at Secondary level. (2) The students having course A in mathematics at Secondary level would achieve higher in maths at +2 level.

Impact of Knowledge of Behavioural Objectives on Achievement in Mathematics Taught Through Programmed Instruction Material

M.Ed., C.I.E., D.U., HARPREED, 1994

The study conducted on 25 students of VIII standard kept the objective of studying the impact of knowledge of behaviours objectives on learning the topic of sets in mathematics and developing a linear programme on the topic of seats. Two schools were selected randomly. Two groups were formed, one was the experimental and the other control. The tools administered were the Intelligence test, Programmed Instructions Material and the Criterion test. The study revealed the difference in the mean performance of learner taught with the knowledge of behavioural objectives and that those learners taught without the knowledge of behavioural objectives.

To Study the Effect of Goal Setting on the Performance of the Child

M.Ed., C.I.E., D.U., BHARTI SALWAN, 1993

The objectives of the study were to compare the performance of the three groups of students: the ones who have decided about their goal; the ones who have not decided about their goal; and the ones who are confused and need career guidance to see the effect of social class and parental qualification on the performance of students.

A sample of 180 students comprising 93 boys and 87 girls was taken at random from the Air Force Golden Jubilee Institute, Subroto Park, Cantonment Area, Delhi. A questionnaire containing questions on their decided goal, subjects chosen, hobbies, parental qualification and earnings was constructed by the investigator.

The major findings of the study were: (1) The performance of students who have decided about their goal is much better than students who have not decided about their goal as well as students who are confused and need career guidance. (2) After comparing the performance of students of the lower, middle and upper class, it can be concluded that most of the students who have performed well belong to middle class.

(3) After seeing the effect of parental education and qualification on the performance of children it was seen that most of the high achievers have highly/very highly educated parents.

A Comparative Study of the Vocational Aspiration of High Achiever and low Achiever Students of Class XI of Senior Secondary Schools of Delhi Territory

M.Ed., C.I.E., D.U., 1983

The objectives of the study were to provide suitable opportunities, openings and facilities to both high and low achievers (Academic) in view of their aspirations and abilities, to make useful suggestion and provide guidance to the students and parents and even teachers in respect of vocational choice, to provide facilities for their vocational placement and follow up work.

As sample of the study, 147 students were selected through a stratified random sampling to whom two types of questionnaires were administered.

The study revealed significant changes in the vocational aspirations of low achiever students and differences in vocational aspirations between low and high achievers, low achiever boys and low achiever girls, low achiever students belonging to the different income level groups, and high achiever students belonging to different socio-economic groups. Educational factors too exerted influence on both the low and high achiever students to a great extent but there was a difference in the degree of influence. The low achiever students were more influenced by the general standard of education and not much by education of parents and siblings.

A Study of Academic Achievement in Relation to Adjustment and Achievement Motivation

M.Ed., C.I.E., D.U., 1984

The main objectives of the study were to find out the relationship between academic achievement and achievement motivation, between academic achievement and adjustment in its varied context such as home, society, emotional hostility, masculinity and femineity. The sample consisted of 220 Ninth class boys from two government schools. The tools used in the study were marks obtained by the boys in final examinations,

Projective tests, Thematic Apperception Test, Bell's Adjustment Inventory and Prayag Mahta's Achievement Inventory. The major findings of the study revealed that students who had good home adjustment were adjusted well in other areas as well like health, social and emotional adjustment. Children with good adjustment got high percentage of marks or good academic achievement led to better adjustment in all areas. Children with good adjustment and high percentage gave more achievement related responses. Students who gave more achievement related responses were found to be better adjusted than children who gave more task related and unrelated response.

Stress in Relation to Academic Achievement: A Study of Secondary and Higher Secondary Class Students of a School in Delhi

M.Phil., JNU, R. DAS, 1989

The present study has attempted to ascertain whether there is a difference in the academic performance of students in terms of different types of school organizational climates, teacher effectiveness and teacher's job satisfaction, as well as whether the interaction of the above three factors in any way influences the academic performance of students.

Four types of schools were taken and 309 students from both classes IV and V from different schools, and 40 teachers were taken as sample for this study. The tools used were: Organizational Climate Description Questionnaire (OCDQ) devised by Sharma (1973) to assess the climate that exists in the school. Teacher Characteristic Description Form (TCDF) devised by Aurora (1973) to measure the effectiveness of teachers, Job Satisfaction Investor (JSI) devised by Indiresan (1973) to measure the job satisfaction of the teachers. The Academic Performance of students was considered in terms of the marks obtained by the students of classes IV and V in their annual examination conducted by the schools from the school record.

The results obtained show that: (1) The Academic Performance of public school students in both classes IV and V were significantly better than those from missionary, government and municipal school (in class IV). (2) The Academic Performance of students varied in terms of the Organisational Climate of the school in both the classes IV and V, that is, students from the open climate schools had shown significantly higher academic performance than those from the closed climate. (3) The academic performance of students differed significantly in terms of the effectiveness of the teacher (in class IV). That is, students taught by Highly effective (HE) teachers showed better academic performance. (4) The academic performance of the students from classes IV and V differed significantly in terms of the job satisfaction of the teachers (in class IV, and in class V). In other words, students taught by the teacher having High Job satisfaction (HJS) showed better academic performance than those taught by teachers having Low Job satisfaction (LJS). (5) The teacher effectiveness combined with the specific type of climate in the school led to differential level of academic performance amongst the students of classes IV and V respectively. In other words, students of open climate school taught by the highly effective (HE) teachers scored high in academic performance than any other combination of school climate and teacher effectiveness. (6) Differential level of job satisfaction of the teacher combined with certain type of school climate led to a differential level of academic performance amongst the students in class IV. That is, students of the open climate school taught by the Highly Job satisfied (HJS) teacher showed better academic performance, than any other combination of school climate and the job satisfaction of teachers. (7) A combination of high level teacher effectiveness and job satisfaction of the teachers and the type of school (public school) in which the pupil studied led to a significantly high academic performance among the classes IV and V students respectively as compared to any other combination of teacher effectiveness, job satisfaction and the type of school. (8) A differential level of Organisational climate combined with certain type of effectiveness and job satisfaction of teachers lead to a differential level of academic performance among the students (in class IV and in class V), that is, in an open climate school the students, who were taught by the highly effective teachers and having high job satisfaction also showed significantly better academic performance. (9) A positive correlation was found among the teachers in terms of teacher effectiveness and job satisfaction in the public school and missionary school respectively (r=.41 and .45), whereas a negative correlation was obtained between these two factors in the government and municipal schools respectively (r being -.38 and -.39). That is, as the effectiveness of the teacher increased and reached higher level job satisfaction also increased linearly in the case of public school and missionary school, was in the case of government school and municipal school the relationship was in opposite direction. That is, as the effectiveness of teacher increased and reached higher level, the job satisfaction decreased and reached a lower level.

A Study of Some Factors Related to Scholastic Achievement

Ph.D., C.I.E., D.G. RAO, 1965

The study was undertaken to find out the relationship of intelligence, study habits, socio-economic status, and certain attitudes towards the school with the academic achievement of the grade VIII pupils of Delhi. 500 boys of twelve higher secondary schools of Delhi formed the sample. The scholastic achievement of pupils was measured using the Jamia Achievement Test Battery which included three important school subjects, *viz.,* social studies, general science and mathematics. The CIE Group Test of Intelligence was used to measure intelligence. An inventory was developed on the pattern of the Wrenn's Study Habit Inventory to measure the study habits. The Kuppuswamy's inventory was used to study the socio-economic status. For measuring attitude towards school, a new tool was developed.

The major finding of the study reported that the three independent variables — intelligence, study habits and school attitude were significantly related to the prediction of scholastic achievement, while socio-economic status was not.

A Comparison of the Attainments of Children of the C.I.E. Basic School with those of Other School Children in Delhi

C.I.E., D.U., S. SHUKLA and D.N. TUTOO, 1959

The purpose of the study was to compare the achievements of the CIE Basic School children with those of children from other schools — Basic and traditional. The sample consisted of grade VI children from CIE Basic School and other schools — Basic and traditional of Delhi. In all, nine schools of Delhi having different structure and nature were sampled. Out of these nine, one was the CIE Basic School. A sample of about 400 students were picked up. Four achievement tests for the subjects of Hindi, social studies, arithmetic and general science were prepared. The data were subjected to statistical techniques like mean, SD, CR and ranking.

It was found that the mean scores of CIE Basic School in Hindi, arithmetic, social studies and general science ranked third, fourth, first and second respectively. Comparison with the help of significance of difference between mean scores of CIE Basic School on one hand and the other schools individually on the other, gave a mixed pattern of information.

A Study of High Achievers with Respect to their Needs and Interests

M.Ed., C.I.E., D.U., SUMAN DAS, 1988

The objectives of the study were to study the socio-economic status of the high achievers, average and the low achievers, to study and compare the interest pattern of the high achievers, average and the low achievers, to study and compare the needs of high achievers, average and the low achievers.

The sample was drawn from two girls schools of Hindi medium. 99 and 83 students of class VIIIth were selected consisting of high achievers, average and low achievers. The tools administered on them comprised of socio-economic scale developed by Jain, interest Inventory by Jain and needs inventory constructed by the researcher.

The findings show that the high achievers have interests in academic and intellectual areas and high order needs than the average and low average achievers. The socio-economic status of school and family did affect the achievement, interests and needs of students. Similarly the high achievers showed maximum needs for achievement and acquisition. The high achievers of two schools had same interests, same intensity and extent of needs pattern.

To Investigate Cognitive and Affective Correlates of Academic Achievement in Social Studies

M.Ed., JMI, SHASHI BHALLA, 1974

The objective was to study the relationship that exists between the affective and cognitive correlates of students with their achievements in social studies. One higher secondary school for girls was selected as sample for the study. It was concluded that the variance in affective development cannot account for variance in academic achievement in social studies.

A Study of the Relationship of Some of the Personality Traits Associated with Academic Achievement of Students at the Higher Secondary Stage

M.Ed., JMI, KAMALA MADHAVA, 1971

The study was carried out with the objectives of finding out the relationship of some of the personality traits associated with academic achievement of students at the higher secondary stage. The sample was drawn from four higher secondary schools. The major findings reveal that personality characteristics are associated with academic achievement. The higher neuroticism, the poorer is performance. The higher emotional stability, better the performance and less tense are better achievers in academic subjects.

A Study of Relationship Between Adjustment and Academic Achievement of Students of Higher Secondary Level

M.Ed., JMI, KHALID MOHD ABRAR KHAN, 1988

The objectives of the study mainly confined to finding out the adjustment of class XI arts group students, finding out the academic achievement score of class Xth and the relationship between adjustment and academic achievement of class XI/X Arts students.

The sample consisted of 50 Arts students of class XI in Higher Secondary school of Jamia Millia Islamia. The tools employed for data collection comprised of the adjustment inventory for school by N.M. Bhagia, academic achievement of students of class XI on the basis of final result and the measurement of school adjustment by N.M. Bhagia (1966).

A Study of Relationship Between Socio-metric Status of Pupils and their Performance in Academic and Non-academic Areas

M.Ed., C.I.E., D.U., POONAM CHOPRA

The objectives of the study were to compare group structure of different classes, to find out if there is any difference in sociometric status according to different criterion, to find out the relationship, if any between socio-metric status for each criteria and academic achievement, between socio-metric status for each criterion and non-academic performance, to compare the teachers' ratings on non-academic performance with academic achievement and to compare teachers' ratings on non-academic performance with students' socio-metric choices on various criteria.

Children's Perception of Teachers' Attitude Towards them and its Relationship with Self-perception, Home Environment and School Achievement

Ph.D. Edu., JMI, DEBAS, J.K., 1979

The objectives of the study were to know the attitude of teacher (as measured in terms of their perception of the pupil's characteristics) towards students belonging to different cultural backgrounds, how students perceived their teachers' evaluation regarding the same characteristics, the relationship between students' perception of their teachers and self-perception regarding the same characteristics, and the relationship of the attitude of teachers and students' self-perception to school achievement.

The sample consisted of all male students of Class IX studying in government boys' higher secondary schools of Delhi in north district, having Hindi as medium of instruction and belonging to different cultural backgrounds. The tools used for the study were Advanced Progressive Matrices for measuring intelligence. A Cultural Status Scale was developed by the investigator for measuring home environment or cultural status of students as well as the Pupil's Characteristics Rating Scale to assess three kinds of perception, namely, pupils' own perception about themselves regarding some of their personality characteristics, pupils' perception of teachers' evaluation on the same characteristics and teachers' evaluation on the same characteristics and teachers' attitude as measured in terms of their perception of pupils' characteristics.

The findings of the study highlighted: (1) Children's perception of teachers' attitude towards them was significantly related with pupils' self-perception, teachers' perception of pupils' characteristics and school achievement (in physical sciences), whereas it was not significantly related with the cultural status of students. (2) Teachers' attitude towards children coming from advantaged homes was more favourable than towards children coming from disadvantaged homes. (3) School achievement (in physical sciences) was not significantly related with the cultural status of students whereas teachers' attitude (as measured in terms of their perception of pupils' characteristics) towards students was likely to affect their school achievement (in physical sciences).

Correlation of Academic Motivation in High School Students

M.Ed., JMI, H.C. ARORA, 1970

The main objective of the study was to find out how for academic motivation is correlated with academic achievement, whether, socio-economic status plays a vital part in motivation and achievement or whether age and intelligence correlates with academic motivation. The study was conducted on two government (boys) higher secondary school from Shahdara zone and New Delhi public school. They were administered Inventory, Intelligence test, socio-economic status scale. The major finding revealed that academic motivation is significantly correlated with academic achievement in high school students. It is least correlated with intelligence.

A Study of Factors which Students Think Have Good or Bad Effect on their Scholastic Attainment inside the School

M.Ed., JMI, SUNDER DAS CHHOKRA, 1970

The main objective of the study was to identify the factors which the students think have good or bad effect on their scholastic attainment inside the school. The study revealed: (1) Separate rooms for separate classes and subjects are needed. (2) The school should always be away from the noise of the town. (3) The school equipment such as furniture, separate comfortable seating arrangement for every student, cemented and whitewashed walls decorated with charts, maps and inspiring mottos. (4) An able principal with impressive and dynamic personality. (5) Timely medical check-up helps in maintaining good health. (6) The students think religious education should not be imparted in schools. (7) Importance of games should not be minimised. (8) Financial help in the form of books, money and clothes, fee-concessions and maintenance of grants etc.

An Investigation into the Academic Performance of Students (Boys and Girls) at the Secondary and the Senior Secondary Stage in Schools Under Different Managements in the Union Territory of Delhi

Project Report, DEPA, NIEPA, KRISHNA GADI, 1986

The objectives of the study were: To find out if there is any significant difference, in the respective overall performances of boys and girls in the secondary school, and the Senior School Certificate Examinations and if so to further identify such differences in performance, streamwise at the Senior Secondary Stage, subject-wise at the Secondary Stage; to find out, if there are significant differences: in the overall respective performances of schools under various managements *viz.*, Govt., Govt.-aided and Private (unaided schools) to identify the factors responsible for variations in the respective performances of boys and girls; to find out, if there is any significant difference in the respective roles and attitudes of teachers, working in schools run by different managements; to study the role of managements in creating the right type of educational climate and to measures which can be taken by the managements to improve educational standards in schools and thus safeguard the interest of students in general.

Sample consisted of the 12 Senior Secondary Schools in all the break up which is one Girls and two Co-educational public schools, government-aided schools, government schools one boys, two girls and one co-educational government-aided school, two boys, two girls, one co-educational government schools. Two separate boys and girls' cohorts were developed. The results in respect of the Std. of IX and X classes were on specified proformas taken subject wise and category wise . The results in respect of the Std. of XI and XII classes were taken streamwise, subject wise and category wise. Questionnaires were developed for students, teachers, principals, education officers, educationists. Interviews were conducted of students, teachers, principals and parents, educationists, the chairman, Central Board of Secondary Education, Deputy Controller of Examinations, CBSE, Additional Director of Education and other Senior Officers of the Directorate of Education, Delhi Administration.

Secondary data was collected from two sources results of the Senior Sec./Sec. Examinations (for the years 1983, 84 and 1985) conducted by the CBSE, through their journals and supplemented with additional information from the Board's office and publications of Directorate of Education, Delhi Administration from educational Statistics Cell 1983-84 list of schools — Union Territory of Delhi — 1984-85.

On the basis of data collected, its interpretation and analysis, the following findings have emerged: (1) An analysis of the overall results of the All India and Delhi Examinations conducted by CBSE over the last three years, shows that the girls have always excelled the boys in both the Senior School Certificate and Secondary School Examinations. This is also true of the overall streamwise (Humanities, commerce and science) results of the Senior School Certificate Examination, Qualitatively as well as Quantitatively. (2) The performance of girls, falling in different groups based on marks, is also superior to that of boys. However, the position of top achievers, placed in the category obtaining above 75% marks, in the Senior Secondary Certificate Examination (All India as well as Delhi Schools) goes in favour of boys. In the Secondary School examinations, girls apparently seem to have an edge over boys, but in absolute terms, the number of boys appearing for the examination is higher than that of girls; so no significant conclusion can be drawn as far as this category of distinction holders is concerned. (3) In order of merit, the results of Private Schools are at the Top, followed by aided schools. Government schools come last.

In each type of schools, girls have invariably been found to have an edge over the boys. The results of boys in Govt. and Govt.-aided schools, present an extremely depressing picture, being more pronounced and noticeable for Govt. schools. Of the total number of candidates appearing at the Delhi Sec. School Exam, 60% are boys. The pass percentage of boys in this exam is only between 50 to 55% (after being moderated by the C.B.S.E. at their level) of those passing; farther, their quality of results is substandard. The number of those in the 75% and above category is almost negligible. Approx. 80% to 85% of the boys secure marks less than 50%, and of these too a large number fails in the 33 to 40% pass percentage category.

The low pass percentage and poor quality/substandard results deprive the students of a chance to take admission in XI class of science and commerce streams. The poor quality of results at the Senior Secondary stage is again due to the poor academic base over the last 10 years of schooling. It is due to this fact that Govt. school students have to opt for Humanities/ Commerce and Science in order of preference.

The order of preference for students under All India Scheme is Science, Humanities and Commerce. (4) Analysis of students, teachers' and Educationists' Questionnaires reveals that no single school could boast of good teachers exceeding 13% (ranging between 10 to 15%) of the total strength of its staff. 50 to 55% of the teachers in every school can be termed as average: they take their jobs merely as a routine and display no zeal for work unless goaded by rewards. The remaining 40% of the teachers are a blot on the profession: they are late comers; slip away from the school, take their classes irregularly and they indulge intrigues and other undesirable activities. These teachers have a baneful influence on the institutions they serve in and they are incorrigible. (5) Most of the Principals, E.O's and Educationists commended the attitude of most of the lady teachers towards their work. According to them, female teachers are conscientious, sincere and hardworking. At the same time, they are imbued with fine qualities like patience and perseverance. Moreover, lady teachers adopt the teaching profession by choice, and not under the force of circumstances

(73% of the lady teachers gave their responses to this effect). Female teachers in every type of school are giving better results in examinations than their male counterparts. (6) To a great extent, poor results of boys and boys' school, are ascribable to the indigenous quality of the average male teacher, as only 27% of them stated that they had come to this profession voluntarily; others came over, when they found other doors in the employment market closed on them. Their attitude to work is non-serious and of indifference. A fairly large percentage of male teachers in every school (Govt./aided/private) take little interest in their teaching work. Most of them are interested only in supplementing their incomes through private tuition work or some side business. A few of them are activists of official or unofficial teachers' organisation and neglect their own duties towards students and their schools; their discussions centre around the prospects of their career advancement; they never bother about their own professional growth or the welfare of the children put under their charge. They perform their duties without an interest of enthusiasm. (7) In co-educational schools, male teachers, at times, succeed in infecting their female colleagues with their views of indifference to work. This attitude of male teachers is plaguing each type of school in Delhi. (8) There is a general state of indiscipline found in Govt. schools, Boys' schools in particular. They lag far behind the other types of schools in respect of quantity as well as quality of their students' performing. Govt. schools suffer from a bad image in public eye with regard to the standard and quality of education imparted therein. One feels that much of the money being spent by the Govt. on these schools is going waste. There is much to be desired as far as the performance of these schools is concerned.

The graphic profile of schools, under different managements, concerning students' academic performance, as viewed by students themselves brings out fairly well the strong and weak points of each type of school.

There is only one point in favour of Government schools that the boys attend the classes regularly, showing their inner desire and keenness to study, but there are 16 weak points which highlight the apathy, indifference and casual attitude of teachers in these schools. Principals, Education Officers, and teachers themselves support the view that teachers neglect the general, yet most essential duties of day-to-day teaching work *e.g.* writing diaries, planning lessons, use of teaching aids, correction of written work, full coverage of courses in a systematic manner on time, conducting science practicals regularly, discouraging students from copying in examinations and taking due interest in the organisation of extracurricular activities.

Aided schools are doing comparatively better. Points favouring these schools are that students and teachers come to school punctually and that teachers take classes regularly and cover the courses systematically. However, the negative points are that teachers depend for their planning and preparation on keys and guides, do teaching work in a routing manner, without using any teaching aids. The deficiencies in the school programmes are made good by educated parents hailing from middle income group by arranging for private tuitions/ coaching for their children, though these schools are no higher than average yet they are definitely better than Govt. schools.

There are 9 points in favour of public schools. Their teachers are better prepared, go to classes punctually and remain busy teaching till the end of the period, pay special attention to the students, from the examination point-of-view, encourage students to ask questions and appreciate their pupils' good work. Science practicals are conducted fairly regularly. Exposure of students to a large number of activities helps in building up their personality.

The weak points of these schools are that the students do not attend the classes regularly. A large number of students join coaching classes and take tuition in more than two subjects on payment of heavy fees. This serves them as a sort of vitamin, toning up the level of their academic preparation for the examinations. Hence the better academic performance of the students of these schools is not entirely to the credit of schools or their teachers. (9) The ultimate responsibility of running the schools efficiently whether run by Govt. or private agencies, lies on their managements. Private schools functioning under good managements, are progressing by leaps and bounds; while those controlled by commercially inclined people, are exploiting the public as well as their own teachers. (10) Educationists have nothing but praise for good well-established public schools managed by enlightened citizens. These schools have distinct characteristics listed as: (i) They lay emphasis on institutional planning, setting out clear-out goals both for teachers and students, (ii) They permit freedom of experimentation and innovation to teachers, which ultimately helps in raising the standard of performance, (iii) In these schools a system of monitoring, based on continuous appraisal of the teachers' performance and the students' achievement, keeps all concerned on their toes and injects a seriousness of purpose in all the activities of the school, (iv) They provide physical facilities on a lavish scale, thus creating a congenial work climate, (v) They appreciate, good work done by teachers, keeping the letters morale and motivation high, (vi) They strive for an all-round development of the child's personality and character building by an abundant provision of co-curricular activities, (vii) They enable students to learn good manners and etiquette, which are a *sine qua non* for success in life.

In short, these schools (not numbering more than 10 in the capital) are run on sound educational lines. Simultaneously the educationists have denounced the so-called public schools run on commercial lines. These schools are ill-housed and ill-equipped, and employ unqualified teachers. They charge exorbitant fees from the children on their rolls, but render poor service in return. Every month they withhold from their teachers part of their salaries. Thus these schools are exploiting the public as well as their own teachers. They succeed in attracting students by labelling themselves as English-medium schools. (11) Aided schools maintain a high tone of discipline among teachers as well as students. They are doing better in the field of co-curricular activities as well. All this is attributable to their autonomous character, though only partial because of a measure of control exercised over them by the Directorate of Education. (12) These schools are characterised by a system of centralised decision-making. Implementation of decision is regulated by excessive emphasis on hierarchical status and ritualistic adherence to rules and procedures. The education department lacks an effective system of monitoring. The Director of Education, who is usually an I.A.S. Officer keeps on changing frequently. The Education Secretary who shares the responsibility of running the Department with Directorate of Education is also an I.A.S. Officer. Since the I.A.S. incumbents of these two posts do not stay long in the Department, they are not in a position to give proper direction to the working of the Department. Because of the poor monitoring of the efficiency of the Departments' functioning at various levels, people have developed almost total immunity to accountability. A general deterioration in the work atmosphere is noticeable. Casual attitude of employees and indifference to work are in evidence every where in the working of the administrative machinery. Educationists even go as far as to say that a steep decline in our national character over the years is reflected in the working of all Government Departments, Education Department being no exception. Teachers, principals, Education Officers and others who are willing to work, are feeling totally demotivated and demoralised. Some people in the department are refuting promotion to higher posts as they are afraid that they will be incapable of exercising their authority, while working on higher posts, because of political pulls and pressure and the obstructionist attitude of Teachers Association.

A Study of Teacher Effectiveness, Job Satisfaction Organisational Climates and its Relationship with Academic Performance of Primary School Learners: A Comparative Study of Public Missionary and Municipal School

Specifically, the study had the objectives of (i) identifying the level of stress amongst 10th and 12th class students and if this differs amongst them as well as between them and those who are in the 9th class and do not take the board examination, study the relationship between stress and academic performance, (ii) studying the relationship between stress and academic performance in the context of class, sex, subject stream and previous academic performance of students. Students from three classes, namely, XIIth and Xth who appeared for the Board Examination, and students from IXth class who did not appear for the Board examination comprised the sample for this study. From each class 80 students taken randomly and the stress was studied at 2 "high" stress and "low" stress likewise sex factor studied at two levels *viz.*, boys and girls. Finally, the relationship of stress and academic performance with class, streams was studied.

Stress was measured by using a stress questionnaire specially designed for the purpose.

Academic performance of students was adjudged by the percentage of marks they obtained in the selection examination. The previous academic performance was taken as the percentage of marks obtained by the students in the final examination of their previous classes respectively. The students were administered the stems scale specially devised for this purpose and the analysis was carried out on the obtained information from students in all the three classes.

The result obtained were as follows: 1. (a) Stress was found to differ significantly between the students of classes 12, and 10 as well as between students of class 9 and 10 respectively. To be more specific class X students had significantly greater stress than the students of class XII and IX in that order. However, stress did not vary significantly amongst students of IXth and XIIth class, (b) There was a significant difference in the stress scores of boys and girls of X class, but not between any other class students, (c) There was a significant difference in the stress scores of science and arts, and commerce and arts group of 12th class students. To be more specific commerce group had significantly greater stress than the science and arts group in that order. However there was no significant difference in stress scores of science and commerce group students respectively. 2. (a) Academic performance was found to vary significantly in terms of the 3 classes. The academic performance of 9th class appeared to be the highest followed by the 10th and 12th class in that order, (b) The academic performance of students varied in terms of stress factor *viz.*, high stress and low stress, that is, low stress students had secured significantly higher academic performance than those who had higher stress score. Such differences were obtained only in regard to students of class XII on academic performance between high and low stress students and not to the other two class students, (c) Boys and girls were not found to differ in terms of their academic performance. Academic performance also varied in terms of the interaction between class, stress and sex factors. To be more specific students of IXth class with low stress and belonging to male sex had significantly high academic performance than other.

Stress and Academic Performance

3. Stress and academic performance were found to be significantly negatively related. In other words higher the stress, lower the academic performance of students.

4. In the study it was found that the degree of correlation between stress and academic performance among XII and IX differed significantly, but not in terms of other classes.

5. In the study it was also found subject streams opted by students appear to affect the relationship between stress and academic performance, which may be attributable to the difficulty level of the subject matter students' interest and aptitude for the subject concerned.

Stress in Terms of Previous Academic Performance

Stress was found to vary significantly in terms of classes and previous academic performance (above mean and below mean academic level).

6. To sum up it may be stated that stress varied significantly between the students who appeared for Board examination and those who did not. More specifically, students who appeared for Board examination of 10th class had significantly greater stress than those of 12th and 9th class. Again the students of 12th class who appeared for Board examination significantly greater stress than those of 9th class who did not appear for Board examination.

7. Stress was significantly higher among students who were in the commerce stream as compared to those in science and arts stream respectively. Again, the stress amongst the students of science stream significantly greater stress than those in arts. Thus stress significantly related both class and subject stream factor. There was no significant difference in the boys and girls stress except among 10th class.

8. The academic performance was found significantly but negatively correlated with stress. That is higher the stress, lower the academic performance.

9. When the previous academic performance of students considered by dividing it, into above mean and below mean performances, there was significant difference in the mean stress scores of those who had above mean performance and below mean performance. In other words, the stress scores were significantly lower for those who had high mean previous academic performance as compared to the low mean previous academic performance.

From the above results one may conclude that stress appears to act as a positive influence in enhancing the academic performance of students in large number of cases. It would be worth-while to find out the exact level of stress which may be needed to induce or bring about the best performance among students. By highlighting the relationship between stress, class, subject stream, previous academic performance and academic performance as such, the present study may be considered as having contributed to a relatively difficult area, that is of the influence of stress of the academic performance of students particularly in 10th and 12th that is in Board examination.

Learning Strategies and Learning Outcomes of Senior Secondary School Students

M. Phil, ZHCESSS, JNU, SANDHYA, 1991

The present study was undertaken to explore the under stream specific differences among learning strategies and learning outcomes, the values, school adjustment and academic performance of the students. Matching variable were gender (Male and Female) and stream (arts, commerce and science).

Learning strategies, values, school adjustment and academic performance were taken as explanatory variables. A 2×3 factorial design and quota sampling was used. The sample consisted of 180 students (90 Boys and 90 Girls) from Senior Secondary classes of a large government school in Delhi. The students selected were from three streams (arts, commerce and science). The tools used were Ramsden's Approaches to Study Inventory (ASI), modified by Sen, Super and Neville's. The Value Scale (modified by the present researcher) and Saxena's Adjustment Inventory.

The major findings were: (1) Gender differences are significant on deep strategy, in that the female students use deep strategy more frequently and give more importance to values. (2) Stream differences are significant on learning strategies and learning outcomes. Arts students use surface strategy more frequently. Commerce and science students gave more importance to values than arts students. Commerce students showed better school adjustment. Science student achieved better in academic performance. (3) Learning strategies and learning outcomes differ across gender and stream. Surface strategy is used by male students from science more frequently. Female students from commerce and science give more importance to values. (4) For male students, deep strategy is related to high score on values and school adjustment. (5) For female students, Deep strategy is related to values and academic performance. Surface strategy is negatively related to academic performance. Strategic strategy led to a high score on school adjustment. (6) For arts students, deep strategy is related to values and school adjustment, to school adjustment for commerce and to values for science students. (7) The factor analysis of items on the value scale yielded 10 factors. After clubbing 5 factors namely peer-group influence, personal competence, creative values, achievement value and being helpful to others were found meaningful and interpreted.

A Study of Maladjustment of Mentally Exceptional Children and its Effect on their Scholastic Achievement at the Higher Secondary Stage

M.Ed., JMI, ASHOK KUMAR, 1972

The study mainly restricted itself to find out the nature of personality deviations and factors that cause maladjustment among mentally exceptional children. 500 children from 4 different schools were selected for carrying out the study and Cattell's Culture fair Test of General Intelligence. Cattell's 16 P.F. Test, Socio-economic status scale and aggregate scholastic achievement scores were used as tools of the study. It was reported that there were wider prevalence of personality deviations among the mentally exceptional children and in certain cases it may be rather severe.

Perceived Control, Self-esteem and Academic Performance of Orthopaedically Handicapped Adolescent in Integrated and Non-Integrated School Settings

M.Phil., JNU, SUJATA, 1993

The focus of this study has been on the impact of school setting (integration and segregation) and educational level of the orthopaedically handicapped adolescents on their perceived control, self-esteem and academic performance. Two groups of pupils from integrated school (27 from class 5th and 6th and 16 from class 7th and 8th) were taken. Another two groups of pupils from the non-integrated schools (24 from class 5th and 6th and 13 from class 7th and 8th) were selected for comparison. All the 80 students selected from integrated and non-integrated schools for orthopaedically handicapped students situated in Delhi.

The study assumed that orthopaedically handicapped students may have lower perceived control and higher self-esteem in integrated schools than their counterparts in non-integrated schools. Secondly, their perceptions of control may be related to their academic performance. It was also assumed that different background factors may relate differently to their perceived control, self-esteem and academic performance.

The study was taken up to examine the effect of educational level and school setting. To measure explanatory variables (perceived control, self-esteem and academic performance) appropriate scales were traced out. The Kanungo's learned helplessness questionnaire was used to measure perceived control and Coopersmith's self-esteem inventory for self-esteem.

Both the scales were translated into Hindi version using back translation method, since the medium of instruction in all the selected schools was Hindi.

The findings were: (1) In both the school settings orthopaedically handicapped adolescents in educational level II showed significantly higher personal control than the students lower education level. (2) Students in integrated schools showed higher personal control and lower universal control feelings than their counterparts in non-integrated schools. (3) All the factors inherent, personal loss of control and universal loss of control, showed inverse significant correlations with academic performance. (4) Self-esteem found negatively correlated with perceived control and positively with academic performance. (5) Socio-Economic-Status had positive relationship with perceived control, self-esteem and academic performance. (6) Students in both the school settings and educational levels did not differ significantly in their self-esteem and academic performance. (7) 70% of the integrated school students and 65% of the non-integrated school students attribute their outcomes to internal factors, and students at both the educational levels were equally internal. (8) Those having higher personal and universal control attributed their outcomes to internal factors their success than those having lower personal and universal control.

Effectiveness of Token Economy Procedures on the Academic Performance of Students with Learning Disabilities

M.Ed., JMI, SIMRAN DHILLON, 1994

The objectives of the study were identifying children with learning disabilities, identifying problems in the area of spelling, implementation of the token economy programme and evaluating the effectiveness of the token economy procedures. The sample comprised of 5 boys and 3 girls from Modern Schools Vasant Vihar of age group 5 and half to 6 years. They were administered Assessment tools and Intervention tools.

The findings revealed: (1) Accuracy on letters of the English alphabet improved with token economy procedures. (2) The accuracy rate was over 50% for all children thereby strengthening the effectiveness of token economy. (3) Speed in the academic task writing improved with token economy procedures. (4) The speed increase was over 30% for all children, thereby maintaining the effectiveness of token economy. (5) The post intervention scores revealed that the speed and accuracy on task dropped on cessation of token economy.

A Study of Effectiveness of Self-instruction Training on the Academic Performance of Young Bearing Disabled Children

M.Phil., JMI, P.S.S. SEKHER, 1994

The main objectives of the study were to identify children with learning disabilities, identify problem areas in the academic task, implementation of self-instruction training strategy and evaluate the effectiveness of self-instruction training. The sample of the study consisted of 16 children of 5 to 10 years from various SES families taken from St. Columbus School from the primary sections. The tools consisted of the Assessment and Intervention tools.

The major findings revealed: (1) Self-instruction training enhances academic performance of children. (2) Even though the change in arithmetic performance of four children were found not to be significant using chi square but there was a definite increase in their performance during intervention phases thereby supporting the effectiveness of self-instruction training.

Predictive Efficiency of an Inductive-deductive Reasoning test, an Intelligence Test and Middle School Examination Marks to Predict Academic Success in Maths in IX Class

M.Ed., JMI, RADHEY SHAYAM AGGARWAL, 1974

The study envisaged to find out the predictive efficiency of an Inductive-Deductive reasoning test (developed by investigator) and an intelligence test (Raven's Progressive Matrices Test) to predict academic success of middle school examination (class VIII) in mathematics. It was found that middle school examination marks in maths gave best prediction with the midterm marks. Reasoning and intelligence test scores did not predict as good with the criterion as middle school examination marks in mathematics. As far as combination of the predictor is concerned it was found that the middle school marks combined with the reasoning test scores gave better predictors than the middle schools examinations alone.

A Study of Adjustment and Academic Achievement of Class XI Students Involved in Various Co-Curricular Activities

M.Ed., JMI, SEEMA KHAN, 1989-90

Mainly the study concentrated on examining the extent of participation of students in co-curricular activities, identifying the least and most popular co-curricular activities among students and the difference in academic achievement and adjustment of participants and non-participants of co-curricular activities.

The study designed to analyse the relationship (if any) between the academic achievement and adjustment of participants and non-participants in co-curricular activities revealed that there was no general trend of liking of a particular type of activity between those students who participated in maximum activities (80%) as compared to those who took part in fewer activities.

A Study of Factors Associated with Problem solving Ability in Physics

M.Ed., C.I.E., D.U., V.R. SOMAN, 1990

The study centred around intelligence, achievement, achievement in mathematics, physics, reading comprehension and problem-solving strategies. It envisages following objectives: (1) to study the relationship of problem-solving ability in physics to intelligence as measured by scores in Advanced Progressive Matrices, (2) to develop a programme to enhance problem solving ability, (3) to study the effect of this programme.

The sample comprised of 32 students of class XI (Science) of Kerala Education Society Senior Secondary School, New Delhi of average age of 16 years were selected. The study proceeded mainly with administration of a pre-test in physics numericals and progressive matrices to all students. On the basis of obtained scores the students were divided into experimental and control groups. On the basis of post test after teaching through different methods, their ability to solve problems in physics were explored. A questionnaire was developed by the investigator to study the factors.

On the basis of analysis, following major findings emerged: (1) There is an almost significant positive correlation between Raven's test score and problem-solving ability in physics. There is a low positive correlation between achievement in mathematics and problem-solving ability in physics. (3) There is moderate positive correlation between achievement in physics and problem-solving ability in physics. (4) There is negligible correlation between reading comprehension skill and problem solving ability in physics. (5) The programme designed by the investigator produced a substantial gain in score in problem solving in the experimental group. In the number of students scoring more than 50% in problem-solving the experimental group showed an improvement while the control group remained static.

A Study of Achievement Motivation in Relation to Personality Dimension (Extroversion-Introversion) and Scholastic Achievement Among the High School Pupils

M.Ed., C.I.E., D.U., AMARJEET KAUR, 1986

The main objective of the study was (1) to find out the distribution of achievement motivation items among the students; (2) to find out the distribution of personality traits like extroversion and introversion; (3) to find out the distribution of how variables like extroversion, introversion are related or influence n-achievement and (4) to find out the distribution of the Pearson correlation among the variables like achievement motivation, extroversion-introversion, scholastic achievement.

The study was confined to 392 pupils studying in XI and XII class from six higher secondary schools from urban area of Delhi.

They were administered the Mukherjee's Sentence Completion test and Maudsley Personality Inventory.

The major findings were: (1) The v-Ach (HS) score in the case of girls is higher than that of boys. (2) The v-Ach (FF) score is higher in the case of boys than in the case of girls. (3) The

Extroversion-introversion score is higher in the case of boys, than that of girls. (4) The Extroversion-introversion score and v-Ach (HS) score are related to a high degree than Extroversion-introversion and v-Ach (FF) score. (5) The extreme groups on the Extroversion-introversion scale differ on n-Ach (HS) and n- Ach (FF) score significantly, (6) Scholastic achievement score is higher for girls than that of boys. (7) The v-Ach (HS) score and scholastic achievement score are positively correlated. (8) The v-Ach (FF) score and scholastic achievement score are negatively correlated.

Some Correlates of Underachievement in Mathematics

M.Ed, CJ.E,, D.U., JYOTI SHARMA, 1995

The objectives of the study were to (1) explore the concept of underachievement in mathematics, (2) identify problem-solving strategies in mathematics, (3) development of a test to identify underachievers in mathematics, (4) explore errors in problem-solving strategies used by underachievers, (5) explore the attitude of underachievers towards mathematics, interest in mathematics among underachievers and academic self-concept of mathematics underachievers and (6) build up a theoretical model depicting underachievement in mathematics.

In order to conduct the pilot study, ten students of Class IXth were taken up which was later extended to 36 from one school and 60 from other. Groups of underachievers were formed by grouping students who secured marks ranging from 40% less in mathematics and more than 60% based on the teacher evaluation of their performance in mathematics.

The major findings as reported in the study were: (1) Underachievers have no sound knowledge of basic skills and lack of proper understanding of mathematical concepts. (2) Negative attitude towards Mathematics — Most underachievers score low in mathematics because they had negative attitude. (3) Mathematics concepts need proper logical thinking with a sound knowledge of basic concepts students found difficult to understand. (4) Some students suffer from Attential Sequential Dyscalculia. Number of such students is very low (only 5 found in this study). These students sometimes skip the steps or sometimes forget to complete the question — ignored by signs of addition, substruction etc.

A Comparative Study of Some Factors Responsible for High and Low Achievements

M.Ed., C.I.E., D.U., SH1VE KUMAR MUNJAL, 1980

The study mainly was carried out to know the effect of anxiety on academic achievement and the difference in the anxiety and extroversion of high and low achievers in chemistry. Dutt's Personality Inventory and Mausley Personnel Inventory were used as tools in the study on 60 low and high achievers (30+30) from four schools. The study reported that high achievers are significantly lower in anxiety as compared to low achievers. High achievers in Chemistry do not differ significantly from low achievers on Extroversion.

A Study of Academic Achievement in Relation to Adjustment and Achievement Motivation

M.Ed., C.I.E., D.U., 1984

The main objectives of the study were to find out the relationship between academic achievement and achievement motivation, between academic achievement and adjustment in its varied context such as home, society, emotional hostility, masculanity and femineity. The sample consisted of 220 Ninth class boys from two government schools. The tools used in the study were marks obtained by the boys in final examinations, Projective tests, Thematic Apperception Test, Bell's Adjustment Inventory and Prayag Mahta's Achievement Inventory. The major findings of the study revealed that students who had good home adjustment were adjusted well in other areas as well like health, social and emotional adjustment. Children with good adjustment got high percentage of marks or good academic achievement led to better adjustment in all areas. Children with good adjustment and high percentage gave more achievement related responses. Students who gave more achievement related responses were found to be better adjusted than children who gave more task related and unrelated response.

A Study of Measured Creativity and Scholastic Achievement Among High and Low Intelligence Group at the Higher Secondary Stage

M.Ed., JMI, SURESH C. AHUJA, 1973

The study attempted to measure the creativity and scholastic achievement of high and low group of students by selecting a sample of 500 Class XI students from 3 non-government higher secondary schools for boys and one government higher secondary school. The tools used were Cattell's Group Test of Mental Ability, designed by R.B. Cattell and A.K.S. Cattell and High School Personality Questionnaire. The findings revealed that those having low intelligence test score may have moderately fair creative output.

A Comparative Study of Reading Attainment Across Various Types of Schools in Delhi

M.Ed., C.I.E., D.U., 1985

The primary objectives of the study were to find out the differences if any between student samples drawn from two schools in terms of overall Reading Attainment and in terms of factual, interpretive and evaluative comprehension and the number of references made to the given passage, to study and assess to what extent the Language Programme in the sample schools is geared towards the development of higher order reading skills.

R.B. Cattell's Scale III, Form A Culture Fair test and a group of three reading comprehension tests were administered on a sample of 10 students of Grade XI that out of these 10 students, 5 were from the privately run English medium public school and the remaining five were from a state-run English medium school.

❑❑❑

CURRICULUM AND INSTRUCTIONAL MATERIAL

An Investigation into the Working of Vocational Stream in Delhi Schools

M.Ed., C.I.E., D.U., NARESH KUMAR SALIVAN, 1985

The objectives of the study were to study the problems and reactions of the teachers who conducted these courses, to study the problems and reactions of the students who offered these courses, to follow up the present educational and vocational courses of the students who had offered these courses and to study the reactions of the parents whose wards offered these courses.

The sample of the study constituted 163 students pursuing different vocational courses from different schools in Delhi. The parents of all these students more approached. 30 teachers teaching vocational courses in different schools of Delhi were also taken up as part of the sample.

Threesetsofquestionnairesforstudents,teachersandparents were administered. The major findings of the study revealed: (1) Majority of students opted for vocational courses either of their own will or the teacher played an important role in encouraging students to choose their vocational courses. (2) All students felt teachers to be well qualified and competent. (3) Majority of students enjoyed the courses and would like their brothers and sisters to opt for vocational courses. (4) 75% of vocational students joined academic stream after completing higher secondary school. 25% went for job and other vocational courses. (5) Majority of teachers have not been given regular appointment which is bound to decrease effectiveness of these courses. (6) 50% teachers did not feel any need for preparation to teach these courses. The rest preferred to use textbooks and lesson plans. (7) Majority of teacher enjoyed teaching vocation courses. They found maturity level of students satisfactory. (8) Majority of parents did not take any initiative to advice their wards to offer vocational courses. (9) Around 75% of parents checked the progress of their wards regularly. (10) Majority of parents felt satisfied into the teaching of these courses.

An Investigation into the Problems Hampering in Implementation of Physical Education Programmes in M.C.D. Primary Schools of South Zone in N.C.T. of Delhi

SCERT, New Delhi, N.K. GHAI

The objectives of the study were to assess the present status of physical Education in M.C.D. Primary schools in South Zone in N.C.T. of Delhi, to ascertain the problems and difficulties faced by Headmasters/Headmistresses in implementation of physical education programmes in their schools and to suggest strategies for proper implementation of physical education programmes in M.C.D. Primary schools.

In order to gather data for the Investigation, a questionnaire was developed and interviews conducted. The sample comprised of 80 M.C.D. Schools selected on a random basis.

The major finding as highlighted in the study were: (1) There is an acute shortage of funds in organising physical Education programmes in the schools. (2) There is no qualified physical Education teachers in 78% schools. (3) There is shortage of infrastructural facilities in organising physical Education programmes. (4) In 22% schools, where qualified physical education teachers are appointed, they have been given work to teach other subjects too because of shortage of other staff in the school. (5) The pupil fund collected from the students in the school cannot be utilised as per need of physical Education activities for the students due to cumbersome administration procedures. (6) The decision taken by civil work department M.C.D. to convert play field of the school into brick flooring (kharanja), as per data collected 43% of schools have already converted into the same, this is dangerous for students to play on such flooring. (7) As per the scheme of operation black board where the minimum facilities for any school is given, which includes a physical education kit also. But as per data 52.5% schools do not have O.P. kit in physical education. (8) The students are deprived of having any experience of playing those games which involves lot of space, money and time. Therefore these students have limitation to play the games and have no choice according to their interest. (9) The in-service teachers training in physical education is not given to all the physical education teachers as well as to those assistant teachers given additional responsibility of physical education in the school. (10) There is no provision to take the services of any coach or expert to train students in particular physical education activities, since one person cannot be expert in all the areas of physical education.

There is no encouragement from the parents for promotion of their children towards games and sports. (12) There is no proper guidelines provided by the authorities to the schools for organisation and implementation of physical education programmes in the schools. (13) The encouragement from the higher authorities for organisation and promotion of physical education activities in the schools is lacking. (14) The pupil fund is not fully utilised for the welfare of the students for which it is really meant. (15) The Indoor games material is available in the schools but the member is very little. (16) There is no transport facility if the students have to go to take part in the competitions.

The Changing Concept of 'Productive Work' in School Education

M.Ed., JMI, FORHAT JOHAN, 1988

The objectives of the investigation were to study the concept of 'productive work' in school education since independence, factors contributing to the varying status and meaning given to 'productive work' during the last forty years, find out the views of teachers regarding 'productive work' (S.U.P.W.) as practised now and the views of pupils regarding 'productive work' (S.U.P.W.) as practised now. The sample was drawn from 4 government schools of class IX to find the views of pupils and 7 government schools for the teachers' view. 140 pupils and 19 teachers were selected as sample. Two proforma were prepared and administered on selected sample.

The findings of the study revealed: (1) Teachers presented their strongly favourable attitudes towards S.U.P.W. (2) It was only in one government school that the 'Productive Work' was chosen standard-wise, *e.g.* in VI class gardening, in VII class candle making and in VIII block painting, batik, meal planning etc. and chalk making for IX, Food preservation for XI and XII. (3) Generally S.U.P.W. was not practised as desired in our scheme of education. There is no proper time-table for it. Even the teachers are not professional.

A Study of the Mathematics Textbook of Grade-five and its Analysis in the Experiential Context of the Learner

M.Ed., C.I.E., D.U.

The objectives of the study were: to understand the teacher's perception of Mathematics textbook in experiential context of the learner, to understand the teachers use of Mathematics textbook in the experiential context of the learner, to arrive at suggestions for the improvement of the mathematics textbook and its use.

The study focussed on the textbook analysis of Grade- Five in the experiential context of the learner. Attempts were made to device situations that elicit open-ended response by the teachers to some already structured questions for interview. The researcher developed his own tools after discussing with the supervisor and some experts in education. Data was mainly collected through discussion and personal interviews with the mathematics teachers of primary classes. The sample for the study consisted of 15 teachers from Government Schools, where only N.C.E.R.T Textbooks are being implemented.

The major findings of the study were: (1) The concepts in textbook were in consonance with the cognitive development of the pupils. (2) The presentation of concept was logical in nature, making a sequence from concrete to abstract. (3) The textbook gives scope for concrete experiences and self-effort by pupils. The teachers help them with one or two activities examples and students follow them. (4) The concepts given are according to the experience of the learner. But speed-distance-time, averages have to be modified a little in introduction. (5) The textbook material is related to the day-to-day life of the pupils. The concepts are introduced and are applied taking examples/activities from general experience. Even the textbook material is quite sufficient in building upon the experiences of the learner. Teachers can do other activities, besides given in the textbook. But because of limited time the teacher is confined to textbook only. (6) To a great extent the teachers are dependent on the textbook for selection of problem teaching a topic as it helps in introducing new concepts by providing suitable learning experiences. (7) The objectives of teaching mathematics at Grade-Five according to different units are mentioned specifically at the end of the book.

A Study of Epistemological Implications of Some Metaphysical Concepts in Modern Physics

M.Ed., C.I.E., D.U., PREM SINGH BUTH, 1988

The objectives of the study were: (1) To identify the concepts of modem physics which raise philosophical issues. (2) To analyse the metaphysical concepts raised by modern physics. (3) To study the epistemological implications of these metaphysical concepts. (4) To highlight their close bearing on teaching of physics at senior secondary level.

A descriptive-cum-analytical method to analyse logically the concepts of modem physics was used. The study makes use of deductive reasoning to arrive at generalisations, inferences and implications.

The major findings of the study were: (1) Existing curriculum at 10+2 level which incorporates new concepts of physics shows faults and fractures and cementing of it is imperative. A serious thought is to be given to the reconstruction of physics curriculum at 10+2 stage. (2) It does not attract students. The curriculum has to be redesigned in the manner that it motivates them. Piecemeal handling of concepts serves no purpose.

A Study of Curriculum in Home Science at +2 Level of Schooling

M.Ed., C.I.E., D.U., MANJULA KHANNA, 1985

The objectives of the study were: (1) To decide the aims of teaching Home-Science in consultations with teachers. (2) Examine the extent to which existing curriculum of Home Science meets the objective. (3) Find out teachers' opinion regarding syllabus, method of teaching, laboratory conditions, regarding books, evaluation procedures of Home Science curriculum in relation to objective. (4) Collect and analyse the suggestions for improving the curriculum of Home Science at senior secondary stage.

This study was conducting on 40 teachers from different Government Senior Secondary Schools. The study used both secondary as well as primary sources for collection of information. Secondary sources consisted of draft syllabus of the +2 stage. The primary source was the questionnaire constructed for the purpose by the investigator.

Major findings of the study highlight: (1) Teachers are ignorant of written statements of aims in the course in Home Science. They need assistance and even instruction in formulating and using aims and objectives. (2) The syllabus needs to be restructured in such a way that other subject areas of Home Science like child development, clothing and textiles be included in the syllabus in addition to food and nutrition and home management. (3) The teaching methods need to be modified so that it is made more interesting by resorting more towards discussion, field trips than the usual lecture method. (4) The textbooks be redesigned by involving teachers so that they may know the area depth and quality of the content. Illustrations, logical sequencing, easy language should be given special place. (5) 40% of teachers find laboratory conditions poor. 72.5% have laboratory assistants whereas 37.5% have other teachers for help in the laboratory. There is lack of sanitary facilities, electricity, water supply, exhaust fans and disposal. The funds allocated for laboratories are extremely less. In majority of cases, purchase was made by themselves. (6) The most commonly used technique of evaluation is test followed by periodical tests. 65% of teachers give short answer and 37.5% objective type. In case of periodical test, they give 67.5% short answer type and 32.5% essay type. (7) The system of assessment should be continuous one. Credit should be given for regularity.

A Critical Study of the Existing Curriculum in Home Science at the Plus two Stage in Delhi Schools

M.Ed., C.I.E., D.U., RITU VERMA, 1983

The objectives of the study were: (1) To study the extent of job satisfaction among home science teachers. (2) To conduct a comparative study of job satisfaction between secondary and senior secondary school home science teachers. (3) To analyse the various factors that bring about the element of dissatisfaction among home science teachers. (4) To study the difference in job satisfaction amongst teachers working in rural and urban schools. (5) To examine the extent to which the existing curriculum of Home Science meets the objectives of teaching Home Science at the plus two stage. (6) To find out the teachers' opinion regarding the aspects of syllabus, methods of teaching, laboratory conditions, textbooks and the evaluation procedures of home science curriculum at the senior secondary stage and (7) To suggest ways and means for improving teaching and learning of Home Science at the Senior Secondary stage.

The sample of the study comprises of 114 teachers drawn from government and private schools from rural and urban areas of Delhi. It is a normative study. The tools used in the study was constructed by the investigator to study the job satisfaction among teachers.

The major findings of the study show: (1) The present curriculum of Home Science at the plus two stage meets the objectives of Home Science only to a limited extent. (2) To meet the objectives of Home Science at the plus two stage, changes are required in the laboratory conditions, syllabus and textbooks of the subject. (3) The syllabus of Home Science at the plus two stage is not adequate. (4) Other subject areas of Home Science, like Child Development and Clothing and Textiles, should be included in the syllabus in addition to the two subject areas, namely, Food and Nutrition and Home Management which are being taught presently. (5) Some of the units in the Part A, namely, Foods and Nutrition of the syllabus are repeated. (6) The most commonly used methods of teaching in the case of the selected sample were a combination of 'Lecture and Dictation Notes' and 'Dictating Notes and Question and, Answer'. (7) There is no prescribed textbook for Home Science at the plus two stage. (8) The available books of Home Science for the plus two stage are not adequate. (9) The faulty aspects of the textbooks are 'lack of depth in the content' and 'difficult language'. (10) The laboratory condition is poor. (11) The problems faced by most of the teachers regarding home science laboratories are lack of continuous water supply, small size of the laboratory, inadequate work centres and lack of funds. (12) The evaluation procedure adopted by most of the teachers are a combination of monthly/weekly test and the terminal examination.

A Study of the Differential Selection Criterion of Work-experience Items Adopted by the Different Categories of Students of Delhi Schools (Secondary Classes)

M.Ed., C.I.E., D.U., ASHOK KUMAR CHAWLA, 1982

The study has been directed towards determining and analysing the differential selection criteria of Work Experience items adopted by various types of students studying in some of the schools in Delhi based on a survey of 254 students belonging to eleven different schools. The sample of students represent a wide cross-section of society. This is ensured by including in sample schools catering to different social groups like working class, business community, rural population etc. A detailed questionnaire was drawn, tested, revised and canvassed for correction of the basic information. In addition, discussions were held with the principals of schools and some of the students and their parents.

The major findings of the study revealed: (1) The choice of work experience items for the student is primarily a school-specific choice. None of the schools offer all the 49 items of work experience. The students have to choose from the items of work experience offered by their respective schools. (2) Some of the schools have a very limited choice resulting in the concentration of students in the items offered by the school. For instance, tailoring and embroidery and meal-planning preparation and preservation are the predominant choice offered by some students because of the availability of this item alone in their school. (3) The list of work experience items offered by any school is further conditioned by the nature of the school and the type of families that it is catering to the work experience items offered in government schools in the rural areas and urban areas. Similarly, public schools, model schools, schools in government colonies, etc., have such specific lists which probably reflect the choice of the school administration more than the choice of the students. (4) The students' personal traits like their interest in extra-curricular activities, vocational plan, and employment prospects are quite often more influential in determining the choice of work experience item than factors like family background or financial constraints. (5) Parents education seem to influence the choice of the work experience items through the choice of school. Rich parents tend to send their children to public schools which offer a larger variety of work experience items than the other schools. However, the direct influence of parents' education on the choice of work experience items cannot be denied. (6) The parents' education and their income are mainly influencing the choice of work experience items only indirectly. (7) There appears to be some significant difference between rural-based students and the urban students. This again may be largely due to the difference in the school curricular with respect to work experience items. (8) The concentration observed in some of the work experience items is not necessarily due to deliberate choice made by the students but is a consequence of the list offered by the schools in which they are studying. (9) Students' personality factors, their vocational plans and employment opportunities influence their choice of work experience items more than the other factors like family backgrounds, and financial conditions. Thus, within the limited range of choice made available by their schools the students make a conscious choice giving more weightage to the future than the background. (10) Even within the same school the actual work experience item that a student is learning, is not necessarily his first preference. In one of the schools the number of students who offered electronics far exceeded the size of a section to which this work experience item could be made available. The number was curtailed by such an academic criteria like marks obtained in science subjects, etc. (11) The students have a clear plan of future vocations and their work experience items. They have to link these plans and choose work experience items which are related to the future vocations. (12) Some of the items of work experience remain sex-based items. Girls have preferred items like tailoring and embroidery and meal-planning preparation and preservation more than the other items available in the schools. (13) There does not appear to be a very clear association between the choice of extra-curricular activities and the choice of work experience items. Majority of the students have selected sports as their favourite extra-curricular activity. All the students are distributed almost evenly amongst the different work experience items. (14) Some schools are providing vocational guidance which in turn influences the choice of work experience item. (15) Some of the subsidiary conclusions that emerge from the above conclusions are that the school administration obviously finds it difficult to organize training in all the items of work experience. The problem of timetable adjustment, the engaging of work experience teachers for these items is so complicated that unless there are sufficiently popular and full of utility, introduction of these in a school becomes uneconomical. Even where the schools are willing to enhance their list of available items they are not able to get suitably trained teachers for this purpose.

Evaluation of Present Environmental Studies (Science) Syllabus

M.Ed., C.I.E., D.U., JYOTI JYOTSNA, 1993

The objectives framed for the study were to identify the difficult concepts introduced to the students of III, IV, V standard, the difficult concepts recognized by the teachers teaching EVS to these classes and to compare and finalise the list of difficult concepts. The sample was drawn from students response of two schools of Delhi, one public having English as medium of Instruction and the other one the MCD school having Hindi as medium of Instruction. 20 students were selected for the purpose. Their opinions, interviews and performance test. The major finding as revealed in the study was that the concepts based upon everyday life and repeated in lower grades are easily comprehended by students. But the concepts either abstract or complex or lengthy or need a previous base to be understood have been regarded as difficult concepts.

Effectiveness of Concept Mapping in Science Education

M.Ed., C.I.E., D.U., VANDANA GUPTA, 1995

The study intended to develop concept maps of some topics in the chemistry syllabus of class IX and to examine the relative effectiveness of teaching through concept mapping and traditional method. 76 students of class IXth were taken up as sample from one senior secondary school, formed into two equivalent groups, taught through two approaches, one using the concept maps and the other which does not envisage the use of concept maps. An achievement test was administered to find the difference. It was found that although science teachers should make use of concept mapping method while teaching concepts of science but traditional method is equally effective.

Towards Bridging the Curricular Gap Between the Secondary School Science and Mathematics and Senior Secondary Physics Curriculum

M.Ed., C.I.E., D.U., BYOMKESH MISHRA, 1995

The objectives of the study were to obtain the opinion of the teachers regarding the overall adequacy of physics curriculum for +2 level, to find out the reaction of teachers to the presentation and co-ordination of subject matter, to find out the content area where the teachers find themselves not adequate, to decide the adequacy of physics curriculum in consultations with experts and teachers, to find out to what extent aims and objectives are being achieved, to find out the teachers point of view regarding the existing curriculum in physics (theory only) at +2 level with reference to secondary level science curriculum, to find out the students points of view regarding the existing curriculum in physics (theory only) at +2 level, to find out the difficulties faced by students in coping the +2 level curriculum (specific area of difficulty), to take suggestion of teachers and expert for the changes in curriculum, to analyse the performance of students on the curricular objectives of class XI Physics with a view to bringing out the areas of difficulty, to analyse the physics portion of curriculum of grade XI with a view to compare with secondary level physics, to discover to what extent, there is a gap between +2 level physics and secondary level physics and to suggest improvement in curriculum.

The sample comprised of XI Class students from nine public schools, 10 selected for individual interview, 10 for group discussion and 10 for the interview from nearby, schools. Course material for IX, X and XI grade and an analysis of students' response in examinations were used as tools for the study. The study was based on three components, namely opinion survey, content analysis of the curriculum for XI Standard Physics and analysis of students response in Examination. The three components are quite distinct in nature.

The overall results reveal that there is a link between X and IX Class Physics but X Class Science has no relation with XI

Class Physics. There are also some topics of higher abstraction level which are difficult to the students not because of the level but for the missing link. There is also a very high level of abstraction.

Development of Teaching Material of a unit of Taxonomic Botany for +2 Stage and Comparing its Effectiveness with the Traditional Methods

M.Ed., C.I.E., D.U., VARINDER MOHAN, 1980

The study was conducted by forming two equivalent groups of a class and given different treatments by teaching them a unit of taxonomic botany through traditional and programmed methods. It came into view that the programmed group, had made a significant progress in learning of the unit under investigation. It was observed that teaching through programmed learning could bring better results in comparison to the teaching through traditional classroom methods. Programmed learning may not be superior to ordinary teaching methods but it definitely adds a tool to the professional armoury of the educational instructors.

A Critical Appraisal of the New Syllabus in Chemistry at +2 Level

M.Ed., C.I.E., D.U., VIJAY PAL SINGH, 1992

The objectives of the study were to evaluate the present chemistry syllabus at +2 level in terms of its systematic progression from secondary IX and X level, in terms of relevance of new syllabus for the vocation studies take printing, dying and photo taking, in terms of suitability of the syllabus for pursuing professional courses like Engineering, Medical etc., to find out the problems faced by students and teachers dealing with new syllabus and to suggest measures for improvement of present form of syllabus at both levels based on the reaction of teachers and students.

Questionnaires for students and teachers were developed and administered on 76 students of classes XI and XII and 60 PGTs in chemistry from government, aided, private and Kendriya Vidyalayas.

The major findings of the study revealed that at the time of entry in XI class, the students did not have adequate knowledge of basic concepts in chemistry. There existed large communication gaps in the chemistry content at secondary and senior secondary stage. Syllabus did not provide relevant material useful for vocational courses like photography, ceramics and paintings etc. but was quite appropriate for developing manipulative and experimental skills in the students necessary for investigation of materials in their own. There was a need for regular and intensive in-service teachers of chemistry teachers as they found difficulty in teaching certain topics.

A Status Study of the Implementation of Work Experience Programme at Primary Level in District North, Delhi

SCERT, New Delhi, RITU KALANI, 1994

The objective of the study was to study the present position of the subject of Work Experience in Municipal Corporation Schools of North District, Delhi. 'Present position' includes time allocation, funding aspect, types of work experience activities conducted, suggested work experience syllabus followed, methods of planning and organisation, evaluation; to find out whether Work Experience is considered as an essential subject at primary level; to study the opinion of parents, teachers and students regarding teaching and learning of the subject 'Work Experience'; and to suggest measures for better implementation of Work Experience at primary level.

The study was conducted on 83 Municipal Corporation Primary Schools. Data was collected by administering questionnaires and interview schedules to the primary teachers as well as the heads of the schools respectively in Hindi language.

The picture that came to light was as follows: (1) The primary teachers are suitably qualified but it was found that nearly half of the teachers had not undergone any type of In-service training in the field of Work Experience. (2) The subject of Work Experience was not an essential part of the school curriculum at the primary level. It has been observed that 'Art' and 'Sewing' are two subjects in option carrying 100 marks. In some schools work experience activities are being conducted under the subject 'Art' or the subject 'Sewing' but subject of Work Experience does not enjoy the status of the compulsory subject and find no place in the Report Card. (3) A Syllabus Guidelines dated August, 1981 has been provided in some of the primary schools while others are following their own syllabus in the subject of 'Work Experience'. 4. Time allocation for Work Experience shows a great deal of deviation from that suggested by the 'National Curriculum for Elementary and Secondary Education — A Framework' (1988) published by N.C.E.R.T. It varies from school to school. In majority of the schools, two periods per week are allocated to this subject, whereas it should be 20% of the total instructional time *i.e.* at least 8 (eight) periods per week. (5) Since Work Experience does not enjoy the status of a compulsory subject so its planning is not done in the proper perspective by all schools at par with other subjects. (6) At primary stage of education emphasis be laid on the development of good health, environmental sanitation, creativity and beautification practices through work experience activities. It is observed that amongst the types of activities conducted at the primary level paperwork was the most popular activity. Sewing, knitting, embroidery and clay modelling were some other popular activities. (7) As the subject of 'Work Experience' does not figure in the Report Card, evaluation in most of the schools, is not being considered seriously. It is in a small percentage of schools that 'Work Experience' as an essential subject in all primary schools is recognised.

A Study on Work Experience Activities in the Primary/ Elementary NDMC Schools

SCERT, New Delhi, MADHULIKA S. PATEL and PAWAN SUDHIR, 1994

The main objective of the study was to evolve an understanding about imparting education to the children and also to know about the status of W.E. being imparted to children in the schools.

A questionnaire was developed for the purpose. The data was obtained from 80 teachers of 45 schools out of 57 schools of NDMC at primary/elementary level.

The major findings of the study were: (1) The self-assessment by teachers reveal that Mini Tools kit is used by 36 per cent teachers only. The self-assessment or by peers indicate that the science kit is used by 42 per cent of teachers. (2) 29 per cent of teachers are trained in the use of the kit, the per cent of teachers using these kits is significantly higher than the percentage of teachers trained. Teachers have also indicated that there is a need for fresh training or retraining of teachers in the use of kit. This will update their knowledge and skill in this regard. Since the number of teachers using the kits is significantly higher than the teachers trained in the use of this kit, it may be concluded that the teachers are favourably inclined towards the use of this kit in the classroom. The availability of kit and training of teachers appear to be important for the popularization of kit in schools. (3) The obstacle/hindrances as visualised by the teachers in the use of the kit are related to non-availability of kit (67 per cent), discouragement by peers (39 per cent), inadequate competence (58 per cent), inadequate availability of time (53 per cent), improver maintenance (50 per cent), unavailability of support services (47 per cent). (4) The work experience activities are conducted in all the primary and elementary NDMC schools included in this study. The activities for imparting work experience to the children carried out in schools include paper making (Greeting Cards), paper flowers, charts clothe printing clay modelling, chalk making, tree plantation, drawing, book binding, use of waste material, knitting, cleanliness, doll making, rhymes and folder making etc. The periods allocated per week for the work experience activities in these schools are not uniform. It may be noted that in 36 per cent of the schools no allocation of periods has been made in the timetable and the organization of Work Experience activities is solely dependent on the personal initiative of the concerned teachers. In 8 per cent of the schools two periods per week are available for the Work Experience activities. There are two per cent of the schools with 4 periods per week for Work Experience activities and five per cent of the schools provide 5 periods per week for these activities. It appears that no definite guidelines exist about the amount of periods/time per week to be allocated for the work experience activities in the schools. (5) 65 per cent of the teachers in the schools feel that the available time is insufficient or less, the remaining 35 per cent feel that the time is sufficient. Since 49 percent of the schools have two periods per week for Work Experience activities and 36 per cent of the schools have no allocation of time for these activities, it may be inferred that in schools having the allocation of the periods, the teachers have mixed views about the sufficiency or the insufficiency of the available time. (6) More than 90 per cent of teachers desire to have systematic training in various WE related activities. (7) The availability of budgetary support for the work experience related activities in the schools is far from satisfactory. While 22 per cent of the teachers have opined that they receive funds for WE activities, the remaining 78 per cent have opined that the support for such activities is not available in the schools. In almost all (99 per cent) the schools the students bring material from their homes for these activities. (8) The schools also do not have uniformity in respect of the scheduling of activities. While 5 per cent of the schools prepare the calendar of their activities, the other 95 per cent do not prepare the activity calendar.

An Investigation into the Problems of Teaching New Mathematics in Middle Classes Under UNESCO Scheme in Higher Secondary Schools of Delhi

M.Ed., JMI, B.S. AHUJA, 1969-70

The main objective of the study was to know the difficulties that the teachers face in teaching and students in learning new mathematics in class VII under UNESCO experimental science project in higher secondary schools of Delhi. The sample consisted of teachers who were teaching new mathematics to VII grade in all the 30 experimental schools. A Questionnaire was used for both Teachers and students separately.

The findings of the study revealed introduction of New Mathematics as a part of middle school syllabus was justified because of its advantage over the traditional Mathematics in spite of some difficulties experienced both by the teachers and students of experimental schools in teaching/learning programmes of New Mathematics.

Aspects of Creativity in Methodology of Teaching English

M.Ed., JMI, B.V.V. LATHA, 1995

The main objective of the study was to critically examine the creative element in the prescribed materials, the methods and practice adopted by the teacher for fostering creativity in English language learning and the institutional arrangement for fostering creativity. The descriptive survey method was used in studying ten government schools and Class VIII was taken up for study. A questionnaire was administered. The major findings revealed: (1) 90% of public school teachers were post graduate with training, 70% of government-aided school teachers were post graduate with training, 40% of government school teachers were post graduate with training. Public school policy of recruiting highly qualified staff is bound to pay them dividend. (2) 50% of public school teachers possess 10 or more years of experience, corresponding figures for government aided schools at government schools are 40% and 80% respectively. (3) 70% of public school had undergone language training while 50% and 30% of Government aided and government school teachers had in-service training. (4) Public school teachers were more prepared to handle creativity culture in classroom. (5) Most of Government schools followed English Reader while Aided school communicate in English, Oxford University Press. (6) Public schools also prescribed Interact English, Macmillan publication.

A Study of Investigation of Problems in Implementation of Work Experience in the South District of Delhi

Project Report, DEPA, NIEPA, L.P. SINGH, 1990

The tools used in the study questionnaire developed by investigator and Interview of 35 Government and senior secondary schools in urban, semi-urban and rural areas.

The major findings of the study: (1) Most popular elective area in girls' school is meal planning and food preservation and in boys school is commercial art/paintings. (2) Essential (core) area of work experience is neglected by both boys' and girls' school. (3) Girls school in comparison with boys schools are comparatively getting lesser funds but 60% of schools are not getting sufficient funds. Although girl's schools are getting less fund but still they are doing better in work experience programme. Funds are received at the end of the year, because of this purchase of raw material is also delayed, effecting the work experience activities. (4) Insufficient accommodation both in boys and girl's school. (5) Insufficient availability of raw materials and storing capacities of raw material. Products produced during work experience activities also lack facilities for storing them. (6) Lack of qualified staff for elective areas of work experience programme affects the efficient working of. (7) Training of teachers in work experience for various area is required. (8) There is only 51.42% schools having school committee as such for planning the whole year woke experience activities. Only in girls school, they do have these committees. (9) There is proper monitoring of woke experience activities by girls school principal and because of this their programme is better than boys school. Monitoring and evaluation cell is in only 18.75% of boys' schools. (10) Publications and printing material for work experience is also very less available to schools. The related literature only received in the form of guidelines and syllabus from CBSE was in 1989. (11) Co-operation from non-Government agencies is almost nil. Co-operation from local expertise is also nil. If ever any help was taken, this was discontinued later on. (12) It is very interesting that student's attitude towards work experience programme is positive, they only need proper guidance and motivation. (13) Parents are not against this programme. Many of the raw materials of certain activities are costly and hence parents may not be so much inclined towards work experience programme, especially in boys' school. (14) According to teacher responses work experience do develop some occupational skill. (15) The pattern of evaluation procedures is quite variable; but all these schools in the end allot grades in final examination on the nine point scale, which is statistically valid for large set of students. (16) Incentives provided by organising various activities to students in girls school is comparatively better than boys school, but overall it is negligible and hence it affects the motivation of students towards work experience activities. (17) Girls school provide more incentives to poor students than boys school, but overall, all the government schools do provide material help to poor students. (18) The percentage of organising fair is only 26.6%. (19) The pattern of periods per week is different in girls and boys school, but girls schools are getting more periods than boys school. Almost negligible periods per week are given to essential (core) activities. Work Experience periods are being utilised for teaching other subjects. (20) Number of teachers taking two elective areas is 13 out of 35 indicating that school teachers have to teach other subjects of their relevant field, along with work experience subjects and hence there is lack of interest in them for teaching work experience. (21) Methods adopted in doing WE activities is group work. In boys school, this percentage is higher than girls school, indicating that they are more students per teacher. It is may be due to higher number of students per class. Teacher is unable to give due attention to each student. In the process students loses interest in the WE activities.

A Study of Determinants for Successful Implementation of Work Experience Programme in Delhi Schools

Project Report, DEPA, NIEPA, B. TIRKEY, 1995

The study had the objectives of analysing the factors responsible for success of work experience programmes, to know whether location of schools in slums Walled City, Rural, Urban, Semi-urbanised, areas have an influence on the choice of work experience activities in the school. Is there any need in the evaluation system, what modification can be done in providing financial grants to the schools, how work experience activity can be correlated to subject areas. Information was collected from 33 schools. (1) The role of controlling administrative and academic agencies is important for the successful implementation of Work Experience programmes. (2) In-service teacher training is a regular feature and about 500 teachers are given training every year. During 1993-94, in all 469 teachers were provided training. In addition to this 10 study circle meetings for the teachers and 2 one day workshops were arranged for the Principals to provide necessary orientation at six stages. (3) Though the data and thrust areas selected for training are laudable but the training programmes have not succeeded in the areas of providing necessary motivation to teachers evaluation by the teacher and the system of grading, the system of maintaining proper records of the work done by the students and cumulative records of evaluation done by teachers.

Developing and Trying out an ELT Package For Class IX

Project Report, DEPA, NIEPA, SHASHI KOCHAR, 1990

The package was tried in one school with the objective of developing ELT package trying out the package in schools and assessing the effectiveness of the package.

The present study entitled 'Preparation of ELT package for Class IX students' was a systematic, scientific and methodological attempt to evolve relevant and interest based instructional material for students of Class IX. As per opinions obtained the material appeared to be very suitable intended to enrich students and lead to their personal development.

The effectiveness of the material established that any teacher in the field of education can take up the project of developing reading material or material of any type for purpose of research and innovation in the field of education.

Impact of Knowledge of Behavioural Objectives on Achievement in Mathematics Taught Through Programmed Instruction Material

M.Ed., C.I.E., D.U., HARPREED, 1994

The study conducted on 25 students of VIII standard kept the objective of studying the impact of knowledge of behaviours objectives on learning the topic of sets in mathematics and developing a linear programme on the topic of seats. Two schools were selected randomly. Two groups were formed, one was the experimental and the other control. The tools administered were the Intelligence test, Programmed Instructions Material and the Criterion test. The study revealed the difference in the mean performance of learner taught with the knowledge of behavioural objectives and that those learners taught without the knowledge of behavioural objectives.

A Survey of Co-curricular Activities in Learning of Science in South Delhi Schools

M.Ed., JMI, JAMINI GEORGE, 1986

All the twenty schools surveyed in South Delhi had co-curricular activities in science. Although the most popular activity seems to be project making but other activities such as quizzes, debates, essay competitions on science topics also took place at the convenience of the school.

All the schools participated in the annual science exhibitions. Yet the general attitude of the school's administration towards science activities is that of having to do one more job which they have been asked to do by the school establishment. They have not realized the importance of co-curricular activities in the learning of science. This attitude was reflected in the projects the students carried out under their guidance and the responses to questions put to them regarding their project.

There was usually a common fund for all the co-curricular activities in the government schools. Other than that there was no separate fund for co-curricular activities in science and all schools do not have a fixed timing for it in their time-table. By and large all classes from Primary to Secondary participate in these activities. Though participation class wise varies from school to school.

It was found that in all the schools' students were not able to answer questions which were not directly related to their projects. They did not ask questions which could have clarified their understanding of concepts. And one gets the impression that most of their projects were carried out as tasks to be completed rather than as opportunities for further exploration.

In almost all the cases projects did not help students understand concepts they may have come across in their regular science classes. It seems projects work did not motivate students to ask many questions. Everything was taken for granted (reflector was thought to provide a support in the electric radiator whereas its actual purpose is reflection of heat into the room).

There was no attempt to do simple experiments to test their own device and to try to make use of something they may have learnt in science classes (did not measure temperature inside the solar cooker). For most of them learning science was simply gathering a lot of information without really understanding its implications. So the thrill and the excitement of doing science was lost.

It is unfortunate that there is little or no realisation, amongst teachers as well as students of the potential of project work in learning of science and so much time and effort of teachers and students is lost.

An Evaluation of the Hindi Supplementing Readers Prescribed for Secondary Classes VI, VII and VIII in Government Schools of Delhi

M.Ed., C.I.E., D.U., MOONISHWUR LALL CHINTAMUNEE, 1980

The objective of the study was to analyse and evaluate the academic and physical aspects of Gyan Rashmi I, II & III. The present study is related to the evaluation of supplementary readers. A Rating Scale was prepared on the basis of Gyan Rashmi I, II & III and evaluated by 40 teachers selected from government schools.

Effectiveness of Task Analysis Techniques in the Designing of Instructional Units for Teaching English to Class Nine Students

M.Ed., C.I.E., D.U., RODRICK RAJIVE LAL, 1994

The study stresses the point that effective, systematic and scientific planning of instructional units can result in effective instruction. It is an effort to study the effectiveness (in terms of a significant difference of learning outcomes indicated by the difference between the pre-test and post-test (scores) of instructional units designed with the help of Task analysis in teaching English to class 9 students.

The design adopted for the study was that of the single group pre-test part test pre-experimental design. Two criterion tests in the form of pre-test and post-test were used in the study. One opinionnaire after the post-test was administered to measure their attitudes towards the lessons taught in experiment.

The major findings revealed: (1) No significant difference between the pre-treatment and post-treatment achievement scores of the learners as a result of the implementation of instruction units designed with the help of Task Analysis techniques. (2) Instructional Units designed with the help of Task Analysis Techniques help develop a positive attitude among learners towards their lessons.

Evaluation of English Textbooks for Class VIII

M.Ed., C.I.E., D.U., NEEMU BHATIA, 1994

This simple evaluation study compares the five textbooks of English, ER, GR, OE, RIF and EXP for class 8th on the basis of a systematic analysis of the various aspects of content and the physical artefact of the textbook.

The objective of the study was (1) to analyse and compare the content in the textbooks selected for the purpose of study from the point of view of (a) thematic selection & presentation, (b) Vocabulary selection and (c) learning tasks pertaining to comprehension, composition and linguistic structures set out for the learners; (2) To analyse and compare the presentation of illustrations and physical artefacts in the textbooks selected for the study. Various English medium public schools of Delhi were selected for the conduct of the study.

The major findings of the study were: (1) Almost all the text consist of a variety of themes. (2) The organisational pattern in all text levels excepting ER, exemplifies a mixed approach where prose and poetry lessons follow one another. In EXP the content has been organised following a thematic approach which is more systematic and appealing than in the other textbooks. (3) The thematic analysis of the selection of poems too, reveals a wide variety of themes, particularly in EXP. These satisfy all criteria while those in the other four textbooks have been found to be lacking on one count or other. In EXP the presentation is more systematic. It also provides a list of books under 'References' at the end of the each thematic unit. (4) The variety of exercises and the use of dictionary in all the textbooks guide pupils to develop their vocabulary on their own through a variety of sources. Indeed, it is an important aspect as it affects readability and comprehension. (5) In RIF no exercise on linguistic structures has been included while in OE it has been taken care of in the 'Language Book', the analysis of which is, however outside the scope of this study. The list of structures being taught in ER, GR and EXP reveal no consistency, ER consisting of discrete items primarily attempts to teach these through pattern practise, based on sentence frames. This in keeping with the Behaviourist theory according to which habit formation is the way of learning. In GR the rules of grammar as such are not taught but the pupils are 'told' the manner in which to attempt the exercises. EXP deals with language structures thoroughly. Practice in structures has been focused upon in each textbook of the three textbooks, which is very important for second language learning. (6) It is only in RIF that the aim is to 'test' the 'understanding and memory' of pupils. While the emphasis in all other books has been found to be on providing guidelines to understand the text, which is a more desirable approach in context of language learning. OE and EXP focus on 'inferential' questions and ER is concerned primarily with 'direct reference' questions. (7) EXP primarily, and GR to some extent, consist of exercises to develop the creativity of pupils. (8) GR has set its purpose in teaching poetry, as 'appreciation' which is higher than that envisaged by NCERT. The collection of poems too, are lull of poetic imagery. The poems in ER are simple to follow yet meaningless. OE and EXP, particularly, seem to present a more satisfactory collection of poems. (9) The illustrations of GR and RIF have been found to be the best in all respects. While OE is satisfactory, those in EXP though better than ER, have not found to be good enough. (10) RIF has been found to be most satisfactory on the physical artefact and the rate is also not too high. However, a marked distinction in the price of ER and the four textbooks is also noteworthy. ER is priced at Rs. 9/- while the others are three times more expensive. (11) While discussing about the relevance of the title, the title Reading is Fun seems to be a very well chosen one. A need to revise textbooks regularly is felt in the context of textbook being a tool for learning. EXP first published in 1985 has been revised 8 times, while ER has been reprinting its first edition brought out in 1971 over the years. Thus, EXP is quite up to date in choice of contents, language study, while ER is still stuck on to the Sentence pattern and practice drills for teaching the structures of the language. A textbook should also contain guidelines for teaching/learning and these have been found to be most systematically expressed in EXP.

A Critical Review of Integrated Science Textbook (Learning Science Part II) for Class VII (Developed by NCERT)

M.Ed., C.I.E., D.U., VED MITRA ARYA, 1980

The study intends to evaluate the integrated science textbook for Class VII developed by the NCERT.

The study involved 34 Government-aided, NDMC and public schools. It took up 34 teachers, 490 students and 60 parents and administered self-devised questionnaires for teachers, students and parents followed by discussions and personal interviews with teachers at a workshop organised by Directorate of Education, Delhi.

The major findings show: (1) The general planning of textbook is satisfactory. (2) The selection of subject matter is adequate. (3) The book has the provision for developing scientific attitude. (4) The number of useful illustrations included in the textbook are sufficient but each of the illustration needs a thorough review so that only needed portions be focussed. (5) No sufficient time to arrange for demonstration/practical or to correct students work in classrooms. The allotted time for teaching textbook is not in accordance with the philosophy of integrated science programme. (6) The book contains printing mistakes.

Evaluation of the Social Studies Textbook Part-III in Secondary Schools for Class VIII Published by N.C.E.R.T, New Delhi

M.Ed., JMI, ANOKHEY LAL, 1975

The study was carried out with the objective of evaluating the objectives of Geography teachings, subject matter, mode of presentation, language, maps, diagrams, exercises, activities and physical features of the book and develop the criteria for selecting proper geography textbooks specifically for middle classes. A qualitative and quantitative analysis was done and it was revealed that the book was qualitatively good.

Backwardness in Mathematics and Basic Arithmetic Skills

Ph.D., C.I.E., DU., R.C. GUPTA, 1972

The purpose was to provide a standardised tool to the teachers and research workers whereby they would be able to diagnose the weak areas in mathematics. 180 boys and 176 girls were selected for the final study. The important findings were: (1) low achievers in mathematics have poor command, whereas high achievers have good command over basic arithmetic skills; (2) basic arithmetic skills can be quickly and conveniently mastered by the course of self-help in basic arithmetic skills.

An Analysis of the Context of History Textbook Prescribed in Union Territory of Delhi for Classes VI, VII, VIII in the Light of National Integration

M.Ed., JMI, BLAKTI SINGH, 1985-86

The main aim of the study was to analyse the Indian history textbook prescribed for middle classes in Delhi and to find out how far the subject matter included in the textbook is likely to promote the concept of National Integration among students. The findings showed that they were not likely to promote the concept of National Integration.

Evaluation of Physics Textbooks (Part-I) Prescribed for Middle Classes in Schools of Delhi

M.Ed., JMI, KUSUM CHOPRA, 1971-72

The study mainly emphasised on analysing the content of the textbook for some of its aspects *viz.*, subject matter, illustrations and exercises in the light of the objectives of new science curriculum and objectives of new science curriculum and of teaching physics. The study was conducted to appraise the book for its worth in the light of the objectives of the new science curriculum and the principles of textbook preparation recommended by the UNESCO experts. Qualitative and quantitative analysis was carried out. The teachers rated the book qualitatively as 'good' but it was only slightly above "average".

A Critical Study of the Ideational Content in Hindi Textbook of Class VI in Delhi

M.Ed., JMI, GEETA VERMA, 1970

The study mainly concentrated on the kinds of (ideals) values, attitudes and concepts reflected in the textbook, the extent to which ideational content of the book is desirable by its reflection, gradation and presentation in the context of the aims and objectives of education in Indian Society. It was found that the book did provide good and enough material for its ideational context.

A Study of the Contribution of Project Work at the +2 Level in Biology to the Development of Certain Inductive Aspects of Scientific Thinking

M.Ed., C.I.E., D.U., 1983

The objective of the study was to assess the ability of science students of senior secondary classes.

The sample comprising of 94 students were taken from class XII biology group of four public schools in Delhi. All schools selected followed the All India Senior Certificate Examination System. The study is an *ex post facto* study where experimental and controlled groups were formed on the basis of marks obtained in the test of scientific thinking.

The major findings of the study were as follows: (1) Investigatory projects done at the +2 level in biology are not contributing significantly towards the development of scientific thinking in the students of schools under study. (2) The existing methods of conducting and doing project work are not up to the mark. This influences the poor performance of students in the test. (3) The conditions in the school classroom, library, laboratory are not congenial for effective planning and execution of projects. Students and teachers are not satisfied about the conditions under which they have to work and feel strongly that the evaluation is also not proper.

Development of Remedial Course in Mathematics for Raising the Standard of Low-achievers of Grade VI

M.Ed., C.I.E., D.U., AJEET SINGH MALIK, 1995

1. To find out the reasons of deficiencies in the achievement of the course content in the grade VI. 2. To develop a remedial course

for the low-achievers in mathematics at the level of grade VI. 3. To find out the ways and means of communicating the content of remedial course to low-achievers. 4. To study the effect of the material course communicated to the low-achievers.

The main cause of deficiencies in the achievement of the course-content in the grade VI, is the poor command over computational skills, which are learnt at primary level. The analysis of errors made by the students in Brueckner's diagnostic test, shows that 54% students did wrong operation; they multiplied instead of dividing a fraction by another fraction. 54% students were deficient in computational skills. Majority of students were lacking in comprehension of the process of division. 34% students faced difficulty in reducing fractions to lowest terms. 68% students faced cancellation difficulties.

The remedial course improves the performance of the low-achievers, by remedying the defects. The difference between the means of pre-test and post-test scores, is significant at .01 level, which further shows that the group had made significant improvement in mathematics.

Aims and Objective of Teaching Chemistry: A Critical Appraisal

M.Ed., C.I.E., D.U., ANAND MOHAN MISHRA, 1995

The study framed the objectives of deciding the aims and objective of teaching chemistry in consultations with experts and teachers, finding out to what extent these aims are being achieved by teachers and students, finding out the teachers' and students' point of view regarding the existing curriculum in chemistry (theory and practical) at +2 level, finding out the difficulties faced by chemistry student, finding out the working conditions of chemistry teacher and taking suggestion of the teachers towards the future changes in curriculum.

Questionnaire for teachers and students of chemistry, Interviews, draft syllabus at +2 stage were administered on Classes XI and XII students from government, aided and public schools. 25 students of below average, 51 students of average, 24 of above average were selected for the study. Total sample consisted of 100 students. Data collected from secondary sources consisted of reports of NCERT and annual reports of CBSE.

The study identified certain aims and objectives of teaching chemistry as suggested by teachers and experts at +2 level. It also revealed: (1) Majority of students preferred to be taught theory by discussion method than textbook method. (2) Majority of students preferred the combination of project and lab method for practicals than only the routine lab method. (3) Teachers and students feel that curriculum should have objective outlook suited to train students for professional studies and employment potential. (4) Majority of teachers get sufficient charts to make teaching effective but models and other teaching aids are not provided in sufficient numbers. (5) Most of the students feel that their teachers were instrumental on developing their interest in chemistry. They feel that their teacher and teaching methods were able to motivate them in taking interest in subject matter. (6) Most of the students are satisfied with the teaching methods while teachers feel that the teaching methods in theory achieve the aims of teaching chemistry up to an extent of 58.33% and methods of teaching practicals achieve the aim up to an extent of 64.56%.

An Investigation into the Causes of Problems in Teaching Geography in Secondary Classes of Delhi Schools

M.Ed., C.I.E., D.U., SHRIKRISHANA CHANDREPAL SHARMA, 1982

The specific objectives of the study were to find out the causes of basic problems of teaching Geography *e.g.*, lack of qualified teachers, teaching aids and suitable textbooks, to find out the number of teachers adequately qualified to teach Geography at secondary level, to investigate the number and types of courses available for teachers and their utilisation for adding to their qualification and to suggest measures to solve the problems of Geography teachers in Delhi.

A sample of 50 boys and 65 girls from 120 schools was drawn. All kinds of schools — government, aided, unaided were taken up from rural and urban areas of Delhi. The questionnaire developed by the investigator was administered on the selected sample.

The main findings and conclusions as reported by the study were: (1) The Geography teachers were poorly qualified. Only 28% teachers fulfil the eligibility conditions of minimum requirement *viz.*, having Geography as one of the subjects at bachelor's degree level. (2) One out of every four teachers were found to be unqualified to teach Geography in Secondary classes. They devote more attention to teach History or Civics, which are counterparts of Geography under the social science paper. Thus they create disinterest among students towards Geography. (3) Only 23% teachers are professionally equipped to teach Geography to IX and X classes as remaining 77% did not have Geography as one of the teaching subject at B.Ed. or B.T. training. (4) Institutions like NCERT and S.I.E. etc. are conducting sufficient number of orientation courses and seminars to equip the teachers to meet the challenges of this subject, 81% Geography teachers have attended such courses. (5) Teachers generally do not take initiative to hold and attend seminars/lectures by experts at inter school level. (6) Teachers could not acquire requisite qualifications in the subject for the reason that Geography was neither a popular subject nor it was considered a paying subject during the days they did their graduation *i.e.* in the fifties or sixties. (7) The task of teaching Geography is not assigned on any sound basis like qualifications etc. Sometimes teachers volunteer to teach the subject. Sometimes they have to teach it because they do not have sufficient number of periods in the subjects of their specialization or when no other teacher is ready to teach the subject. (8) Teaching aids like globes, maps and charts are available in most of the schools but meteorological and survey instruments which are all the more needed for the enhanced courses in Geography are hardly available in schools. (9) Most of the available teaching aids are outdated. In few schools, there are teaching aids as old as 20 or 25 years. More often than not these teaching aids are out of order as well. There is lack of space to store or display the teaching aids. Most of the teaching aids are dumped in dark stores. (10) Though Directorate of Education has provided T.V. in about 90% schools of Delhi and 82% teachers find the T.V.

lessons help in teaching of Geography, yet 45% schools have not provided for Geography T.V. periods in the timetable. It is really sad that only 30% classes go to watch T.V. programmes in Geography. Moreover there is no proper place to accommodate all students to watch such programmes. (11) Parents and teachers feel that the subject matter is not relevant to instructional objectives, two out of every three teachers find that enough additional content is not given for brighter learners. (12) A little more than half i that the textbook is capable to suitably promote the desirable attitudes. (13) Only 35% parents and teachers find that the statistical information in the textbook are up-to-date conversely two-third teachers realize that the statistical information are not up-to-data and need to be revised. (14) The content items are not properly organised. The arrangement neither suits the age level of learners not the organisational divisions are suitably arranged (15) 65% teachers find that the treatment in the textbook is not made interesting through variety and novelty.

❑❑❑

INSTRUCTIONAL METHODOLOGY/CLASS-ROOM PRACTICES

A Case Study of Selective Delhi Schools with Special Reference to Innovative Classroom Practices

Ph. D., JMI, M. ASHRAF, 1988

The study was carried out with the objective of examining some schools in Delhi sociologically with a view to understand the sociological context of the innovations introduced in their classrooms, to study the on-going as well left-over innovative practices in their classrooms' to study the impact of those innovative classrooms practices on students, teachers, school tone and community and to make generalizations about the factors facilitating and obstructing innovations in schools.

The present study was concerned with the investigation of going as well as educational innovations that ware carried out in the past in senior secondary schools of the Union Territory of Delhi. The teachers teaching in 32 senior secondary schools and the students studying in the same schools were involved in this study. In order to light upon the concrete position of the educational innovations, the schools were personally observed by the researcher and some facts from the school documents were also recorded. 32 educational innovations prevailing in the schools were identified.

The major findings of the study were: (1) All the innovations were not introduced in all the schools. Further, all of them were not of the same nature. Moreover the introduced innovations had no effect on the functioning of an innovative classroom practice. (2) Location of the school (in New Delhi or Old Delhi) had not been an effective factor for the functioning of an innovative classroom practice. (3) The management of a school had played a very crucial role in the functioning of an innovation. In the government aided schools and unaided schools the degree of the achievement of the objectives was comparatively higher. In the government schools, the degree of achievement was always lower and more often, it was almost nil.

The sex of the students and teachers was also an important factor for the success or failure of an innovative classroom practice. For example, if meal planning was introduced in a girl's school the chances of success were bright. And if the same innovation was introduced in a boy's school it would be totally rejected. On other hand, if economic survey of railway coolies for which the students had to go to railway station at nighttime for data-collection, it would have been totally rejected, while it would have been quite successful in a boy's school. (5) The degree of achievement of the objectives of innovations introduced was not so high in only Hindi or Urdu medium schools as it was in other types of school *i.e.* English medium schools and the schools where both Hindi and English had been adopted as a medium of instruction. Medium of instruction of the school had been an important factor for the success of an innovation. (6) The planning of an innovation counted a lot for its smooth functioning. If the innovation was planned within a school it had been according to the nature of the school and the students. Therefore, there was no need to motivate the principal and teachers because they were already self-motivated, and the success was certain.

On the other hand, if it was planned from the top, it was not essentially been according to the nature of the school and the students. Lot of efforts were needed to motivate the principal, teachers and the students for that kind of innovation. Thus the success was not sure. The on-going innovations belonged to different categories *i.e.* curriculum, extra-curricular, evaluation and teaching method. It was not sure whether all innovations percolated from the top would be totally successful or totally unsuccessful. In the same category some innovations were perfectly successful while others were not. (7) The innovations were comparatively more successful in such schools where the teachers were not transferred in comparison to those where the teachers were frequently transferred. Though the teachers in central schools were also transferred, yet the innovations introduced were going on successfully inspite of the fact that teachers in these schools were transferred to far off places. Therefore, the teachers of central did not like to be transferred and they felt the transfer as a disadvantage or punishment. The teachers however tried to make their performance better in the school in which they were working. The frequent transfer of the teachers had an adverse effect on the success of the innovation. (8) Shortage of time had been a very serious hurdle in the path of success of an innovative activity. Besides this, long vacation also had an adverse effect on an innovative practice. Long vacation and less than one period per day in the school timetable created discontinuity in the smooth functioning of an innovative classroom practice. (9) The absence of syllabus had been major cause for the failure of an innovative activity. (10) Non-availability of funds had a direct and adverse impact on the smooth functioning of an innovation. (11) No teacher was promoted or demoted on the basis of his or her good or bad performance for an innovative practice. Even then some innovations such as 10+2 scheme achieved success. This was due to the policy of the government. It was observed by the investigator that if some teachers had been promoted on the basis of their good performance, more innovative practices would have been successful. (12) No effect or negligible effect of an innovative practice on the annual results of the students became the major obstacle in the path of success of an innovative classroom practice and *vice versa.* (13) Other hurdles that came in the way of successful implementation of an innovative practice was shortage of proper space, lack of competition, formal examination, large number of students and very few equipment, lack of coordination and cooperation among the staff, blind copying of the called modern behaviour, lack of properly trained staff, lack of application facilities and lack of cooperation from parents.

A Case Study of an Alternative School in Delhi: Focusing on the Teaching Learning Process

M.Phil., JNU, MEENA

The methodology used *viz.* participant observation was one most applicable for this case study especially since alternative school emphasized on interactive approach students functioning, including the teaching/learning process.

The present study has been an exploratory study into the functioning of an alternative school. It can serve as a useful reference point for those researchers who are interested in studying the other alternative schools and/or in using participant- observation in the classrooms of even the regular schools. For those interested in designing and/or implementing alternative schools and curricular programmes, the present study can point out the problems that can be anticipated and the possible strategies that can be adopted to deal with them.

The major findings of the study were (1) The school is characterised by informal and open interactions among its members. Even, the hidden curriculum *i.e.* the rules, regulations, room-layouts, informal norms and processes laid an emphasis on co-operation, independence, harmony and integration of the physical-vital mental and psychic aspects of ones being. (2) The teachers, though espousing the free progress ideology were sometimes unable to deal with practical problems that arise in the practice, and at some of these times tend to resort to the traditional use of autonomous authority. The teachers pre-service training programmes needs to be improved and the in-service training to be extended so that the teachers can find a way to resolve their inconsistencies, The teachers at the school have a very demanding job and heavy duties to perform, and although the satisfaction of service is considerable, the lack of momentary enumeration tends to add to their frustration. The school needs to review their decision of no-payment to the teachers, since each year their trained personnel leave them and are replaced by an inexperienced bunch of newcomers, who may or may not be sensitive to the ideology of the school. (3) Regarding the teaching/learning process, planning needs to be taken more seriously. The teachers, rather than drafting out concrete activities, prefer to let the topic evolve on its own. They rely on their intimate contact with the children to respond spontaneously to their needs and interests. If they invested this knowledge in their planning and devised sets of activities suitable to each child's needs and interests, the topics could prove more beneficial to each child. Evaluation too, along with emphasising the positive, needs to point out areas for improvement and relevant suggestions both with regard to the topics and individual child reports, Training in the three R's needs to be taken more seriously and not neglected. (4) Examining the functioning of the school with regard to the criteria of parental discontent, loss of key staff member ideological conflicts, funding problems and "staff burnout" it was seen that parental discontent seems to be a permanent feature. However, it has never reached magnified proportions, and could (at least in the past) be alleviated by reassurances from the school authorities. Staff burnout is linked to the school's policy of not providing monetary enumeration, and needs to be tackled by the school authorities.

The ideological conflict, may be examined best by using Deal and Nolan's classification. The school seems to espouse the "school as a garden" ideology to some extent where plants are a metaphor for the children. Here, the main task of the school is to create an environment in which the innate qualities can unfold since the source of knowledge exists inside the children.

The school is revolutionary in its ideology to the extent that it believes that the world is preparing for a big change and the school can help in it by giving the necessary importance to psychic education.

As the mother says, "From beyond the frontiers of form, a new force can be evolved, a power of consciousness which has not yet manifested and which, by its emergence, will be able to build a new world."

In its functioning, the school often resembles a "negotiation" school since it is a mixture of authority, autonomy and consensus. Some schoolwide decisions are made by consensus, others by hierarchical superiors. In the classrooms, the teachers expand options although the children ultimately decide objectives, activates and evaluation criteria. The informal norms emphasize cooperation and interdependence.

Thus, the school combines the ideologies in a specific way yielding an eclectic approach. Perhaps, this is to be expected since the school, as any other organization, is a loose collective (Meyer and Roman, 1975) and thus contains individuals who operate from different ideological perspectives. For a harmonious development of the child, it is important that the teachers and parents come to some mutual understanding and agreement. The school does recognise this and asks for a conscious involvement from the parents.

A Comparative Study of Teaching by Different Methods of Programming of Different Levels of Pupils DPTT of PSYL Foundation, NCERT

P.V. KULKARNI and M.S. YADAV, 1966

The study attempted to know which method of programming could have better impact on instruction for the development of an ability for a given group of students.

Branching, linear and simple programmes (*i.e.,* without providing immediate knowledge of results) were tried out on below average, average, and above average students to study the relative effects of different types of programmes on the development of knowledge, comprehension and application objectives for 'Solving Simple Equations'. The sample consisted of class VI students of an English medium school in Delhi. Three matched groups were formed on the basis of marks obtained by students in mathematics in their last examination. These groups were then administered the different styles of programmes on 'Solving Equations'. The treatment lasted for a week. The main findings showed that the treatment effects did not seem to be significantly different. With so many missing cases, with school marks not very much dependable as criterion variable and the sample size being also quite small, no sound conclusions could be drawn.

A Comparative Effectiveness Study of Self-paced Instructional Method in Teaching Accountancy at plus two Stage

M.Ed., C.I.E., D.U., NARENDER KUMAR JAIN, 1982

The study was undertaken with the objective of finding out whether this new technique can be successfully employed in teaching accountancy; to observe the actual use of self-paced instruction material and traditional method and to compare their effective so that it may be even helpful in finding out if self-paced instructional material and traditional method can be supplemented as a better method of teaching than only traditional method of teaching.

The sample of the study comprised of 40 students of XI class from one school divided into two groups of 20 each — one experimental and the other one controlled. Based on the pre- and post-test, of both the groups, the major findings of the study showed (1) Instruction to pupils through traditional method was more effective. (2) Programmed Instruction was found to be slightly more effective as compared to traditional method although the difference is non-significant. (3) No significant difference between programmed instruction and traditional method was found.

Effectiveness of Programmed Lessons as a Remedial tool for low Achievers in Learning Some Geometrical Concepts (VIth Class)

M.Ed., C.I.E., D.U., 1983

The study was taken up to investigate into the effectiveness of programmed lessons as a remedial tool for low achievers in learning some geometrical concepts among Class VI. The study was confined to one government school. The students who achieved below 30% in pre-test were taken up as low achiever. Initially 40 students were selected. Later based on their average percentage in the pre-test of Geometry, they were matched score- wise to form Group A and Group B. Group I was taught through programmed instruction and Group II was taught through the routin-wise classroom instruction.

The major findings show; (1) Teaching and learning through programmed instruction can definitely help students and teachers. Students receiving programmed lessons as a help, remove their deficiency in learning of the unit under investigation. (2) Most of the students were not able to do questions of completion of diagrams. So it can be said that drawing skill cannot be improved by programmed lessons.

A Comparative Study of Effectiveness of Personalised System Instruction and Traditional of Method in Teaching Physics at +2 Level

M.Ed., C.I.E., D.U., SURAJ PRAKASH, 1982

The main objective of the study was to observe personalized system of Instruction and Traditional Method Physics Teaching to compare their effectiveness so that it may be helpful in finding out if PSI may be supplemented, as a better method of teaching.

In order to study the effectiveness of both the methods, the study was carried out in NDMC Navyug School, I Avenue, Sarojini Nagar. Two sections consisting of 28 students each were selected from this school and two groups were formed. One group was taught through traditional method and the other one through PSI system.

The findings reveal the following: (1) Instruction to pupils through PSI is not more effective than through traditional method up to 1st test. (2) There was significant difference between the PSI and Traditional method shown by the 2nd test. The students achieved higher score through PSI that showed the effectiveness of PSI over traditional method. (3) Total Score (T1 + T2) shows that PSI system is more effective.

Effectiveness of Task Analysis Techniques in the Designing of Instructional Units for Teaching English to Class Nine Students

M.Ed,, C.I.E., D.U., RODRICK RAJIVE LAL, 1994

The study stresses the point that effective, systematic and scientific planning of instructional units can result in effective instruction. It is an effort to study the effectiveness (in terms of a significant difference of learning outcomes indicated by the difference between the pretest and post-test (scores) of instructional units designed with the help of Task analysis in teaching English to class 9 students.

The design adopted for the study was that of the single group pre-test part test pre-experimental design. Two criterion tests in the form of pre-test and post-test were used in the study. One opinionnaire after the post-test was administered to measure their attitudes towards the lessons taught in experiment.

The major findings revealed: (1) No significant difference betweenthepretreatmentandposttreatmentachievementscores of the learners as a result of the implementation of instruction units designed with the help of Task Analysis techniques. (2) Instructional Units designed with the help of Task Analysis Techniques help develop a positive attitude among learners towards their lessons.

Effectiveness of Hilda Taba Model in Teaching Certain Concepts of Biology at Secondary Level

M.Ed., C.I.E., D.U., CHANDRA BOLI GHORAI, 1996

Hilda Taba Model is a means of teaching concepts through selective framework, supplemented by the concrete examples. This helps the learner to achieve maximum information about the concepts. The students develop the concept by their active involvement and processing of information.

The study highlighted that the teaching of biology through traditional method has been effective. This method has been quite successful in attaining the concepts of biology by the students.

Effectiveness of Concept Mapping in Science Education

M.Ed., C.I.E., D.U., VANDANA GUPTA, 1995

The study intended to develop concept maps of some topics in the chemistry syllabus of class IX and to examine the relative effectiveness of teaching through concept mapping and traditional method. 76 students of class IXth were taken up as sample from one senior secondary school, formed into two equivalent groups, taught through two approaches, one using the concept maps and the other which does not envisage the use of concept maps. An achievement test was administered to find the difference. It was found that although science teachers should make use of concept mapping method while teaching concepts of science but traditional method is equally effective.

A Comparative Study of Bruner's Approach and Lecture Method for Teaching Certain Concepts in Maths

C.I.E., D.U., 1984

In the study, effort was made in constructing programmes on three different topics of mathematics in Bruner's Idea and their effectiveness is compared with the lecture method.

24 students were selected in the final sample consisting of 5 below average, 14 average and 5 above average students. No pretest was administered to groups, instead average of five class tests were taken into account. The equivalent groups were divided on the basis of this average. Post-test was administered at the end of treatment period lecture method and programme developed on Bruner's approach.

To Study the Effectiveness of Programmed Lesson as a Remedial Tool for Low Achievers in Biology (Xth Class)

M.Ed., C.I.E., D.U., MADHU KUMAR, 1982

The main objective of the study was to examine the effectiveness of programmed lesson as a remedial tool for low achievers in Biology (Xth class).

The sample consisted of class Xth students of Kulachi Hansraj Model School, Ashok Vihar, Phase I who had Biology at 'A' level or higher level. All the students achieving below 45% in the biology terminal test were taken as low-achievers and were included in the sample. They were 32 in number. Later, they were classified into two groups, almost equivalent in their achievement, based on their average percentage in biology. They were matched percentage-wise to form Group A and Group B. The groups were randomly assigned to two different treatments, the programmed lessons classroom teaching and second group having only traditional teaching with no programme lessons.

The major findings of the study revealed that teaching and learning through programmed Instruction can definitely helped the students. Both the programmed lessons and traditional classroom teaching can be utilised for an effective teaching of programmed lesson. To generate at the index level, it can be interpreted that programmed lesson cannot replace classroom teaching but adds a tool to the professional army of the educational Instruction.

Effectiveness of Jurisprudential Inquiring Model of Teaching in Developing Values

M.Ed., C.I.E., D.U., 1991

The study mainly deals with the kind of effect of intervention strategies, attitude scale and Jurisprudential Inquiring Model based instructional material lays impact on values of sixty students of Class IX. The study proceeded by formation of two equivalent groups control and experimental group based on the results of an attitude scale. The control group was taught by traditional method. After teaching three lessons (one each on pollution, population and drug-addiction) to both the groups, post-test was administered. It was found that Jurisprudential Inquiry Model was more effective as compared to traditional approach in inculcation of desired values in pupils.

Development of Teaching Material of a Unit of Taxonomic Botany For +2 Stage and Comparing its Effectiveness with the Traditional Methods

M.Ed., C.I.E., D.U., VARINDER MOHAN, 1980

The study was conducted by forming two equivalent groups of a class and given different treatments by teaching them a unit of taxonomic botany through traditional and programmed methods. It came into view that the programmed group, had made a significant progress in learning of the unit under investigation. It was observed that teaching through programmed learning could bring better results in comparison to the teaching through traditional classroom methods. Programmed learning may not be superior to ordinary teaching methods but it definitely adds a tool to the professional armoury of the educational instructors.

Effectiveness of Inductive and Deductive Approaches in Teaching Concepts of Economics

M.Ed., C.I.E., D.U., 1984

The study was carried out with the objectives of preparing a criterion test to measure the achievement of pupils, inductive based instructional material for teaching pupils following inductive approach, and to prepare deductive based instructional material for teaching the pupils following deductive and approach.

The sample consisted of one school where from 64 class XI pupils in commerce stream and all of them studied economics as a main subject. Two equivalent Groups were formed. They were taught by two approaches of teaching *i.e.* inductive and deductive approaches and matched on the basis of previous achievement.

The major findings show that the teachers of Economics should make use of inductive and deductive strategies while teaching concepts in Economics. Inductive approach has been more efficient in teaching concepts on demand.

A Study of the Comparative Effectiveness of Traditional and Experimental Methods of Developing Pupils' Vocabulary in English in Hindi Medium Schools

M.Ed., C.I.E., D.U., SHANKAR MUKHERJEE, 1982

The main objective of the experimental study was to observe the extent to which carefully designed exercises based on linguistic principles can be helpful in improving the English vocabulary (in respect of meaning, spelling and grammatical function) of students learning English as a second language.

The sample consisted of two sections of the same school which were chosen as the control and experimental groups. Pretest and post-test were conducted and the scores of only those students were used in calculations who fulfilled the criteria of equivalence in terms of age, intelligence and previous achievement and attendance. As part of the tools used, the textbook "Learn English Book III," A dictionary, tables, charts and diagrammes were used.

The findings of the study were as follows: (1) There is significant difference in the effectiveness of experimental and traditional methods of developing pupils' vocabulary in English. The mean performance of the experimental group is significantly higher than the mean performance of the control group. (2) Different experimental techniques have different degrees of effect on pupils' vocabulary competence. The semantics technique appears to be the most effective and the only technique which is able to bring about a statistically significant difference in the mean performance of the two groups.

Study the Effectiveness of Ruleg and Egrul Approaches in Teaching Concepts of Physics

M.Ed., C.I.E., D.U., NAND KISHORE, 1987

The objectives of the study were expressed as: to find out whether or not the pupils taught through Ruleg approach obtain significant gains in the mean scores on the criterion test, to find out whether or not the pupils taught through Egrul approach obtain significant gains in the mean scores on the criterion test, to find out whether or not there is significant difference in the mean scores of the pupils taught through Ruleg approach and those through Egrul approach on the criterion test.

The major findings to the study revealed: (1) The teachers of physics should make use of Ruleg approach while teaching concepts in physics. (2) Though Egrul approach seemed to have an edge over the Ruleg approach, but the difference was found to be statistically insignificant at .05 level of confidence.

A Study of Relative Effectiveness of Some Information Processing Models of Teaching on Mental Process and Attitude Towards Science

Indian Educational Review, Vol. 30(2), 156-161,
NARESH KUMAR GUPTA, 1995

The study attempted to make a study of relative effectiveness of some information processing models of teaching on mental process and attitude towards science. A purposive sample of 140 students in the form of three non-equivalent intact sections of Class IX in the same government senior secondary school of Delhi, drawn with the help of incidental sampling technique was used. Tools used to collect data included The Group General Mental Ability Test by S. Jalota, Reasoning Ability Test (RAT) by K. Bayati, Verbal Test of Scientific Creativity by V.P. Sharma and J.P. Shukla, Part test of Passi Test of Creativity (Verbal and non-verbal) and Science Attitude Scale by Anvinash Grewal. Quasi-experimental method was employed for the study in a natural setting with pre-test and post-test parallel group design. The major findings revealed that the concept attainment model, inductive thinking model and inquiry training model were found to be equally effective in promoting attitude of students towards science.

A Study of the Comparative Effectiveness of the Information Processing Models of Teaching in Developing Certain Concepts in Chemistry at the Secondary Stage *Ph.D., JMI,* TALAT AZIZ, 1990

The study was carried out mainly to compare the teaching programmes based on information processing models with the traditional teaching programme in chemistry with respect of concept attainment.

The sample consisted of 280 students of class IX of four different central schools of Delhi out of which 140 students formed the control group and 140 formed the experimental group. An achievement test, the concept attainment test developed by the investigator and the group test constructed by Dr. S.S. Jalota were used.

The major findings reported that the boys and girls exposed to teaching programme based on information processing models of teaching performed significantly better on the concept attainment test than the boys and girls taught through traditional lecture method. (2) Chemistry can be effectively taught through model approach. (3) Models approach of teaching is better than the traditional approach of teaching. (4) Concept attainment model and Inductive thinking model are effective for teaching science concepts. (5) Binner's concept attainment model is effective for attainment of concepts.

An Investigation into the Effectiveness of Humanistic Activities for Teaching English *M.Ed., JMI,* ARTI NARANG, 1989

The study mainly aimed at studying the effect of humanistic activities used for the teaching of English on the self-concept of the learners, to ascertain the effectiveness of humanistic activities on the self-esteem of learners, to measure the development of language creativity of the students taught English through humanistic activities and to study the effect of using humanistic activities for teaching English on the level of classroom environment.

The sample consisted of students of class IX of a privately managed secondary school recognised by Delhi Administration. They were grouped into two, 50 students that formed control group and 50 students forming experimental group in the age group 13-14. The tools administered Saraswat's self-concept questionnaire, one self-esteem inventory, Language creativity test in English by Mr. S.P. Malhotra and Ms. Sucheta Kumari and Classroom environment scale by Rudolf H. Moos and Edison J. Trickett.

The major findings showed: (1) There was improvement in the level of concept of the students who were taught English through humanistic activities. (2) Humanistic activities increased the level of self-esteem in the learners. (3) The language creativity in English of the students of the experimental group was higher than those of the control group because of the use of humanistic activities. (4) The level of classroom environment increased in case of students using humanistic activities. (5) Students possessing higher esteem had greater creative ability in English language. (6) A better classroom environment increased self-concept of students.

An Investigation into Effectiveness of Graphic Organizers on Cognitive Achievement in Biology of Ninth Grade Students of Kendriya Vidyalayas of Badarpur in Delhi

M.Ed., JMI, MADAN MOHAN JOSHI, 1991

The objective of the study was to investigate whether cognitive achievement amongst students of 9th grade will be better when they undergo instruction with graphic organizers or with verbal organizers. Three equivalent group of students were formed, one was taught through graphic organiser and the other one through traditional programme and the third one verbal organiser programme.

The findings of the study revealed that the graphic organiser programme method of instruction was better and more effective in terms of cognitive achievement in Biology than the verbal organiser programme method of instruction and traditional programme method of instruction.

Effectiveness of Peer Interactive Learning (PIL) in Improving Scholastic Achievement and Retention

M.Ed., C.I.E., D.U., MAUSUMI MANJIT, 1996

The following were the objectives of the study: (1) To examine the extent to which PIL is effective in improving scholastic achievement in science. (2) To examine whether PIL is effective in improving retention. On the basis of random sampling a control group and an experimental group were chosen. 45 students of class VIII were taken as sample for the control group and the same number was taken up for experimental group. In the experimental group, nine small groups were constituted for instructional experiment on the basis of their performance in the pre-test. Each group was a mixed ability group. Each group had at least one student from each quartile of distribution of mark.

The study was experimental in nature and was based on pretest, post-test control group design. After taking the pre-test the investigator taught the control group in the usual method of lecture-cum-demonstration. But in the experimental group instructional experiment was conducted for eleven working days. The instructional experiment was based on peer interactive learning. At the end of the instructional experiment, the achievement test was given as post-test, to both control group and experimental group and students' response were scored. A sociogram and a group acceptance questionnaire were used for the experimental group students. The achievement test was administered as retention test, to both control and experimental groups. The major findings of the study were: (1) PIL is significantly effective in improving scholastic achievement. (2) PIL is significantly effective in improving retention. (3) PIL is effective in incorporating positive transformation in the group dynamics of the class. (4) PIL is significantly effective in improving retention.

The study highlighted that given an opportunity, the pupils are able to assume responsibility and carry out a task successfully and interact purposefully helping each other to learn and be mature in the learning process. The study also indicated that a pupil should never be branded as average or below average because this status is not permanent. Certain situational factors place a student at certain level at a particular time period. When the situational factors change, the performance and achievement of the pupil also change. The study established that managing one's own learning and assuming responsibilities goes a long way in helping the students become not only task oriented, but also disciplined. Finally, the study established that not only older students are able to manage their tasks by themselves, young learners of pre-adolescent stage can also learn from experience and need not be spoon fed every time.

Comparative Effectiveness of Pupil Participation Through Micro Teaching and Traditional Teaching

M.Ed., C.I.E., D.U., P.L. VALMIKI, 1987

The objective of the study was to study the comparative effectiveness and retention of the acquisition of general teaching competence by the two groups of teaching through conventional method of pupil participation and micro teaching skill of pupil participation, skill of increasing pupil participation acquired through traditional method of teaching and through micro teaching. In order to increase pupil participation, a questionnaire, rating scale and an observation schedule was administered on selected sample.

The major findings revealed that the micro based teaching has been effective in improving general teaching competence and its retention for in-service training significantly whereas traditional method has not.

A Comparative Study of the Effectiveness of the Traditional Programmes and the Structured Learning Programme on the Degree of Conceptualization of VII Grade Hindi Medium Boys Students of a Government School of Delhi

M.Ed., JMI, GAJRAJ S. DABAS, 1982

The objective was to investigate whether conceptualization of congruence of triangles of seventh grade students will be better with structured programmes amongst the equivalent group of students of VII grade with instructions in the traditional programmes. It was found that the 'structured programme' of instruction was better and more effective in terms of conceptualisation of 'congruence of triangles', than the traditional one.

Effectiveness of Computer Software in Teaching English Grammar at Middle Level

M.Ed., C.I.E., D.U., ANJALI AGARWAL, 1995

The objective was (1) to find out the effect of CAI in teaching of English Grammar to students of Class VII. (2) to find out the reaction of students towards software approach to English Grammar. (3) to find out the retention level of students taught through traditional method and those taught through CAI after a period of one month.

20 students from one school were selected as sample of the study. In order to check the performance of students' achievement criterion test was administered on them as tool for investigation.

The major findings of the study highlight: (1) Traditional method of teaching is effective in the teaching of English Grammar. (2) Teaching of English Grammar should continue with traditional method of teaching for teaching English Grammar. (3) Teachers of English Grammar can use CAI in combination with traditional method only. (4) Teaching of English Grammar through CAI can lead to better scores only if this approach is used with traditional method of teaching. (5) Teaching of English Grammar through CAI has no effect on the retention as compared to the traditional method of teaching.

Comparative Effectiveness of Video Tape Based Teaching and Normal Classroom Teaching on Academic Achievement in Chemistry

M.Ed., C.I.E., D.U., RAJENDRA PRASAD, 1985

The study proceeded by keeping the following objectives in view: (1) To investigate the effectiveness of video tape based teaching as compared to normal classroom teaching executed through lecture-cum-demonstration method. (2) To familiarise oneself of the problem one faces with regard to video film recording of actual classroom teaching and how they can be solved in general to make video as popular audio-visual aid for effective classroom communication. (3) To experience and to suggest to what extent video can successfully be employed as supplementary aid for classroom communication.

The study was carried out by forming two groups of 20 each. One group was the control and the other was the experimental group. The former was given normal classroom teaching and the other was imparted video film based teaching. After the different treatments, pre-test-post-test was administered.

The study reached the following major findings: (1) Video teaching was quite beneficial to students for clarification of basic concepts of chemistry. (2) Good video teaching is of great help in teachers pre-service and in-service training. (3) Those students who were taught through video films did very well in the annual examinations especially in the question related directly as well as indirectly with the topic taught through video film.

Comparative Effectiveness of Video Tape Based Teaching and Normal Classroom on Academic Achievement in Chemistry

M.Ed., C.I.E., D.U., HARPAL SINGH, 1985

The main objective of the study was to compare programmed instruction and traditional method in teaching physics at 10+2 level (IX).

The sample consisted of XI class Science (one section) students. They were grouped into two equivalent groups and assigned to two treatments respectively (Programmed instruction) (traditional method). The means of the games of two groups were tested on the basis of pre-and post-test.

The major finding of the study was that the programmed learning was more effective than traditional method.

A Correlation Study of Communication Effectiveness of T.V. Programme Classroom Environment and Social Studies of Class X Students in Delhi *M.Phil, ZHCESSS,* 1987

The present study was undertaken to ascertain the relationships among different (mediating) variables namely, communication effectiveness of ETV programme, psychosocial characteristics of classrooms environment and student's performance in science and social studies.

110 boys of Government Boys' Senior Secondary School and 110 girls of Government Girls' Senior Secondary School were chosen as the sample subjects. The selection of the sample was made on the basis of quota method of sampling.

The instrument includes the communication efficacy scale and classrooms environment inventory to assess the psychosocial characteristics of the classroom's environment.

The major findings of the study revealed that (1) regular exposure to ETV programme results in higher post ETV scores both by boys and girls in science and social studies; (2) boys' ratings show low but positive association between the perceptions of communication effectiveness of ETV programme and classrooms environment in science and social studies; (3) girls ratings show moderate but positive association between the perceptions of communication effectiveness of ETV programme and classrooms environment in science and social studies; (4) the predictability of student's performance in science and social studies by using communication efficacy and classroom environment scores in science and social studies do not reveal positive results.

Besides, the home TV environment contributes directly/ indirectly to the perception of communication effectiveness of ETV programme and classrooms environment in science and social studies. It does not directly relate to student's performance in different academic subject.

The findings show positive association between the perception of communication effectiveness of ETV programme and classrooms environment. This in turn, is expected to contribute to academic performance.

A Survey of Co-curricular Activities in Learning of Science in South Delhi Schools

M.Ed,, JMI, JAMINI GEORGE, 1986

All the twenty schools surveyed in South Delhi had co-curricular activities in science. Although the most popular activity seems to be project making but other activities such as quizzes, debates, essay competitions on science topics also took place at the convenience of the school.

All the schools participated in the annual science exhibitions. Yet the general attitude of the school's administration towards science activities is that of having to do one more job which they have been asked to do by the school establishment. They have not realized the importance of co-curricular activities in the learning of science. This attitude was reflected in the projects the students carried out under their guidance and the responses to questions put to them regarding their project.

There was usually a common fund for all the co-curricular activities in the government schools. Other than that there was no separate fund for co-curricular activities in science and all schools do not have a fixed timing for it in their time-table. By and large all classes from Primary to Secondary participate in these activities. Though participation class wise varies from school to school.

It was found that in all the schools' students were not able to answer questions which were not directly related to their projects. They did not ask questions which could have clarified their understanding of concepts. And one gets the impression that most of their projects were carried out as tasks to be completed rather than as opportunities for further exploration.

In almost all the cases projects did not help students understand concepts they may have come across in their regular science classes. It seems projects work did not motivate students to ask many questions. Everything was taken for granted (reflector was thought to provide a support in the electric radiator whereas its actual purpose is reflection of heat into the room). There was no attempt to do simple experiments to test their own device and to try to make use of something they may have learnt in science classes (did not measure temperature inside the solar cooker). For most of them learning science was simply gathering a lot of information without really understanding its implications. So the thrill and the excitement of doing science was lost.

It is unfortunate that there is little or no realisation, amongst teachers as well as students of the potential of project work in learning of science and so much time and effort of teachers and students is lost.

The NCERT and Eklavya Approaches to the Teaching of Social Studies With Special Reference to Economics

M.Ed., C.I.E., D.U., MANISHA MINOCHA, 1987

The present study was undertaken to examine the approaches of the NCERT and Eklavya with reference to: (a) The pedagogical principles involved with regard to; the activity and involvement of the pupils; whether there is a logical presentation of the subject matter according to the disciplines they are based on and whether the curriculum is connected with the environment of the child, or not; the rural or urban bias, if there is any.

The major findings of the study revealed: (1) On the whole, a more or less uniform connection with the environment has been found in the Eklavya books, which is in accordance with their focus and aims, as shown by their documents. The books have a rural bias, as the books are taught mostly in rural areas, which is in accordance with their wish to connect lessons with the environment. (2) There is little connection with the environment in the NCERT books. They have stated in their documents that they wish to have an environment based curriculum at the primary stage and at the secondary stage. According to them the curriculum must be broad based with reference to the amount of knowledge available, previous knowledge of the child and the needs of society. Though they mention that at the secondary stage, the curriculum must be linked with the experiences of students in the non-formal sector, they have not given priority only to environment at the stages above the primary stage. (3) The NCERT books have some bias towards the urban areas, especially in the VI standard civics book and in the kinds of activities they suggest which require at least a well-equipped library and access to books and magazines. On the other hand, we can say that it has a more national outlook and has included the history of the kingdoms of the South, which is an improvement over the previous history which remained confined to the history of North India. (4) Both the NCERT and Eklavya lessons are based on the logic of the discipline though there is a difference in the method of its presentation or education. (5) In the Eklavya books involvement of the child is constant and plentiful. The NCERT books also have a provision for activities but mainly at the end of the lessons (except in geography). Much depends here on the actual teaching, which we could not observe due to lack of time. (6) Connection with experience of the child is desirable as long as it does not interfere with the voyage beyond experience wherein we must also travel along with the child. But too much emphasis on vast amounts of subject matter that is not related with experience of the child is equally undesirable. The curriculum must strike the difficult balance between the two. (7) The approach towards the curriculum of two institutions is different. The Eklavya group have in their documents stated that the framework of the existing textbooks is not something they have adopted — they have worked within it for the sake of conducting a preliminary exercise, and whole lot of questions regarding the nature of the curriculum are still wide open for consideration. They do not claim to give any generalisations or recommendations but have shared with us their limited experiences and the questions before them.

A Study of the Methods of Imparting Value Education at Senior Secondary Level in Some Selected Schools of Delhi

M.Ed., C.I.E., D.U., NEERJA DHANKAR, 1996

The objectives of the study were: (1) To identify the formal and informal methods of imparting Value-education at Senior Secondary Level in some selected schools of Delhi. (2) To identify values which are being imparted and are relevant to present changing scenario, in the country and world at large. (3) To identify values which must be imparted but are not being imparted at Senior Secondary level. (4) To analyse the specific features of the methods adopted by each school to impart Value Education at Senior Secondary level. (5) To compare methods adopted for imparting Value-education by different schools. (6) To study the effectiveness of methods adopted by different schools. (7) To examine the assumption that various curricular and co-curricular activities taken up by the schools are being effective in inculcating necessary values in the students. (8) To study methods as suggested by different educational bodies from time to time. (9) To give relevant suggestions on the methods for imparting Value-Education at Senior Secondary Level.

The sample consisted of three schools selected under different managements: D.A.V. School Vikas Puri, M.C.L Saraswati Bal Mandir, Hari Nagar, Government Composite Model Co-educational Senior Secondary School, Vikas Puri. 30 students were selected from each school. The tools used in the study were in the form of two checklist prepared by the investigator.

The major findings of the study were as follows: (1) Awareness of students in all the three schools confines to their own country. They do not know anything about International days. The students are not aware of Human Rights as being given by U.N.O. (2) Cultural values are also limited to the students' own culture. They do not come to know much about other cultures through school. Only folk dances are done belonging to other cultures. (3) Aesthetic values are given upmost importance in all the three schools. (4) Teachers are no longer role models for the students for simplicity, punctuality, non-violence and other necessary values. (5) Non-violence is not totally practised in the schools. (6) Private schools celebrate religious festivals of North India and Hindus. Government schools do not celebrate any religious festivals. (7) National days are celebrated in all the three schools. (8) Environment Day is not celebrated in any of these school. (9) Healthy physical development is emphasized by all schools through various activities. (10) Community service is taken up by these schools. (11) N.C.C., N.S.S., Boys scouts, girls guide training are losing their importance in the schools. (12) Martyr's Day is not observed. (13) Vana Mahotsava is not celebrated in any of the three schools. (14) Democracy is not practised. Only theoretical knowledge and explanation is given. (15) Mode of punishment is not well thought over before practising it. (16) Students value intrinsic qualities of the teachers and not looks. (17) Students consider it their duty to keep the school clean. (18) Value of manual work is being emphasized by the school. (19) Students are taught to make best out of waste and economic use of resources. (20) Reading news in morning assembly is practised in all schools. It is the main source of their national and international news awareness. (21) Current problems of society are not discussed frequently with senior students. (22) Teachers do not remain simple is the complaint by the students. (23) Only D.A.V. school has separate guidance and counselling cell. (24) D.A.V. school conducts Havanas and Pujas according to Arya Samaj customs on special days. (25) M.C.L. Saraswati School's total atmosphere is laden with Hindu culture based values, necessary social values are embedded. Sanskrit is taught from second standard onwards. (26) Govt. School's emphasis is on values as enshrined in the Constitution of India (National Values). (27) Govt. School's Principal believes in Total Atmosphere Approach to impart necessary values in the students.

Aspects of Creativity in Methodology of Teaching English

M.Ed, JMI, B.V.V. LATHA, 1995

The main objective of the study was to critically examine the creative element in the prescribed materials, the methods and practice adopted by the teacher for fostering creativity in English language learning and the institutional arrangement for fostering creativity. The descriptive survey method was used in studying ten government schools and Class VIII was taken up for study. A questionnaire was administered. The major findings revealed: (1) 90% of public school teachers were post graduate with training, 70% of government aided school teachers were post graduate with training, 40% of government school teachers were post graduate with training. Public school policy of recruiting highly qualified staff is bound to pay them dividend. (2) 50% of public school teachers possess 10 or more years of experience, corresponding figures for government aided schools at government schools are 40% and 80% respectively. (3) 70% of public school had undergone language training while 50% and 30% of Government aided and government school teachers had in-service training. (4) Public school teachers were more prepared to handle creativity culture in classroom. (5) Most of Government schools followed English Reader while Aided school communicate in English, Oxford University Press. (6) Public schools also prescribed Interact English, MacMillan publication.

Effect of Computer Education on the Reasoning Ability, Mathematics and Languages *M.Phil*, ZHCESSS, JNU, 1986

The present study was formulated to study the effect of computer studies, which has been introduced as an applied subject at the secondary school level, on verbal and abstract reasoning of students. It was also proposed to examine the transfer effect, if any, of learning of computer studies on the learning of other related subjects like mathematics and English. The sample consisted of 100 students from St. Columbus School, Delhi, who had completed class 8 or class 9 in the 1984-85 sessions.

Pre-post research design in a matched group framework was adopted for this study. Two groups were formed: (1) experimental groups who had undergone computer studies course for one year either in class 8 or in class 9. (2) Control groups who had not undergone it. The results of this study show that the computer students (students of experimental groups) scored slightly lower scores than their matched control group in English. Further, the difference was more in class 8 than in class 9. Though the difference was not significant, it cannot be ignored.

This study was an evaluative study. The main findings were that a positive transfer effect of learning computer studies was visible on mathematics; and a slightly negative transfer effect was visible on English, reasoning of computer students was slightly superior to their matched control group.

Cognitive Achievement in Algebra of Sixth Class Students Comparing Structural and Traditional Programmes

M.Ed., JMI, SHASHI MAKKAR, 1995

The main objective of the study was to investigate whether cognitive achievement amongst students of sixth standard will be better with structured programme or with instructions as in the traditional programme. The sample was drawn from one government senior secondary school and two equivalent groups, controlled and the experimental group. The tools comprised of Age and Past Academic Achievements, the Numerical Ability Test for measuring numerical ability, Coloured Progressive Matrices Test for measuring Intelligence.

The major finding highlighted that the structured programme method of instruction was better and more effective in terms of achievement in handling all the four operations involving algebraic polymials in the fields of algebra as compared to traditional methods.

❑❑❑

TEACHER AND TEACHING ISSUES

An Investigation into the Effectiveness of Various Supervising Techniques for Better Science Teaching in Delhi Municipal Corporation Schools

M.Ed., C.I.E., D.U., KHEM CHAND SHARMA, 1982

The study was carried out by keeping the following objectives in view: (1) To identify certain supervisory techniques which are applicable in present situation. (2) To try out experimentally these supervisory techniques in some primary schools and know about the effectiveness of such techniques on the achievement of children in science subject. (3) To know, whether these techniques have the same effect on a different group of children; and (4) To suggest various techniques of supervision that can be employed by the science supervisors during their visit to schools for better science teaching.

In order to study the effectiveness, it has taken up 2 matched groups (control group and experimental group) of students studying in Class V in six Municipal Corporation Primary schools of one educational zone of Municipal Corporation of Delhi. After giving them different treatments, the major finding arrived at revealed that supervisory techniques applied by the investigator as very effective for the betterment of science teaching in Delhi Municipal Corporation Primary Schools. Achievement of students of experimental group is higher than the achievement of control group students.

Teaching Strategies in Pre Schools Comparative Case Studies of American, British and Indian Schools in Delhi

M.Ed., C.I.E., D.U., SIMMI BATRA, 1992

The main objectives of the study were to examine the nature of the difference and the similarities in the techniques and the strategies that teachers in their school's use.

The sample of the study comprised of children of 4-5 years age group selected from American Embassy school and British school and one public school at New Delhi.

The major findings as highlighted in the study were: (1) The incidence of negative strategies is very high in Delhi schools. (2) Use of positive strategies that aid affective development is most frequent in all the three schools. But the frequency of touching the child is lesser because it is used in too casual manner. (3) Encouraging competition within was rarely done by teachers of all the three schools. (4) Strategies aimed at promoting cognitive development often by most of the teachers of American School and least often by Delhi School teachers. Encouragement of creativity and fantasy was not observed even once in Delhi School. On the contrary discouragement was more common. (5) The overall use of negative strategies is done by Indian School teachers, American School and British School teachers respectively.

A Study of Democratic Authoritarian Attitude of Teachers Towards Education With Respect to Extroversion, Introversion and Some Other Variables

M.Ed., C.I.E., D.U., SEEMA GAIROLA, 1985

The main objective of the study was to understand the attitudes of teachers on democratic authoritative dimension in relation to extroversion, age, sex and the teaching subject.

The study was conducted on 120 teachers teaching at secondary level from six government higher secondary schools. The tools used were Maudsley's Personality Inventory (E Scale) Minnesota Teachers' Attitude Scale Adapted by N.K. Dutt. Descriptive statistical analysis was done to arrive at conclusions.

Themajorfindingsofthestudyshowed:(1)Introvertsaremore democratic than extroverts in their attitudes towards education. (2) No difference in attitude towards democracy on the basis of age. (3) No difference in attitude of male and female teachers. (4) The subject of teaching does influence the attitude of teachers since arts teachers have been found to be more democratic than non-arts.

A Study of Use of Reasoning by Teachers in Teaching

M.Ed, C.I.E., D.U., ARBIND KUMAR JHA, 1995

In this study an attempt is being made to understand the role and the use of reasoning which an average teacher makes in his/her daily classroom teaching. The subject is not an end in itself but a means to develop reasoning, understanding and a sense of questioning power in students. How far these goals are achieved and are achievable is the main purpose of the study. Keeping this aspect in view, the following objectives were kept in view: (1) To examine Reasoning *per se,* in conceptual as well as operative modes. (2) To underline the role of reasoning in the process of teaching. (3) To find out the extent (intensity & frequency) to which reasoning or any component of reasoning is being used by the teachers. (4) To identify the techniques and methods used by teachers leading to development of reasoning ability amongst students. (5) To investigate if there is any gap between the practices of teaching and ideal of teaching, held by the teachers. (6) To identify the techniques and methods used by teachers leading to the development of reasoning ability amongst students. (7) To investigate if there is any gap between the practices of teaching and ideals of teaching, held by the teachers.

The sample was drawn from seven schools of West Delhi. It comprises of 40 PGTS and 40 TGTS. In all 80 teachers were observed and interviewed. The tools used in the study were: (1) Observation sheet and (2) Personal interview.

The major findings of the study were: (1) Lecture method is found the most popular among the teachers. (2) Inductive and Deductive methods were popular among Mathematics, Science and Language teachers. (3) Question-Answer method was also popular — with the same groups of teachers. (4) Rest of the thirteen methods *viz.*, Analytic method, Synthetic method, Development method etc. requiring reasoning ability as well as skills were found least popular and were used sparingly. (5) Mathematics teachers were using questioning techniques more frequently in imparting knowledge, building sound concept than teachers of other disciplines. (6) It was found that questioning as a technique of imparting knowledge was most popular among the five techniques along which they were observed and (7) Explanation as a mode of presentation was most popular followed by Description and Narration. Rest of the mode of presentation which require sheer reasoning do not figure prominently. (8) Acquainting the students with subject matter was perceived as the main objectives of teaching by the teacher. (9) Most of the teachers were found democratic in their treatment. (10) Knowledge/ Information was considered as the most prominent expected outcomes followed by understanding and application. (11) Reinforcing (repetitive recapitulation) to be given top priority among the teachers as a follow-up activity. (12) It was found that some PGT's (Who were from science background) were using more reflective questions in teaching social-sciences, in comparison to those PGT's (Humanities) who were from pure humanities background. (13) Through interview as well as observation it was found that some teachers were keen to use various methods and techniques in imparting knowledge but found it difficult to do so due to certain practical difficulties. (14) It was found through interview that there was a deep gap between the practices of teaching and ideal of teaching held by the teachers. (15) Through interview it was found that teachers were more interested in techniques as an effective teaching than in the methods.

Teachers Perception of their Principals Impression about them Related to their Self-perception and their work Behaviour

M.Ed., D.U., MONICA CHECKER, 1990

The objectives of the study were: (1) To find out the relation between teacher's self-perception and teacher's perception of his/her principal's impression about him/her. (2) To find out the relationship between teacher's self-perception and his/her work behaviour. (3) To find out the relationship between teacher's perception about principal's impression about his/her and his/her work behaviour.

The study was conducted on 72 teachers, comprising of 12 teachers from 6 different schools located at Faridabad. Two tools were used: (1) Perception Scale: Teachers' self-perception and of their principal's impression about them. (2) Teachers' Work Behaviour Scale. The major findings as revealed by the study were: (1) There exists a positive relationship between the three variables. That is if a teacher possesses a positive self-perception then her work behaviour would be desirable. If the teacher has a favourable self-perception than he/she would perceive his/her principal's impression about him/her as favourable. If a teacher has a favourable perception of what his/her principal thinks about him/her than his/her work behaviour would be desirable. (2) The teachers' work behaviour can be improved if they possess a positive or adequate self-concept and if they perceive that their principals have a favourable impression about them. By improving the work behaviour, the student's achievement can be improved.

A Comparative Study of Motivation and 'Being' Among Teachers in Delhi Schools with Reference to Age, Sex, Educational Qualification and Related Variables *M.Ed., C.I.E., D.U.,* ALKA BEHARI, 1986

The objectives of the study were to find out whether: (1) men and women teachers differ in Motivation and Being. (2) Teachers in Government and non-Government Schools differ in Motivation and Being. (3) Teachers specialising in different areas differ in Motivation and Being. (4) Teachers having different levels of educational qualification.

(5) Teachers of different ages differ in Motivation and Being. (6) Teachers with different years of teaching experience differ in Motivation and Being. (7) Teachers teaching different classes differ in Motivation and Being. The seven variables under study were: Sex, Type of Institution where teachers work, Area of Specialisation, Level of Education, Age, Years of teaching experience and Level of classes taught.

The study was conducted on 250 teachers from seven Government, four non-Government schools of Delhi. The tools used were standardised tests by Dixit, Panchapak and Devi at CIE. For each of the variables discussed above the total sample of teachers was divided into sub-groups on the basis of the variable under consideration. These sub-groups were then compared and the statistical significance of differences was computed.

The findings of the study reveal the following: (1) The group of teachers under study was definitely superior to the sample of standardisation. This leads to a tentative conclusion that we need not feel dejected about teachers as a group and that they are more intrinsically motivated and self-actualised than the average person of similar educational qualifications. (2) There is no significant difference between men and women teachers as far as Intrinsic Motivation and Being are concerned. (3) The type of school in which the teachers work does not bring about a difference in their Intrinsic Motivation and Self-actualisation. (4) Coming to the area of specialisation, it has been found that neither of the groups — Humanities or Science — has any superiority over the other in Self-actualisation and Intrinsic Motivation. (5) Post-graduates have higher scores than graduates on self-actualization and Intrinsic Motivation. (6) Teachers who are older show a stronger tendency towards Intrinsic Motivation and Self-Actualization as compared to younger teachers. (7) Teachers who have teaching experience of 10 years or below are found to be definitely lower in Being and Intrinsic Motivation than those who have more than 10 years of teaching experience. (8) The teachers teaching class IX and above are more Intrinsically Motivated and Self-actualised than those teaching Classes VIII or lower.

Gender Class and Profession: A Study of Backgrounds and Perceptions of Teachers in Delhi Schools

M.Ed., C.I.E., D.U., VANDANA BHARDWAJ, 1996

The objectives of the study were to examine the relationship between class and gender backgrounds among the selected teachers of the selected schools in Delhi, to explore the perceptions related to themselves and the profession of teaching among teachers of different class and gender backgrounds.

It was found in the study that whether private and government school, females come from a higher socio-economic backgrounds than the males. Most of the females have a higher qualified fathers holding high status jobs while on the contrary males have fathers working as blue-coloured workers or farmers.

It was also found that female teachers do not take up teaching for economic reasons. They teach for the sake of putting their degrees to use or to be independent financially. Many females spent a little of their salary that too on self or for providing luxury to the children. While male spent maximum part of their salary on home and are left with little to save. But male teachers have other sources of income besides their salary. The urban male teachers earn from part time jobs (private tuitions, small business etc.) to provide economic supplement to their families while the rural teachers possess the agricultural income to provide extra financial support to their families. On the contrary, the income of female teachers is just an additional source of income in family. Females take up teaching as a profession mainly to avoid conflict with their family role and it is easily accessible and because of lesser hours of working which does not require an intensive training, therefore suits females. Males choose this profession mostly (70%) to follow their role model or it was their ambition. So far job satisfaction is concerned 95% of teachers (both male and female) are satisfied with their job. Male and female teachers have different reasons for occupational satisfaction. For females the nature of profession (extension of their family role, lesser, hours etc.) brings contentment while for males it becomes the source for another part-time job (tuition) their association with a reputed school attracts more clients for the major source of income (which is much more than the salary). Males work in school (in spite of low output in the form of income) due to other benefits they derive from it. There are significant differences among males and females regarding their continuity in the profession. 95% of males wish to continue till retirement whereas a majority of females will continue to work till their job is in least conflict with their family roles. The perception of teachers about status of teaching profession is that it is moderate. They feel that the present status is declined in the last 2-3 decades. Both male and female teacher hold more or less similar views as far as their choice of career for their children is concerned. None of the female teacher want their children to be teachers while males think it is suited best for their daughters. Teaching is strictly 'no' in case of their sons. 90% of female teachers have to perform the domestic chores while it is not a compulsion for the male teachers. School as an organisation demands less time from their female teachers in comparison to the male teachers.

Study of Effectiveness of In-service Science Teachers Programmes Organized by Directorate of Education, Delhi

M.Ed., C.I.E., D.U., SUSHMA GUPTA, 1988

The study was taken up by keeping the objectives of (i) investigating the provision of in-service education programme for science teachers in Delhi, (ii) finding out to what extent the science teachers have participated in the in-service education programme in the year 1986-87, (iii) studying the reaction of science teachers toward in-service education programme in which they participated, (iv) identifying the needs and areas for in-service education programme of science teachers, (v) finding out if there is any difference between the needs expressed for in-service teachers training programme by teachers teaching in government and non-government schools and the teachers who have attended and those who have not attended these programmes and (vi) making suggestion for future in-service education programme for science teachers of Delhi schools based on the findings.

A total of 164 science teachers constituted the sample from eighteen government schools, five government-aided schools and five public schools. Data was collected from the written records, talks/interview with officials concerned, administration of questionnaires and personal contact with teachers.

The findings as revealed by the study were: (1) 7% of teachers have been exposed to in-service programmes in one year during 1986-87. (2) Discussions during the course of in-service programmes were found to be move effective than the demonstration and practical work. (3) Teachers found to be highly useful in understanding the new topics which are included in the syllabus which they are teaching and information about the journals and reference books. (4) In-service teachers' programmes were found to fulfil the objective to some extent. (5) 45% of teachers preferred programmes to be organized at the interval of 2 years, 55% preferred it to be of 3 days duration and 76% of them preferred programmes to be organised during school hours or in summer vacation for which they also wanted compensatory leave. (6) Most of the teachers were satisfied with the present in-service education and were willing to attend in future. (7) Radio and television broadcasting and video cassettes along with teaching were found to be useful for conducting in-service education programmes. (8) The teachers showed willingness to get oriented with the latest development in the field of science education, review of textual material and on experimental skills but none showed preference of or getting oriented in methodology. (9) No difference was found between needs and preferences expressed by science teachers teaching in Government and Non-Government Schools.

Pre-Service and In-service Teachers in Delhi

M.Ed., C.I.E., D.U.

In this study, the results of the six experiments carried out on pre-service and In-service teachers in Delhi and Haryana without any hardware at all were carefully evaluated and the results compared with those obtained by the In-service teachers in Lancaster, U.K., to see if the Course on "Effective Questioning" is equally effective in India without use of any expensive hardware at all.

By analysis of the pre and posttests, the Attitude Scale towards teaching, and the Post-Course Evaluation Schedule, the results as reported were: (1) In the 2 Groups which the Investigator observed in their classrooms for differences in teaching behaviour before the course and immediately after the course, it was noted that both Groups I and Groups VI had definitely shown improvement in the use of the questioning skills of 'prompting', 'seeking' further clarification, and 'asking' questions that call for a set of related facts. There was also a significant increase in the percentage of 'higher-order questions' asked and the percentage of 'higher-order responses' received by pupils. There was an obvious reduction in the bad habits of repeating one's own questions, repeating pupil's answers and answering one's own questions. The percentage of discussion time taken by 'teacher talk' in both the Group was also significantly reduced. The skill of 'refocusing' had shown improvement in Group I and the percentage of non-volunteers called on showed a significant increase for this Group as well. Group VI had shown no significant improvement in these two skills. Both the Groups I and VI have shown no improvement in the skill of 'refocusing'. (2) 56 per cent of participants have reported an improvement in the quality of answers given by their pupils and in the level of pupil participation. From the observations made in the classrooms of both the Groups, it was noted that there was a significant increase in the percentage of higher-order responses given by the pupils. This corresponds with the reports made by the teachers on the influence of this Course. The results of the 2 Groups, Group I and VI, clearly show that this Course of Effective Questioning had achieved its objective of reducing 'teacher talk', increasing the level and amount of pupil participation, and eliminating habits which disrupt discussions. Though the procedures used in Delhi was different from that used in Lancaster, U.K., the results which were obtained were very similar to the U.K. experiment. (3) The microteaching experiment conducted in Delhi, was without the use of any hardware as videotape equipment is not economical in Indian conditions. Only lectures and live-demonstrations were used to illustrate the questioning skills in contrast to the Lancaster experiment where teachers viewed instructional videotapes and saw Model Lessons on Television. Also for feedback, supervisors and peers gave oral criticism, in contrast to the Lancaster teachers who replayed their microlessons on videotapes for self-evaluation. All that was used was the written Instructional material where the 12 Questioning skills were explained. This consisted of a few pages which could be cyclostyled and duplicated easily for distribution to the teachers. This inexpensive adaptation of the Lancaster Course on Effective Questioning was quite successful as both the Groups, the Student teachers in Group I, and the experience in-service teachers in Group VI, had shown significant improvement in the use of the questioning skills and reduction in the frequency of undesirable habits. As a result of this Course there was a significant reduction in the percentage of discussion time taken up with teacher's talk. There was a significant increase in the percentage of 'higher-order questions' asked by the teacher and the percentage of 'higher-order responses' obtained from the pupils. (4) If the average of all the six groups is taken, it can be said that on the whole 35 per cent of subjects in our experiments were familiar with microteaching before beginning this Course, and on the average 73 per cent of the subjects had a favourable attitude towards it. Twenty-six per cent had a neutral attitude towards microteaching, and only one subject (out of 164) had a negative attitude towards it. On the whole these six groups had shown a more favourable attitude towards microteaching than Perrott's Group of In-service teachers. (5) Comparing the six groups in their attitudes towards teaching, it was found that the teachers began the Course with a high degree of agreement with the objectives of this Course which are to "increase the level and quality of pupil participation". In general, the teachers supported the use of audio-visual aids even before the course began. They are also in favour of allowing their pupil's autonomy in determining their activities and making their own decisions, but are not in favour of giving their pupils too much scope for experimentation. They also do not value the emphasis upon the standards of achievement and classroom discipline of formal class teaching. (6) In Group VI where the change of attitude towards teaching was measured after taking the course, it was found that there was a significant shift away from stress on formal teaching in these teachers. There was also a more positive attitude towards experimentation and pupil autonomy after the course. It was also observed that even though before the course began, the teachers were in agreement with the course objectives, after the course the teachers become more convinced that the Course objectives are worthy to attain. (7) Comparing the results of Group VI with Perrott's Group we find that both the Groups have shown a significant shift away from stress on formal teaching after the Course. Though Perrott's teachers have not shown any improvement in their scores for pupil autonomy and experimentation and no change in their attitude towards the Course objectives, Group VI has shown a marked improvement in these categories. Perrott's teachers, however, have shown a more positive attitude towards new educational media after the Course, while Group VI has not. This is understandable as Group VI did not make use of audio-visual aids. (8) After the Course, 99 per cent participants in all of the six Groups have reported that they were very interested in the material, enjoyed the Course, and found it a valuable experience. Ninety-six per cent of them would recommend this Course to others. These results compare favourably with Perrott's Group of In-service teachers where similar figures have been reported. Ninety-six per cent of the participants in the 6 Groups have reported that this Course has given them confidence in their teaching ability, compared to 57 per cent in Perrott's Group. (9) With regard to the worry about how they were doing in the Course, all the groups reported of being more worried than Perrott's Group. We have an average of 52 per cent compared to 12 per cent for Perrott's Group. This difference is probably due to the fact that our 6 Groups got criticism from their peers which caused them more concern than Perrott's Group of teachers who got feedback through self- evaluation of their teaching by playback of videotapes of their own performance, and not from peers and supervisors. (10) None of the participants in Groups I, III, VI and Perrott's Group, who besides the demonstration and model lessons were given the written instructional material to read explaining the skills reported that the method of instruction was inefficient. Only the subjects in Groups IV and V who were not given the written instructional material to read reported this. Also more subjects in these 2 Groups reported problems with regard to the use of the skills, and a greater percentage asked for further instruction in the use of these skills. Hence, for better understanding of the skills this important step must not be left out. In Group II where the students were not able to practise the skills in small groups first before trying them out with the full class, 2 out of 7 students reported that the method of instruction was inefficient. Hence, for greater proficiency the skills must be practised first in a micro setting. (11) It was noted that only those Groups which were teaching in schools during the period of this Microteaching Course took maximum opportunity to deliberately practise these questioning skills with their pupils. Hence, for efficient practice of these skills, it is advisable that normal school teaching is not suspended during the Course period so that participants take every opportunity to practise the skills they have learnt in a micro setting with normal classes as well. (12) In none of the 6 Groups was a negative attitude towards microteaching shown by the participants after the Course. Though 99 per cent of the subjects have reported that they were interested in the macro-teaching materials, only half the number have said a definite "yes" to taking a similar microteaching Course. No student or teacher has said "yes" to taking the traditional In-service Course, which is an important finding for those in charge of In-service teachers. (13) Out of a total of 129 responses,

111 responses expressed positive views about microteaching, and only 18 responses were negative. The two main positive views expressed are that microteaching is progressive, and that it is rewarding and useful. On the whole, this Course has been well received by participants. (14) All the 4 Groups have reported that the skills are very useful, although

the percentage is lower than Perrott's Group where over 90 per cent of teachers have given this response. (15) There is a remarkable similarity in the results reported by two In-service Groups and Perrott's In-service Group with regard to the use of the skills. Almost 49% have reported confidence in the use of the skills after the Course, approximately the same number have stated that they were already using these skills appropriately and five per cent in all the three groups have reported the need of further instruction in certain skills. (16) In the six groups, the maximum number of participants have reported the need of further instruction in the skill of 'refocusing' and asking 'higher-order questions'. The 2 skills which are considered easy by all the six groups and Perrott's Group as well are 'pausing', 'prompting', 'calling on non-volunteers' and 'redirection'. The two bad habits of answering one's own questions and of giving a punitive response to wrong answers are considered easy to eliminate by all the groups. The habits considered more difficult to eliminate by all the groups are asking questions that call for yes-no responses and repeating one's own questions. (17) Over 90 per cent of the participants in 6 Groups have rated the skills of 'asking higher-order questions,' 'prompting' and 'seeking further clarification' as the most important to retain, while in Perrott's Group 'redirection' was the most popular receiving support from 75 per cent of teachers. The teachers in six Groups and in Perrott's Groups have placed less importance on the sequences dealing with habits to eliminate than those dealing with skills to perfect. This appears to be due to the negative mode of presentation of the habits as against the positive mode of presentation of the skills. (18) With regard to the changes in pupil behaviour due to microteaching, 62 per cent of participants reported an improvement in attention and interest of pupils and 56 per cent in the quality of answers given by pupils and the level of pupil participation. In Perrott's Group a higher percentage, 85 per cent have reported an improvement in the quality of answers given by pupils, and 78 per cent in the discussion skills of pupils. (19) As a result of this Course 18 per cent of participants in six groups have noticed a problem of which they were previously unaware of and 12 per cent are now actively correcting this problem. The maximum number have reported correcting a speech problem or a speech mannerism. Thus, besides improving the questioning skills of the teachers, this is an additional side benefit of the Course. (20) All the 6 Groups and Perrott's Group have felt that the microteaching experience ('preparing the microlesson' and 'teaching the microlesson') was valuable to retain and given it the highest rating. The 'discussion of specific skills in the handbook' and 'preparation time at home' have been rated as important to retain by all the groups. But whereas the self-evaluation form has been given a low rating by Perrott's teachers, six groups which used these evaluation forms to observe and give feedback to colleagues, have given it a much higher rating. Also, these six groups have given a much higher rating to watching other teacher's lessons than Perrott's Group. Since Perrott's teachers played back their own videotapes for self-evaluation, they hardly used these two components. Thus for the procedure that was followed by 6 Groups, these two important steps are necessary for a successful microteaching experience. (21) The maximum number of participants in 6 Groups have reported problems with regard to the skill of 'refocusing'. The main problem reported is 'not having a clear idea of the skill' and unable to distinguish it from other aspects of teaching. This is in agreement with results found earlier where maximum number of teachers have reported the need for further instruction in the skill of 'refocusing'. Also the Investigator had found from observation in the classroom that in the post-test there was no improvement in the teacher's use of the skill of 'refocusing'. The problem which has been reported consistently by all the 6 Groups a maximum number of times for all the 12 skills is that of giving too much attention to the subject matter of the lesson. Most of the teachers and students are so conscious of completing the syllabus that the subject matter of the lesson assumes undue importance and interferes with their effective use of the questioning skills. The next important problem reported by all the 6 Groups is that of being carried away by discussion with other pupils. (22) Comparing all the 6 Groups in the use of the 12 Questioning skills, we note that Group VI has reported the greatest confidence in the use of the skills (82 per cent reported having no problems with the skills). Group IV (B.Ed. students in Rohtak), who were not given any written instructional material to read, have reported more problems than others in the understanding and effective use of these skills. Many have also reported not being convinced of the value of some of these skills. Though Group V, which consisted of experienced teachers, managed better without the instructional material, many of them have also reported not having a clear understanding of some of the skills. Hence, it is important that this important step must not be eliminated. Group VI, which had the benefit of the written instructional material, as well as the facility to practise these skills in their normal classes with real pupils during the Course period, made the best performance among all the 6 Groups.

Sex-stereotyping by Male Teachers Teaching Classes VIII and IX in Government Co-education Schools of Delhi

M.Ed., C.I.E., D.U., BHARATI ROY CHODHURY, 1984

The present study was taken up to investigate the effect of teachers' teaching and questioning behaviour on the students responding behaviour in the classes VIII and IX. The tasks performed by the students also show effects of the sexist behaviour of the teachers and follow a stereotyped pattern in which the boys perform more higher order tasks than girls. Three coeducational government schools were selected for the study and classes VIII and IX were taken up wherein male teachers taught.

The interpretation of the inter-school differences in the frequency distribution over different items reveal a fairly homogeneous pattern that exists in all the three schools, except for a slight variation in school II where the teacher's behaviour is less repressive than in any of the other schools.

It was found that in all the schools, the teacher behaviour tends to be sexist and they give more positive attention to boys in the class as opposed to the girls who seem to get more of the teachers' negative attention. The children behaviour and the tasks they perform show evidence of the stereotyped attitudes that the teachers' sexist behaviour in class have passed on to the children.

Effectiveness of Micro-teaching for Improving the General Teaching Competence of Accountancy Teachers

M.Ed., C.I.E., D.U., GURDITTA RAM ARORA, 1984

The study was carried out with the objective of determining the effectiveness of micro-teaching technique of general teaching competence of Accountancy teachers and to study the effectiveness of micro-teaching technique on the Accountancy teachers' attitudes towards teaching. The study proceeded by selecting 21 in-service post graduate Accountancy teachers, including three teachers from public schools, two from NDMC and two from government-aided schools and remaining from government senior secondary schools. They attended micro-teaching programme at SIE Roop Nagar for a week. The study was based on a single group pre-test-post-test experimental design. The tools administered on them included Ahluwalia's teachers attitude Inventory, General Teaching Competence Scale and Evaluation Proforma for different teaching skills.

The major findings of the study reported that the training of micro-teaching technique in four skills namely skill of probing questions, stimulus variation, reinforcement and illustrating with examples significantly improved the GTC of In-service Accountancy Teachers. The gain scores of GTC attained at post training I stage had significantly been retained at post training II stage. It also came into the picture that training in micro-teaching technique does not significantly improve the accountancy teachers' attitudes towards teaching.

A Study of DTEA Schools with Reference to Teachers Perception of the School Climate, their Satisfaction and the Students Achievement

M.Ed., C.I.E., D.U., NINAN JOSEPH, 1986

The study aimed at finding out whether there was any relationship between perceived climate and satisfaction, whether there was any relationship between teachers' satisfaction and students' achievement.

Two questionnaires on school climate developed by Ahuja and Puri and on Job satisfaction of teachers developed by Bhardwaj were administered on 70 teachers from seven DTEA schools.

The major findings of the study revealed: (1) About 85% of teachers perceived their school climate as good. Nearly 86% of total teachers were satisfied in their schools. In two schools all the teachers participated were satisfied with their schools. In one school the percentage of teachers satisfied was only 67%. (2) Principals should run the schools on perfectly democratic lines and to maintain a climate highly favourable to satisfaction of all concerned. For this there should be both pre-service and in-service training of the principals. (3) The programmes of teachers training institutions must be strengthened and enriched. A need was felt for strengthening courses in Educational Sociology so that the problems of morale and human relations are perfectly tackled. (4) Both school climate and satisfaction levels were inter-related. Besides improving the school climate, the teacher's satisfaction level also should be increased. (6) Satisfaction of teachers and students' achievement were also inter co-related. Dissatisfied teacher can never perform his duties up to the mark. Principals can do a lot in this regard, by involving teachers in the day-to-day working of the schools.

Study of Values Held by Teachers in Higher Secondary Schools of Delhi *M.Ed., C.I.E., D.U.,* R.P. SHARMA, 1965

The study is an attempt to bring to surface the 'dominant' interests of the teachers, which can further be extended to spot-light the gaps, if any, between the proposed and the actual aims of teaching different subjects. This study seeks to unearth the difference, if any, that exists between different values held by teachers and whether the difference between different values is significant. It endeavours to bring to light the difference and the significance of difference between values, on the bases of (a) sex and (b) subjects. Besides, it institutes, an inquiry with an open mind into the nature of correlations that exists between the six values, and determines the significance of those correlations. Like many other research studies, it implicitly tries to cause an awareness of the existence and the operative function of values among the teachers, inducing them to self-criticism and job consciousness.

A tool on values prepared by Allport *et al.*, adopted on Indian conditions was administered on 98 teachers (56 males and 42 females) of six government and aided schools constituting the sample.

The major findings of the study appeared as: (1) Teachers on the whole are theoretical, economic and social values as compared to aesthetic, political and religious values. (2) Male teachers stand higher than female teachers in theoretical and economic values while female teachers scored higher in religious and aesthetic value. Interestingly, female teachers have shown greater consciousness of political value than the male teachers. There is no significant difference between value-scores of Arts and Science teachers. (3) The over-all difference among value- scores of teachers are highly significant. (4) Differences between means of theoretical-aesthetic, economic-social, social-political and social-religious turn out to be highly significant. (5) Most of the values are negatively correlated to each other. There are only two cases of positive correlation. The theoretical and economic values are positively correlated to political value. The aesthetic and social values show completely negative relationship with all the values. The negative relationship of religious value with other values raises our curiosity. But it can be attributed to the fact that Indians are definitely 'religious' from Americans. (6) Most of the correlations (negative) are highly significant. The positive correlation between theoretical-political and economic-political values is, however, not significant.

Comparative Verbal Interaction Analysis of Biology Teachers of Public Schools and Government Schools

M.Ed., C.I.E., D.U., 1985

The objectives of the study were to study the verbal interaction pattern of public school biology teachers, to study the verbal interaction pattern of government school biology teachers and to compare the verbal interactional behaviour of biology teachers of both the groups.

The study, which aims at finding out how much the actual teaching is a two way process, is helpful for more effective work of schools because after knowing the verbal interaction pattern of teachers, one can guide and make suggestions for improving the fruitful participation of both teachers and students. Besides, it will also be useful to find out if teachers of expensive schools (public) are considered to be better, are involving children more in the process of teaching-learning.

The findings derived from this study were: (1) The Biology teachers of public and government schools are found to differ in their verbal interaction pattern with respect to only three categories *i.e.*: Category-7 'Criticizing or justifying authority, Category-9 'Pupils talk in chorus' and Category-11 'Both talk together.' The government school biology teachers use these categories more often than those of public schools. (2) It has been fully affirmed that 'teacher-talk' is the dominant behaviour found in teaching of both the groups. One can easily conclude that in our Indian classes, it is the teacher who speaks most of the times and the method followed is clearly the "Lecture method" where students have a very little opportunity to participate in chain of events happening in the classroom. (3) Direct influence is more pronounced in the teacher talk in both the groups as compared to the indirect influence. The teachers use direct influence much more than indirect influence. In other words, the teachers are more authoritative and do not stimulate the students, much, to participate in the communication.

Characteristics of an ideal Teacher as Perceived by Students at Different Stages of Development

D.U., M.Ed., C.I.E., VANDANA GROVER

The objectives of the study were: to identify the characteristics of an ideal teacher as perceived by children at the primary stage, to identify the characteristics of an ideal teacher as perceived by children at the secondary stage, to explore a relationship between the characteristics of an ideal teacher as perceived and the needs of children at primary and secondary stages, to compare the characteristics of an ideal teacher as perceived by children at these two different developmental stages, to investigate the characteristics of an ideal teacher as perceived at each developmental stage with reference to gender, to identify the personality traits of children at the primary and secondary stages and to investigate a relationship between the personality traits of children and the characteristics of an ideal teacher as perceived by them.

Major findings of the study were: (1) There appears to be a relationship between the characteristics of an ideal teacher perceived at each stage, and the developmental needs at that stage. It can be said children unconsciously try to satisfy these needs through their teacher and thus, perceive such characteristics. (2) While comparing the characteristics perceived at the primary and the secondary levels, it appears that there are differences in the characteristics perceived at both levels. These can be attributed to differences in the students' developmental characteristics and related needs at the two stages. Also, there are some characteristics which tend to be common at both the stages. Some of these have comparable percentages at both the levels implying universality of needs, while in others, there is a major difference in the percentages at the two levels. These differences can be attributed to differences in the dominant needs at these levels. (3) There seem to be no differences in the characteristics perceived at each developmental stage, with reference to gender. However, some differences prevail in the importance given to some characteristics by boys and girls at each stage. These differences can be related to the prevailing gender differences in the society. (4) It appears that students, both high and low on the personality traits identified for the study, tend to have similar perceptions regarding the characteristics of an ideal teacher at each stage. The difference lies in the reasons underlying these perceptions, that is, both categories of students quote different reasons for perceiving those particular teacher-characteristics. (5) Since the personality traits of the children are not well- established at these levels, it cannot be said with certainty that a definite relationship exists between the personality traits of children, and the characteristics perceived by them. But this exploratory study does indicate that the two tend to be related to each other.

A Study of the Relationship Between Social Insight and the Different Orientations of Teachers

M.Ed., C.I.E., D.U., 1983

The objectives of the study were to find out the degree of social insight shown by teachers of different types, to find out if there is any difference between the different orientations to teaching among the teaching community and to find out if there is any relationship between Social Insight and the different types of orientations.

The sample selected consisted of 200 teachers of Delhi schools, 50 male teachers each from government and public schools, 50 female teachers each from government and public schools. The tools administered in the study comprised of a test of Social Insight prepared by Cattell and a self-made tool for orientation to teaching.

The major findings of social insight were: (1) Public school and Government School Male teacher differ significantly in all areas and on total insight. The Government school teachers are more withdrawn, more passive, more competitive and aggressive. Their degree of cooperativeness is markedly lower than that of the public school teachers. Moreover, public school male teachers indicate a higher total social insight. (2) Public school male and female teachers do not differ significantly with regard to withdrawal, cooperativeness, competitiveness, aggression and total social insight. Women teachers are, however, more passive than men. (3) The male and female teachers of Government schools differ significantly on aggressiveness, cooperativeness and total insight. Male teachers are more aggressive and less cooperative, and have a lower overall social insight than that of female teachers of Government Schools. (4) Public school female teachers reflect a higher degree of social insight and are less competitive as compared to Government School female teachers. (5) Men and women teachers do not differ significantly on the different areas, but their scores or total insight reflect significant differences. The women teachers seem to show definitely greater insight than men. This finding verdicts the Gestalt Stand that the "whole" is more than the "sum of its parts". (6)

The Public school teachers are more cooperative less aggressive and competitive, and have a higher total social insight, as compared to government schoolteachers as a whole. (7) The most withdrawn group is of government school male teachers and the least withdrawal are female teachers of public schools. (8) The most passive are women teachers of public schools, least passive being public school male teachers. (9) Most competitive group is of Government school male teachers, and least competitive are the public school female teachers. (10) Most aggressive group is of Government school male teachers, the least aggressive being male teachers of Public schools. (11) Highest total insight is of public school female teachers, and lowest of Government school male teachers. As regards orientation to teaching, the major findings were: (1) The Delhi school teachers appear to be most subject-oriented, followed by exam-orientation. Growth orientation comes next, followed by status orientation. They score least on indifference. (2) The public and Government school teachers differ significantly only with respect to "Growth" orientation, the former group being definitely more concerned with the growth of the students than the latter. (3) The women teachers of Public schools are definitely more concerned with their results in exams, whereas their male colleagues appear more interested in their subjects or fields of specialisation. (4) The male and female teachers of Government schools seem quite homogeneous in respect to their orientation to teaching. (5) The Government school female teacher seem definitely more subject-oriented than their counterparts in public schools. Though this is the only area in which the two groups differ significantly, the difference does approach significance in the case of growth and exam-orientation. In both, the public school women teachers have higher scores. (6) The male and female teachers do not show any statistical differences in their orientations to teaching. However, the women teachers tend more towards growth and exam-orientations, whereas the men teachers seem more subject oriented. (7) Public school teachers are more growth oriented, while the Government school teacher lean, towards subject orientation. (8) Most growth oriented group of teachers are the Public school male teachers, the least concerned for growth being the Government school male teachers. (9) Most subject oriented teachers are the male teachers from Government Schools and the least are Public school women teachers. (10) The most exam- oriented teachers belong to Public school (female), while the least concerned with exam results are the Public school male teachers. (11) Status orientation appears to be the same for all categories of teachers.

Job Satisfaction and its Major Determinants Amongst Primary School Teachers of Delhi

M.Ed., C.I.E., D.U., 1984

The main objective of the study was to find out the differences in job satisfaction amongst teachers with varied experiences, among male and female teachers and lastly among teachers working in different types of schools.

The sample comprised of 90 male and 90 female teachers. They were administered a questionnaire developed by the investigator.

The study revealed the major findings as: (1) The teachers as a whole, irrespective of their sex difference, has a lower level of job satisfaction. (2) There is more job satisfaction amongst beginners in teaching profession which goes down with the increasing number of years of teaching experience. Teaching experience is a determinant of job satisfaction. Also that teaching experience is negatively related to job satisfaction. (3) Job satisfaction is higher in case of female teachers as compared to their male counterparts. Sex is also an important determinant of job satisfaction.

Handbook on Sociometry for Teachers and Counsellors

NCERT, New Delhi, A. SHARMA, 1970

The handbook reported six interrelated studies on different aspects of: A. The first study aimed at investigating the secondary school pupils like the relationship between intelligence, achievement, personality and adjustment, interest patterns, life at home and at school, and the popularity and isolation "Social Skills and Activities and Sociometric Status",

"Personality Characteristics and Sociometric Status", "The Sociometric Seating and Classroom Social Relations", "sharing responsibilities" on developing an atmosphere conducive to group living, "Study of Biographies and Classroom Social Relations".

The sample was drawn from three schools in Delhi — one boys' school, one girls' school and one coeducational school. In the boys' school, seventy-three students of class VII formed the sample. In the girls' school, the sample had 104 students. In the coeducational school, 113 students were in the sample. The various correlates studied were: intelligence, academic achievement, personality and adjustment, interest, family life, school life, and socio-economic status. The research tools used were the Raven's Standard Progressive Matrices, the Vyaktitva Parakh Prashnavali, the Chatterjee's Non-language Preference Record, examination marks, check-lists to measure the different aspects of family and school life.

The findings were: the popular students were of higher intelligence and scored higher on scholastic achievement test than the isolates. They had better personality adjustment. The interest profiles of populars and isolates were almost similar. The three most liked interests of popular boys were scientific, mechanical and technical while those of isolate boys were mechanical, scientific and sports. The three least liked interest of popular boys were outdoor, household and fine arts whereas the least liked interests of popular boys were outdoor, household and fine arts whereas the least liked interests of isolate boys were household, agriculture and crafts. Parents of populars had better education than those of the isolates. B. The second study on the popularity and isolation aimed at providing some understanding into the actual nature and frequency of social skills and activities possessed by adolescent students and to compare the social skills and activities of the popular, neglectee, isolate and rejectee.

The sample consisted of grade IX students drawn from three higher secondary schools of Delhi — one boys' school (N=160), one girls' school (N=80) and one public school (N=96).

The various correlates studied were: social skills and activities and personality development. The tools used were: sociometric questionnaire, Social Acceptance Scale, and social skills and activities scale constructed by the investigator himself.

The major findings were: (i) the populars possess more skills and activities than the neglectees but less than those of the rejectees. The public school rejectees perform largest number of skills and activities and even the neglectees possess more skills and activities than the populars; (ii) there are no significant differences in the percentages of different categories of boys and girls performing various skills and activities; (iii) the proportion of neglectees engaged in ten sections of ninth class of the three schools — one higher than that of populars and the proportion of rejectees engaged in learning music is also significantly higher than that of populars. C. The third study aimed at investigating the personality characteristics of popular, neglected, isolated and rejected students.

Three hundred and twenty-five students reading in ten sections of ninth class of the three schools — one boy's, one girl's and one public school of Delhi were taken as sample. The tool used had the 'Guess Who' technique to get the information regarding the way each member of a large adolescent group was perceived by the group. Thirty-five personality characteristics were included in the scale. Student I test was used to find out the significance of difference between mean trait scores of populars and neglectees, populars and isolates, and neglectees and isolates. Unaccepted pupils comprised three categories, *viz.*, isolates and rejectees and neglectees.

The findings of the study were: (i) the personality characteristics of unaccepted pupils are quite similar, whereas those of accepted and unaccepted students are quite dissimilar; (ii) populars are found to be more aggressive and overt, assertive, courageous and vigorous, confident, playing superiority role, well in group participation and friendly, whereas unaccepted pupils are more submissive, non-confident, coward and weak, selfish and non-cooperative and non-group participating. The characteristics which proved most significant in differentiating between accepted and unaccepted children fall into three syndromes: (i) strong aggressive personality characteristics, (ii) characteristics that count in direct interpersonal contacts, (iii) characteristics that are important in making better human relationship. D. The fourth study about aimed at studying the effect of sociometric seating on classroom social relations.

The sample consisted of the students of class VII of a government boys' higher secondary school located in a central government employees' colony for housing officers of grades I and III in New Delhi. Seventy one students, thirty-seven in controlled group and thirty-four in experimental group were taken as the sample. The Wilcoxon Matched Pairs Signed Rank Test was applied to test that the social status of unaccepted pupils remained unaffected by sociometric seating.

The study found that sociometric seating appears to be a useful technique of improving interpersonal relationships within a group. It appears to weaken the barriers which stand in the formation of a cohesive class. E. The fifty study aimed at investigating the effect of the sample consisted of thirty-five students of class VIIC and all the students of class VIIB taken as the control group. Three choice sociometric questionnaire and Bronfenbrenner's fixed frame of reference were used to categorise students into five sociometric categories. The programme of creating an atmosphere in the class for group living started with the election of two representatives for each of the three responsibilities decided. The representatives started working with the class for framing the rules and procedures to manage library, game activities and day to day class management.

It was found that as the programme advanced, there was marked improvement in the class tone; opposition and aggression had started giving way to cooperation. The democratic method of solving their differences and problems was found to develop a sense of responsibility in the individuals and of the group to individuals. A start for developing respect for reason and willingness to settle issues through an appeal to reason was made. F. The sixth study aimed at determining the effect of study and discussion of biographies of some great men of India and biographical sketches of class fellows in restructuring interpersonal relations within class. The students of seventh class of a government boys' higher secondary school located in a rural area of Delhi State were taken as a sample. The parents of the students taken as sample were in the lower socio-economic level. The students were categorised into sociometric categories, namely, popular, above average, average, below average, neglectees and isolates after administering the three criteria, three choice sociometric questionnaire and also using the Bronfenbrenner's fixed frame of reference. The Wilcoxon Matched Pairs Signed Ranks Test was also taken into use.

The investigator, from an analysis of objective data and from subjective observation, concluded that social emotional climate of the class was improved. A better understanding of a pupil's personality and the circumstances in which it developed coupled with the opportunity to interact, helped in accepting him instead of the fact that the class changed in such a way that conditions of threat were reduced and individuals found satisfaction in participation in class work.

School Teachers in Delhi: Relationship Between their Social Background and Professionalization

Ph.D., JMI, C.L. WADHAWAN, 1980

The study was carried out with the objectives of finding out the socio-economic and cultural background of higher secondary school teachers, the degree of their professionalization and to analyse the relationship between their social background and degree of professionalism.

The sample included teachers from three types of schools, namely government schools, aided schools and unaided schools. Thirty government, thirteen aided and five unaided schools were selected. From these forty-eight schools, 375 teachers constituted the sample.

The findings of the study were: (1) The largest number of teachers, forming 64 per cent belonged to lower middle class; 52 per cent lived in rented houses; 74 per cent had a cycle as a mode of transport. (2) Forty-one per cent male teachers and 64 per cent female teachers had urban background. (3) A majority of the teachers (58 per cent) had nuclear families. (4) The social background of the female teachers was better than that of their male counterparts. (5) The academic and professional achievements of the teachers showed that they were generally of mediocre intellectual status. (6) The teachers were not benefited significantly by the in-service programmes. (7) A sizable number of teachers (46 per cent) considered teaching more satisfying than most other careers, but not the most satisfying. (8) The male teachers were more professional than their female counterparts. (9) About 50 per cent teachers opined those parents did not help their wards in their homework. (10) A majority of the male and the female teachers rated the staff rooms, material aids for teaching, school discipline, academic reputation of the schools in the locality and encouragement to innovative teachers as average. (11) Ninety-nine per cent teachers gave poor evaluation of their principals. (12) Forty-six per cent male and 53 per cent female teachers gave average rating to the general mental ability of teachers. (13) There was positive and significant relationship between professional and general environment of the school and the degree of job satisfaction.

Application of Pedagogical Knowledge and Skills Acquired in Teacher Training to School Teaching by Primary Teacher of Mathematics

PUSHPA VERMA & S. CHHABRA, *SCERT, New Delhi*

The objectives of the study were to find out the extent to which the practising teachers of mathematics at the primary stage are familiar with the skills, strategies and devices learnt during their preservice teacher training programme, to find out the extent to which they are able to employ such teacher training competencies in teaching mathematics in their classroom teaching practice, to investigate which of the competencies and approach to teaching mathematics are popular among the teachers and to enquire into the difficulties and limitations of teachers in using their pedagogical skills and competencies in actual teaching of mathematics in order that teacher training programmes may receive feedback for its restructuring and relevance to teaching situations.

It is a preliminary study based on a sample of 100 primary school teachers. Schools were selected on the basis of the representative sampling of schools in Delhi State keeping in view the rural urban area consideration to which they cater as well as the administrative zones in which they are placed. The Questionnaire was the major device for collecting teachers' opinions on a wide ranging skills and competencies they have learnt and practised over the years of their professionalism. The syllabi of the premier teacher training institutions for Primary and Elementary school teachers were analysed in order to determine the pedagogical skills and competencies emphasised in the teacher training programmes. Such institutions include the DIETS, Maulana Azad Centre for Elementary and Social Education, Delhi, Teacher Training Institute, Jamia Millia Islamia, New Delhi, Punjabi University, Patiala.

Questionnaire constructed by investigators were administered on selected sample. Major findings and recommendations of the study: (1) Teachers with better qualification had a better response pattern than teachers with a lower degree. (2) Majority of teachers could not correctly identify the objectives of teaching in exact behavioural terms. Specific inputs are required during teacher training for teachers to correctly identify the behavioural objectives of teaching mathematics. But all teachers did analyse the course contents. (3) While analysing the methods of teaching used by teachers it was noticed that problem-solving, play way and inductive and deductive techniques were used most extensively. Project work, Laboratory and auto instruction were the least utilised. The restrictive way in which education is being imparted is a relevant point to be considered as all techniques were assumed to be equally important as teaching tools by the researcher. It was also noticed that none of the teachers could come up with a new method of teaching beyond those indicated. (4) Similarly the frequency of usage (teaching techniques) usually hovered around one or two techniques being used predominantly. (5) On the micro-teaching level in terms of skills and competencies of teachers, the teachers are either not aware of all the techniques or the skills were not being fully utilised as the method of teaching is only restricted to the use of one or two techniques. (6) Illustrations and applications and problem skills were the two teaching techniques used most often while dramatisation and audio-visual aids featured as the techniques least used. (7) Teachers with a higher level of education seem to improvise more than teachers with a lower qualification who tend to restrict themselves to their known skills. (8) All teachers tend to give homework on a daily basis. Most of this homework was given from the assigned textbook and rarely does the teacher venture out to other sources. The homework in general terms is checked often by teachers. (9) There was no clear consensus by teachers on the use of diagnostic tools for assessment of pupil's learning capabilities as the responses were varied. (10) Suggestions given by the teachers for remedial action to improve the present state of affairs did not indicate any concrete line of action even though some of the suggestions were good. (11) Most teachers indicated that they did not use any material except the textbook for teaching. (12) When asked to suggest improvements in the syllabus, again the response was low. Most teachers agreed that the present syllabus was good but could not site particular strengths and weaknesses in the syllabus. (13) All teachers could give examples for mathematics as for developing reasoning and imagination. (14) In general most teachers found teaching mathematics interesting and absorbing. (15) Creativity and imagination was sighted as the most important tools to develop interest in the pupil for mathematics. (16) All teachers agreed that teacher training had helped them to enhance their skills but not many could specially point to the micro level skills that it had helped them develop. (17) It must be noted as a footnote that questionnaire was in English and some teachers had problems in answering some of the questions due to lack of comprehension. (18) Contradictions were noticed in some cases which might have skewed the evaluation process.

TEACHER SELF-EFFICACY AND COMPETENCE FOR IMROVING QUALITY OF PRIMARY SCHOOLING

Paper Presented in the 1996 International Seminar on Schools Effectiveness and Classroom Processes at Primary Stage

SUSHILA SINGHAL and RITA SHARMA

The study took up the objectives of examining the effect of training teachers into achieving subject specific competencies in the primary classes on their self-efficacy and competence.

The sample consisted of 116 primary school teachers trained at DIET, Moti Bagh into achieving competencies (MLL) during the last two years. This was treated as the experimental group. Another control group of 110 teachers was identified from the comparable schools in South Delhi who had not been trained so far in achieving competencies.

A questionnaire was used in Hindi to obtain data on a five point response format.

The major findings of the study emerged as: (1) On the dimensions of self-efficacy and competence as well as on the total scores, the means for the experimental group were slightly higher than the controls, the variability was more in case of the controls. Only a few significant differences between the two groups emerged. (2) The experimental group felt more certain about the power and capacity of teachers. Teachers believed that they could do many good things if they so desired. The control group on the other hand had more valued observations made on what teachers cannot do. Thus, while the approach of the experimental group is to proceed on a positive course, the approach of the control group is negative, which in turn reduces the effectiveness of their efforts for capability building. (3) The experimental group was better in the use of strategies to communicate the contents to children, in adopting the questioning and answering method and in moulding the contents to the needs of children but the differences were not significant. The experimental group teachers had significantly longer work experience than the control group which in a way reflected on the policy of selecting teachers for training by schools/DIETS. (4) An item-wise comparison under different dimensions of self-efficacy and competence showed extreme response tendencies of groups on one or the other item. On the teacher can item (focusing on a content facilitating method of teaching), while 93.1% of teachers in the experimental group responded highly positively, only 9.1% of the controls did so. Similarly on a teacher cannot item (focusing on the need of increased parental effort and involvement in child's study), 14.5% more of experimental respond highly positively. On an I can item (knowledge of the method of increasing the learning competence of child), 92.8% of controls responded highly positively against 18% of the experimental. On the I cannot item (training defect to handle learning problems of children) 21.30% less than experimental responded positively. Nearly 8% more of controls responded highly positively to the preparation and planning item (time put in lesson planning), and 12% more on teaching aid item (demonstrations/experimentation). Nearly 10% more of experimental respond highly positively to a teaching strategy item (feedback to students); and a 14% more than controls to interactions with students' item (children come forward to clear their problems/confusions). (5) Teachers having good socioeconomic status see more options and can would themselves easily. (6) The younger teachers in both groups seem to have better socio-economic status. In both the groups age and work experience correlate positively. (7) The self-efficacy had almost no correlation with preparation and planning dimension of competence in any group. The total self-efficacy correlates positively with several dimensions of competence in both groups, but significantly in case of only the control group. The correlation between total self-efficacy and competence are positive for both groups, but significant for the control group (r = .26).

Self-actualization Among Teachers of Higher Secondary Schools in Delhi

Ph.D., IIT, Delhi, AMULYAKANT SATYAPATHY, 1980

The study assumed self-actualization model of a person as efficient and practicable in a working situation. It was carried out with the objectives of exploring the relationship of self-actualization with certain background, personality and organizational factors among the teachers of higher secondary schools in Delhi. Altogether 26 factors, 6 of them classified as background, 4 as personality and 16 as organizational variables, were studied in relation to two important measures of self-actualization such as Time Ratio and Support Ratio.

The sample consisted of 302 teachers (171 males and 131 females) of 65 assorted Government, Private-aided and Public higher secondary schools in the urban and rural areas of Delhi. The teachers were selected on the basis of two-stage stratified proportionate simple random sampling method. Data were collected through a set of 5 tests and inventories and analysed using various univariate, bivariate and multivariate statistical techniques.

The major findings of the study was that self-actualization is a phenomenon which is significantly related to and affected by various background variables such as age, sex, marital status, mother's education background and teaching experience; personality factors like achievement value, consideration and involvement with teaching; and organizational variables such as type of school, type of staff, choice of job and work-place, frankness of opinion-expression, innovativeness, disengagement, hindrance, intimacy and aloofness. A causal model of self- actualization was developed.

Teachers' Performance in Mathematics and Reading Test

Indian Educational Review, Vol. 31(1), 92-104, K.M. GUPTA, 1996

The study mainly aimed at examining the teachers' performance in mathematics and reading test. Forty-two teachers (30 male and 12 female) of class V were identified for the study. The tools comprised Mathematics Achievement Test (MAT) and Language Achievement Test (LAT). The collected data were treated using percentage, mean, SD and 't' test. The major findings highlighted that the trained teachers performed better in mathematics than the untrained ones. They rather achieved higher in language than the untrained teachers. Similarly as for the achievement level of teachers, they possessed poor knowledge about synonyms, majority of them performed poorly in comprehension of idea while 48% teachers could not comprehend the meaning of words in a paragraph.

A Study of Factors Contributing to Commitment to the Teaching Profession *Ph.D., C.I.E., D.U.,* P. MOHAN RAJU, 1992

The study examined the factors which contribute to teachers' commitment to the teaching profession and factors that stimulate and sustain the commitment of teachers to the teaching profession. The main objectives of the study were (1) to identify psycho-social variables that influence teachers' commitment to their profession and determination of factors that can be derived from these influencing variables, (2) to study the differences between more committed and less committed teachers on the factors and psycho-social variables in order to develop a profile of more committed and less committed teacher in terms of the identified factors and constituents psycho-social variables that distinguish the two groups of teachers, (3) to determine the relative contribution of these factors and variables to teachers' commitment to the teaching profession.

The study was conducted on 454 senior secondary school teachers of Delhi, who were drawn from 28 schools. The tools used included adapted scales of Goal Congruence Commitment by Singh and Das, and Affective Commitment by Balaji. The other three remaining psycho-social variables, *viz.* intrinsic motivation, overall job satisfaction and inner direction were measured by adopting the available scales developed by Lawler and Hall, O'Rilly and Caldwell, and Shostram respectively. The collected data were treated with Mean, SD, 't' test. Factorial analysis, Stepwise Discriminant Function Analysis and Stepwise Multiple Regression Analysis.

The major findings as revealed in the study were: (1) More committed teachers were found significantly different from less committed teachers on "Work-related Personality" and on all its six constituent variables. (2) On the factor "perceived characteristics of the profession", more committed teachers were found to have scored significantly higher than less committed teachers; and also more committed teachers were significantly higher on all six constituents variables. (3) Scores on "Professional choice satisfaction" and on its constituent's variables were found significantly more for more committed teachers than for less committed teachers. The constituent's variables were choice satisfaction and opportunity for other jobs. (4) Less committed teachers were found to have significantly lower scores than more committed teachers on "professional satisfaction and importance" and on its constituent's variables. (5) More committed teachers expressed a significantly higher "desire to improve skills" when compared to less committed teachers. (6) More teachers were distinguished by having higher scores on "perceived characteristics of the profession", "work related personality characteristics", "desire for skill improvement" and "Perceived Characteristics of the Profession." (7) Results of multiple regression analysis revealed that 4 out of the 5 predictor factors were found significant. They were perceived characteristics of the profession, work-related personality, professional satisfaction and importance, and desire for skill improvement. Among the psycho-social variables external expectations was the most contributing variable followed by the variables — perceived status, intrinsic motivation, interest in the profession, desire to improve skills, social support, choice satisfaction perceived challenges.

A Study of Attitude of in-service Teachers Towards Cooperative Learning and Collaborative Teaching

C.M. SRIVASTAVA, PRATIBHA SHARMA,
HARINDER YADAV and CHAMPA PANT, *SCERT*

The study is an action research project comprised of two groups of the teachers attending the in-service teachers training programmes at DIET, Rajinder Nagar. The total sample for the study constituted 73 assistant teachers of M.C. Primary School.

They were exposed to different strategies of co-operative learning and collaborative teaching. It was found that for continuous staff development, such exposure and strategies were very suitable and useful for mastery of certain competencies.

Work Motivation of Primary School Teachers and their Understanding of MLL

M.Phil, JNU, RITU, 1994

The present study was undertaken to find out the differences in work motivation and understanding of MLL between teachers implementing minimum level of learning and teachers not implementing it and to examine the relationship between work motivation and minimum levels of learning of these teachers.

The objectives may be summarized as: to assess the work motivation and understanding of minimum levels of learning of primary school teachers who are implementing MLL and who are not implementing it to find out the relation between work motivation and understanding of minimum levels of learning among primary school teacher and to find out the relation of demographic variables (age, education and experience of teachers) with work motivation and understanding of minimum levels of learning.

Purposive sampling was used to select the 50 teachers who were asked to implement the minimum levels of learning programme in their schools, and to select 50 teachers who had completed the MLL orientation programme but were not implementing it.

A correlational research design was used to examine the relationship among the work motivation and understanding of minimum levels of learning and demographic variables of primary teachers.

The tools used for data collection were as follows: (1) Scale of demographic characteristics to obtain information on sex, age, experience, marital status, educational qualification, etc; (2) Work motivation schedule for assessing the magnitude of work motivation generated by need for personal growth, need for achievement, need for self-control, need for monetary gains and need for non-financial gains; (3) Minimum levels of learning questionnaire consisted of 15 questions relating to the usefulness of minimum levels of learning programme.

The scales were formulated and pretested for the study. Using the above scale the data were collected and coded. The analysis of data were done using means, standard deviations 't-tests', correlational analysis, percentages and chi square.

Following findings and conclusions can be drawn: (1) The monetary gains did not emerge as motivator for teachers, the opportunities for advancement, responsibility, recognition and appreciation for work and to achieve goals were found important. The teachers' need for achievement was significantly related to their understanding of minimum levels of learning. (2) All the three groups of teachers, *i.e.* teachers not implementing MLL, teachers who could not implement MLL and teachers implementing MLL, differed significantly from each other on work motivation and understanding of MLL. Teachers who could not implement MLL had highest work motivation but lowest understanding of MLL, on the other hand teachers who were implementing MLL had highest understanding of MLL. Work motivation was significantly related of MLL score of teachers implementing MLL as well as for teachers who could not implement it. (3) Highly motivated teachers did not differ significantly from medium motivated teachers on understanding of MLL. No significant correlation between overall work motivation and understanding of MLL were observed either for medium or high work motivation teachers. The understanding of MLL had significant association with need for achievement of medium work motivation teachers, and with needs for achievement and self-control of high work motivation teachers. (4) Teachers having above mean work motivation did not differ significantly from teachers having below mean work motivation. Teachers having below mean work motivation showed no significant association between their work motivation and understanding of minimum level of learning. Needs for achievement and self-control in the above mean group were significantly related to their understanding of MLL but need for non-financial gains was found negatively related with MLL. (5) Level of education did not make any significant difference to work motivation and understanding of MLL of teachers. Graduate teachers' need for achievement and need for self-control were associated significantly with their understanding of MLL. (6) Age of the teachers had no significant relation with work motivation and understanding of MLL of teachers. Both the younger and the older groups of teachers had their need for achievement significantly associated with understanding of MLL. (7) More experienced teachers experienced significantly higher needs for achievement and self-control.

But no significant differences on overall work motivation and understanding of MLL were found. Both the groups had their need for achievement significantly related to understanding of MLL. Significant negative association was also found between need for non-financial gains and MLL for more experienced teachers. (8) Teachers had no other source of information on MLL other than the training programme and discussions with colleagues. (9) Some of the teachers who were asked to implement MLL could not implement it in their schools, even those who were implementing it modified the information and methodology of MLL according to their own needs and specific conditions of the school. (10) MLL was reported beneficial for teachers, more frequently by teacher implementing it. (11) All the teachers not implementing MLL those implementing it and fifty per cent of those who could not implement it felt MLL to be useful for improving attention, motivation and learning levels of students. (12) All the teachers who could not implement MLL, many implementing it, and half of those not implementing it agreed that MLL programme is not applicable in their schools. (13) Teachers implementing MLL and those who could not implement it, reported it useful for lower primary classes only (*i.e.* I, II and III) while teachers not implementing it perceived it useful for all primary classes. (14) MLL programme was found useful for all types of students irrespective of their level of intelligence, socio-economic-status and other individual differences, by teachers not implementing MLL, and those implementing it, whereas, only half of those who could not implement MLL felt the same. (15) The education system should benefit from MLL programme according to teachers not implementing MLL as well as those implementing it, but only half of the teachers who could not implement MLL agreed to it. (16) Contrary to the expectations the percentage of students covering prescribed eighty per cent of the syllabus, was highest for teachers not implementing MLL and lowest for teachers who could not implement MLL. (17) Certain major limitation of MLL such as non-applicability in large class size, pressure to complete syllabus within time, the social financial and intellectual differences among students, providing incomplete knowledge and material to teachers were reported. (18) The reduction in class size and syllabus, more information on material and methodology of MLL, changes in administrative policies and involvement of parents were suggested to remove shortcomings of MLL. (19) Factors related to the personality of the teacher were found most important by teachers for improving the quality of teaching and learning level of students.

Comparative Study of Inductive and Deductive Approaches in Teaching Management Concepts

M.Ed., C.I.E., D.U.. CHANDER PRABHA, 1989

The study had the following objectives: (1) To enlist the various concepts of management. (2) To find out which of the two approaches, inductive and deductive is more effective in teaching specific concepts of management. (3) To find out which approach is more significant to helping the students in retaining the concepts learnt for a longer period.

The study was conducted on 56 students of class XII from one Government Senior Secondary School. It was a parallel group experimental study. Management concepts were taught to both the groups through deductive approach to experimental group and inductive approach to control group. A common posttest was given to both the groups and after two months a common test was administered to study the effect.

The study arrived at the following major findings: (1) Inductive approach has been more effective as compared to deductive in teaching the concepts of management. (2) Retention of the concepts by pupils through the inductive approach is more over the learning by deductive approach at .05 level.

To Study the Effect of Written Feedback Given by Teachers on Children Self-concept

M.Ed., C.I.E., D.U., NEERAJ, 1993

The objectives of the study were to study the effect of different types of comments on different aspects *(e.g.* academic and non-academic) of self-concept, to find the effect of academic and non-academic comments on the child's self-concept, to find out the effects of teachers' labelling through their comments as intelligent or slow learner on the student's self-concept, to see the effect of comments when directly addressed to the students or parents, to determine whether comments reflect teachers' expectations from the child to show how such expectations effect the child's self-concept and to see if teachers give importance to the individual differences in their comments.

A purposive sample of 90 students of class V were selected from an English medium public school. They were administered an academic self-concept inventory, a perception of teacher's scale, an open-ended questionnaire developed by the researcher and a self report on perception about themselves. In order to see the effect of teacher's written feedback on children's self-concept, the data was collected in the form of comments given by teachers in students' diary, note-books and report cards. A content analysis was done. The outcomes were classified into broad categories of factors affecting self-concept. These factors affected self-concept differently and were important as they correlated to each other *i.e.* one leads to another. These categories were correlated with the scores achieved by students on academic self-concept inventory administered. It was found that students having good parent, teacher and peer relationships achieved high than those whose relationships were not so good with either of these. Students who set high goals and had high aspirations were confident of themselves to achieve these goals. They were found to have high self-concept. Though other students also had high future goals but were not sure to reach their goals and had low self-concept. Students having positive views about their own physique, nature and behaviour showed high self-concept than those who were uncertain about everything. Results when correlated with scores on ASCI concluded that students with high scores had positive view of teachers. They liked teachers on the basis of their teaching. They were also liked by the teachers as they thought themselves to be intelligent, disciplined, answering the questions in the class and completing all the work in time. They always get good remarks and praise helped them to do better. Students having low self-concept liked teachers who were not strict but jolly in nature. Sometimes they were liked by teachers but majority of the teachers did not like them as they did not give answers in the class, did not complete their work in time, performed poorly and disturbed the class. But praise helped them do better to some extent. A child who received largely positive academic comments had high academic achievement than a child getting largely negative academic comments. Students with more positive (encouraging) remarks show high positive self-concept than those who received negative (discouraging) remarks. It was also found that teachers' praise helps the child to develop confidence and feeling of competence in them, in turn affecting the self-concept. Thus, it is reasonable to conclude that encouraging remarks like well done, excellent, etc. helped children develop positive self-concept in comparison to discouraging remarks like poor, very poor, weak etc. which lead to negative self-concept.

A Case Study of an Alternative School in Delhi: Focusing on the Teaching Learning Process *M.Phil, JNU,* MEENA

The methodology used *viz.* participant observation was one most applicable for this case study especially since alternative school emphasized on interactive approach students functioning, including the teaching/learning process.

The present study has been an exploratory study into the functioning of an alternative school. It can serve as a useful reference point for those researchers who are interested in studying the other alternative schools and/or in using participant- observation in the classrooms of even the regular schools. For those interested in designing and/or implementing alternative schools and curricular programmes, the present study can point out the problems that can be anticipated and the possible strategies that can be adopted to deal with them.

The major findings of the study were: (1) The school is characterised by informal and open interactions among its members. Even, the hidden curriculum *i.e.* the rules, regulations, room-layouts, informal norms and processes laid an emphasis on co-operation, independence, harmony and integration of the physical-vital mental and psychic aspects of ones being.

(2) The teachers, though espousing the free progress ideology were sometimes unable to deal with practical problems that arise in the practice, and at some of these times tend to resort to the traditional use of autonomous authority. The teachers pre-service training programmes needs to be improved and the in-service training to be extended so that the teachers can find a way to resolve their inconsistencies. The teachers at the school have a very demanding job and heavy duties to perform, and although the satisfaction of service is considerable, the lack of momentary enumeration tends to add to their frustration. The school needs to review their decision of no-payment to the teachers, since each year their trained personnel leave them and are replaced by an inexperienced bunch of newcomers, who may or may not be sensitive to the ideology of the school. (3) Regarding the teaching/learning process, planning needs to be taken more seriously. The teachers, rather than drafting out concrete activities, prefer to let the topic evolve on its own. They rely on their intimate contact with the children to respond spontaneously to their needs and interests. If they invested this knowledge in their planning and devised sets of activities suitable to each child's needs and interests, the topics could prove more beneficial to each child. Evaluation too, along with emphasising the positive, needs to point out areas for improvement and relevant suggestions both with regard to the topics and individual child reports, training in the three R's needs to be taken more seriously and not neglected. (4) Examining the functioning of the school with regard to the criteria, of parental discontent, loss of key staff member ideological conflicts, funding problems and "staff bum out" it was seen that parental discontent seems to be a permanent feature. However, it has never reached magnified proportions, and could (at least in the past) be alleviated by reassurances from the school authorities. (5) Staff burnout is linked to the school's policy of not providing monetary enumeration, and needs to be tackled by the school authorities.

The ideological conflict, may be examined best by using Deal and Nolan's classification. The school seems to espouse the "school as a garden" ideology to some extent where plants are a metaphor for the children. Here, the main task of the school is to create an environment in which the innate qualities can unfold since the source of knowledge exists inside the children.

The school is revolutionary in its ideology to the extent that it believes that the world is preparing for a big change and the school can help in it by giving the necessary importance to psychic education.

As the mother says, "From beyond the frontiers of form, a new force can be evolved, a power of consciousness which has not yet manifested and which, by its emergence, will be able to build a new world".

In its functioning, the school often resembles a "negotiation" school since it is a mixture of authority, autonomy and consensus. Some schoolwide decisions are made by consensus, others by hierarchical superiors. In the classrooms, the teachers expand options although the children ultimately decide objectives, activates and evaluation criteria. The informal norms emphasize cooperation and interdependence.

Thus, the school combines the ideologies in a specific way yielding an eclectic approach. Perhaps, this is to be expected since the school, as any other organization, is a loose collective (Meyer and Roman, 1975) and thus contains individuals who operate from different ideological perspectives. For a harmonious development of the child, it is important that the teachers and parents come to some mutual understanding and agreement. The school does recognise this and asks for a conscious involvement from the parents.

A Study of Characteristic Differences Between Effective and Ineffective Higher Secondary School Teachers

Ph.D., JMI, KAMLA ARORA, 1975

The study was carried out with the objectives of finding out the characteristic difference between effective and ineffective teachers. The study envisaged to examine this objective by identifying educational background of teachers to find the characteristics distinguishing effective and from ineffective teachers, their occupational background, job motivation and variation in their attitudes.

The study revealed certain teacher characteristics that differentiated effective from ineffective teachers and certain other characteristics that do not differentiate characteristics.

A Study of Attitudes and Expectations of Teachers of Senior Secondary Schools Towards in-service Teacher Education Programmes

M.Ed., JMI, GAYATRI DEVI, 1995

The study mainly concentrated on the attitudes of PGTs towards in-service education of teachers. The main objectives were to study the expectations of Post Graduate Teachers on various aspect of these programmes and to relate the attitude of teachers with such factors as age, teaching experience and teaching subjects. The sample consisted of 50 PGTs of government girls senior secondary schools of south district who attended in-service programme of at least one week duration within last five years. The tools comprised of an attitude scale and expectation questionnaire developed by the investigator. The findings showed that PGTs have favourable attitude towards INSTEPS. Teachers who have earlier attended INSTEPS have favourable attitude. Teachers expect more in-service centres and programmes. They expect number of participants be less. They expect that resource persons be experts in subject with knowledge of pedagogy. Incentives in the form of certificates of merit at appointment as resource person or initiator are the other expectation of the teachers.

A Comparative Study of the Attitude and Awareness Towards Minimum Levels of Learning Programme Between Different Groups of Teachers at Primary Stage in Delhi

M.Ed., JMI, MOHD. ISRAR KHAN, 1995

The study aimed at exploring and comparing the attitudes towards MLLs among primary teachers, to explore their attitude towards MLLs, to ascertain their awareness about MLL's concept and strategy. 100 primary school teachers were selected as sample for study.

The major findings of the study revealed: (1) The PRTs agreed that MLLs is a welcome step. It may bring quality and equality in primary education, since it is child centred and provides the teachers, pupils and parents to decide the learning goals to be achieved. It will help the school system to improve upon itself. They opined that MLLs are not new, in fact, the curriculum one generation ago was somehow, implicitly similar to MLLs, in that it also emphasised the skills of reading, writing and reasoning (arithmetic) and knowing about the neighbouring environment. However they agreed that the present curriculum is specifically designed and delineated from the previous ones. The majority of PRTs seem to accept that MLLs will check and improve the falling standards of achievement by pupils at primary stage. (2) Evaluation in MLLs is broad based and intensive, but practically the process of evaluating, is thought of as very complex by the teachers. The evaluation of non-cognitive areas of learning is all the more complex. Teacher pupil ratio, as is it found now, cannot be allowed to remain so high. MLLs are child activity centred and to supervise the activities of pupils, time and energy are needed. It means we have to reduce the number of students per teacher, otherwise no gain can be attained. With present textbook material, nearly all agreed that they with present textbooks are facing problems in MLLs based pedagogy. They complained that the textbook material supplied to them is incomplete and inappropriate. (3) Training of teachers provided by DIETs was inadequate. It did not however equip the teachers to use and arrange MLL based teaching learning and evaluating techniques. Ten days are not much to train the teachers to bring a change in them. One more aspect highlighted was that the teachers of project schools were not given any incentive. They argued that the teachers be given extra incentives monetary or else to encourage them to adopt MLLs.

A Comparative Study of the Attitude of Male and Female Teachers Towards Punishment in Schools

M.Ed., JMI, VIJAY, 1976

The objectives of the study were to construct a scale for the measurement of attitude of teachers towards punishment, to study the attitude of teachers of government higher secondary schools towards punishment, to compare the attitudes of male and female teachers towards punishment, to see the effect of age and teaching experience of teachers on their attitudes towards punishment, to suggest on the basis of the attitudes of the teachers, whether punishment pattern should be changed and, if so, in what way. It could be concluded that there was a significant difference in the attitude of male and female teachers towards punishment.

EDUCATIONAL CHANGE AND TEACHER'S PERCEPTION: AN INDIAN EXPERIENCE

Paper Presented in NIEPA Conference (DPEP Research Studies Programme) Reforming School Education issues in Policy Planning and Implementation, 1996

JAYALAKSHMIINDIRESAN

The objectives of the study were to elicit the perceptions of teachers regarding the significant educational changes which have had an impact of their work life, the objectives of these changes, their role in the process of change, the factors facilitating or hindering the implementation of the change, the impact of the change on students and their willingness to take responsibility for initiating changes in the future.

The study was confined to the schools located in the metropolitan area of Delhi. Five teachers were selected from each school to represent the different subjects being taught by them to include both men and women teachers from various age groups and experiences. Using the structured interview guide, discussions were held with individual teachers. Some of the interviews were recorded with the consent of the teachers. Where it was felt that the teachers were hesitant and not forthcoming, detailed notes were taken. Data analysis includes both qualitative analysis and content analysis of descriptive answers.

The preliminary salient findings as presented in the study were: In brief, teachers have identified different aspects of educational change as significantly affecting their work life. The major changes identified are: (1) syllabus; (2) evaluation process; (3) teaching methodologies; and (4) diversification of courses. The main objective of these changes has been perceived to have been initiated to improve and enlarge the knowledge of students and made the examination system more objective and reliable. Teachers have reported that these changes have put lot of pressure on their time and effort in implementing the changes. However, the teachers feel that they hardly had any role in the process of change and they were only required to implement the changes. While some teachers had the opportunity to participate in training workshops for implementing the change, other teachers expressed dissatisfaction at the way changes were implemented without any prior information, training or required resource materials.

A Study of Teacher Effectiveness, Job Satisfaction, Organisational Climates and its Relationship with Academic Performance of Primary School Learners: A Comparative Study of Public Missionary And Municipal School

Specifically, the study had the objectives of identifying the level of stress amongst 10th and 12th class students and if this differs amongst them as well as between them and those who are in the 9th class and do not take the board examination, study the relationship between stress and academic performance.

Studying the relationship between stress and academic performance in the context of class, sex, subject stream and previous academic performance of students. Students from three classes, namely, XIIth and Xth who appeared for the Board Examination, and students from IXth class who did not appear for the Board examination comprised the sample for this study. From each class 80 students taken randomly and the stress was studied at 2 "high" stress and "low" stress likewise sex factor studied at two levels *viz.*, boys and girls. Finally, the relationship of stress and academic performance with class, streams were studied.

Stress was measured by using a stress questionnaire was specially designed for the purpose which was indicative of the total number of events present in each student.

Academic performance of students was adjudged by the percentage of marks they obtained in the selection examination. The previous academic performance was taken as the percentage of marks obtained by the students in the final examination of their previous class respectively. The students were administered the stems scale specially devised for this purpose and the analysis was carried out on the obtained information from students in all the three classes.

The result obtained were as follows: 1. (a) Stress was found to differ significantly between the students of classes 12, and 10 as well as between students of class 9 and 10 respectively. To be more specific class X students had significantly greater stress than the students of class XII and IX in that order. However, stress did not vary significantly amongst students of IXth and XIIth class, (b) There was a significant difference in the stress scores of boys and girls of X class, but not between any other class students, (c) There was a significant difference in the stress scores of sciences and arts, and commerce and arts group of 12th class students. To be more specific commerce group had significantly greater stress than the science and arts group in that order. However there was no significant difference in stress scores of sciences and commerce group students respectively. 2. (a) Academic performance was found to vary significantly in terms of the 3 classes. The academic performance of 9th class appeared to be the highest followed by the 10th and 12th class in that order, (b) The academic performance of students varied in terms of stress factor *viz.*, high stress and low stress, that is, low stress students had secured significantly higher academic performance than those who had higher stress score. Such differences were obtained only in regard to students of class XII on academic performance between high and low stress students and not to the other two class students, (c) Boys and girls were not found to differ in terms of their academic performance. Academic performance also varied in terms of the interaction between class, stress and sex factors. To be more specific students of IXth class with low stress and belonging to male sex had significantly high academic performance than other. 3. Stress and academic performance were found to be significantly negatively related. In other words higher the stress, lower the academic performance of students.

4. In the study it was found that the degree of correlation between stress and academic performance among XII and IX differed significantly, but not in terms of other classes. 5. In the study it was also found subject streams opted by students appear to affect the relationship between stress and academic performance, which may be attributable to the difficulty level of the subject matter, students' interest and aptitude for the subject concerned.

Stress in Terms of Previous Academic Performance

Stress was found to vary significantly in terms of classes and previous academic performance (above mean and below mean academic level). 6. To sum up it may be stated that stress varied significantly between the students who appeared for Board examination and those who did not. More specifically, students who appeared for Board examination of 10th class had significantly greater stress than those of 12th and 9th class. Again the students of 12th class who appeared for Board examination significantly greater stress than those of 9th class who did not appear for Board examination. 7. Stress was significantly higher among students who were in the commerce stream as compared to those in science and arts stream respectively. Again, the stress amongst the students of science stream significantly greater stress than those in arts. Thus stress significantly related both class and subject stream factor. There was no significant difference in the boys and girls stress except among 10th class. 8. The academic performance was found significantly but negatively correlated with stress. That is higher the stress, lower the academic performance. 9. When the previous academic performance of students considered by dividing it, into above mean and below mean performances, there was significant difference in the mean stress scores of those who had above mean performance and below means performance. In other words, the stress scores were significantly lower for those who had high mean previous academic performance as compared to the low mean previous academic performance.

From the above results one may concluded that stress acted as a positive influence in enhancing the academic performance of students in large number of cases. It would be worth-while to find out the exact level of stress which may be needed to induce or bring about the best performance among students. By highlighting the relationship between stress, class, subject stream, previous academic performance and academic performance as such, the present study may be considered as having contributed to a relatively difficult area, that is of the influence of stress of the academic performance of students particularly in 10th and 12th that is in Board examination.

Personal Orientation and Stress Among Secondary School Teacher Some Covariates

M.Phil., ZHCESSS, JNU, GAYATRI, 1991

The main objectives of the present study were: (1) to study whether locus of control and stress were affected by variables of gender, experience and subject stream taught by the teachers. (2) to ascertain the relationship among different variables demographic, locus of control and stress.

Tools: (1) Scale of demographic characteristics to obtain information on gender, types of schools, teaching experience, training, income, classes taught and subject stream of the teachers. (2) Locus of control scale; Nine items selected from the Rotors (1966) original scale. The reliability ranged from 44 to 48 for employed and unemployed group respectively. (3) Stress scale: Consisting of 32 items taken from Wilson's test profile for teachers. After the collection of the data individually, the data were codified and then analysed by using ANOVA, 't' test and correlation analysis.

The following findings were observed: (1) There were no significant differences by gender, length of experience and the subject stream of the teachers on their locus of control. (2) Significant gender differences were observed on employee administration relation, teacher-teacher relation, parent-teacher relation, physical symptoms of stress and psychoemotional symptoms of stress, whereas, no significant gender differences were observed on student behaviour, time management and total stress scores. (3) Gender was negatively correlated with physical symptoms of stress as well as with psychoemotional symptoms of stress. But there was no correlation between total stress scores and subject stream. (4) Experience was found to play a vital role in affecting the levels of stress. (5) Middle experienced and less experienced category of teachers differed significantly in their total stress scores. They also differed significantly among themselves on employee-administration relation and teacher- teacher relation. (6) Non-science and science category of teachers differed significantly in their physical and psychoemotional symptoms of stress as well as on total stress scores. (7) The locus of control and total stress were positively correlated with each other. (8) Total stress score was positively correlated with all the dimensions of stress.

Work setting and Psychological Among Teachers — A Part Test of Charniss Model

M.Phil, ZHCESSS, JNU, J. KAUR, 1991

The present study was undertaken to find out the differences in the experience of burnout among teachers of the normal, mentally retarded and deaf schools and to examine the relationship of these to work setting and demographic variables.

Some of the objectives may be stated as: to find out the significance of differences between the teachers of normal schools and special schools (mentally retarded and deaf schools), to ascertain the relationships among various work setting factors and demographic variables and the experience of alienation, greater self-interest, emotional exhaustion, lowered personal accomplishment and depersonalisation in teachers of normal and special schools and to predict the burnout among teachers of normal, mentally retarded and deaf schools using work setting and demographic factors as predictors.

The sample was identified through a two stage procedures. The selection of schools was done using purposing sampling procedures while incidental sampling technique was used in the selection of teachers. For the study 120 male and female, full time teachers from normal, mentally retarded and deaf schools were taken, of these 60 teachers were from normal schools and 30 each from mentally retarded and the deaf schools.

Research Design: An *ex-post facto* research design was used to examine the relationships among the demographic and work-setting factors and burnout dimensions.

Tools: The tools of data collection were: (1) Scale of demographic characteristics to obtain information on sex, age, marital status, years in teaching, etc. (2) Scale for career orientations which included four career orientations (Social activists, Careerist, Self-investors, Artisans). (3) Scale for organisational goals, which included the four most important and foremost goals of schools. (4) Work setting scale measured teacher perception of their setting and included 37 items based on seven dimensions, namely, work overload, stimulation, scope of student contact, autonomy, leadership and participation in decision-making, social isolation, and involvement in extracurricular activities. (5) Scale for role clarity. (6) Alienation scale. (7) Greater self-interest scale. (8) Maslach Burnout Inventory. The scales were formulated and pretested for the study. Using the above scales the data were collected individually and codified. The data were then analysed using 't'-tests, correlational analysis and multiple regression analysis.

Following findings and conclusions can be drawn: (1) Teachers of normal and special schools do not differ from each other significantly in their experience of alienation, greater self-interest, lowered personal accomplishment and depersonalization, but special than the teachers of normal schools. (2) Among the teachers of special education, teachers of mentally retarded schools experience more frequent emotional exhaustion, while teachers of deaf schools suffered greater alienation. However, they showed, similarity on other aspects of burnout. (3) In all the three types of schools, the perceptions of the work-setting as negative, resulted in the experience of burnout. (4) Though no significant intergroup differences were observed in the perceptions of work setting on dimensions of stimulation and social isolation, the teachers of special schools experienced significantly greater autonomy, participation and work overload than teachers of normal schools. (5) Teachers of deaf schools and normal schools perceived their work setting more negative than the teachers of mentally retarded schools. (6) Work setting factors of work overload, lack of autonomy, lack of participation in decision-making and lack of stimulation were highly related to the experience of greater burnout. (7) Male teachers experienced greater depersonalization than the female teachers. On the other aspects of burnout gender did not make any significant difference. (8) Years in teaching played a mediatory role in the experience of burnout, with more experienced teachers, feeling lesser burnout than the less experienced teachers. (9) Marital status was significantly related to burnout for the teachers of normal schools. (10) Years in teaching and lack of participation in leadership and decision-making were found to be the best predictors of burnout. Although, lack of stimulation, autonomy, gender and marital status also made sizeable contribution to the experience of burnout. (11) Part of the charniss model which tested the relationship between the work setting factors and burnout was found valid in Indian school situation as well.

Perceived Teaching Effectiveness in Mathematics and School Motivation in Secondary and Senior Secondary Classes

M.Phil., ZHCESSS, JNU, M. ARORA, 1994

The present study was designed to answer the following questions: (i) Are there significant main and interaction effects of school, gender and grade on the measured variables of perceived teaching effectiveness, school motivation, attitude towards maths and achievement in maths? (ii) Are there school, gender and grade specific differences in the patterns of relationship among perceived teaching effectiveness, school motivation, attitude towards maths and achievement in maths?

The matching variables in the study were types of schools (Public and Government), grades (IX and XI) and gender of students. The variables measured were perceived teaching effectiveness, school motivation, attitude towards maths and achievement in maths. The study used a 2×2×2 factorial design.

The sample consisted of 160 students from the two types of schools. 80 students were tested from each type of school. From each class 40 students were taken up. An equal number (n=20) of girls and boys were tested from each class.

The tools used were: Personal Data Schedule. Perceived Teaching Effectiveness Scale developed by the researcher. School Motivation Inventory (Developed by McInerncy and Sinclair 1993).

Attitude towards Mathematics was assessed by a scale developed by the researcher.

Achievement in Mathematics

The major findings of the study were: (1) There are significant effects of grade and gender on overall teaching effectiveness, teaching as an activity, concern for students and evaluation, as the class XI students and boys perceived their maths teachers as effective on these dimensions. (2) There are significant effects of school, gender and grade on classrooms management style and professionalism. As the government school students, boys and class XI students perceived their teachers as more effective on these dimensions. (3) There is a significant interaction effect of grade and gender on overall perceived teaching effectiveness, as in the government schools, boys perceived the maths teacher as more effective. (4) There is a significant interaction effect of school and gender on concern for students and on classrooms management style, as in the government schools, boys perceived their maths teachers as more effective. (5) School type is found to have a significant effect on overall school motivation, task orientation, competitiveness, striving for excellence, affiliation, social concern, recognition, rewards and sense of purpose for schooling, as the public school students showed a higher level of motivation on all these dimensions. (6) Gender has a significant effect on social concern, as boys showed more concern for others. (7) There is a significant interaction effect of gender and school on task orientation. (8) School has a significant effect on attitude towards maths, as the public school students had a more favourable attitude towards maths. Also, there is a significant interaction effect of school and gender on this variable. (9) School has a significant effect on achievement in Maths, with the public school students being high achievers. Also, there is a significant interaction effect of school and grade, and school, gender and grade on this variable. (10) High perceived teaching effectiveness is related to high school motivation for the public school students, and for class IX students. (11) Government school students, class IX students and boys perceiving their maths teacher as effective have a more favourable attitude towards maths. (12) Public school students, class IX students and girls perceiving their maths teacher as low on effectiveness often take extra coaching in maths. (13) Government school students, class XI students and girls having high motivation have a favourable attitude towards maths. (14) A low school motivation is related to low achievement in maths for classes IX and XI, and for male and female students. (15) Class IX and class XI students, both girls and boys coming from a higher socio-economic status showed a higher level of school motivation. (16) Government school students, class IX students and girls having a favourable attitude towards maths do not take extra coaching in maths. (17) Girls from the high socio-economic status have a more favourable attitude towards maths. (18) High achievement is related to the little extra coaching for public school students. (19) High socio-economic status is related to high achievement for government school students, for class IX students, for class XI students, for boys and girls.

A Correlation Study of Communication Effectiveness of T.V. Programme Classroom Environment and Social Studies of Class X Students in Delhi

M.Phil., ZHCESSS, 1987

The present study was undertaken to ascertain the relationships among different (mediating) variables namely, communication effectiveness of ETV programme, psychosocial characteristics of classrooms environment and student's performance in science and social studies.

110 boys of Government Boys' Senior Secondary School and 110 girls of Government Girls' Senior Secondary School were chosen as the sample subjects. The selection of the sample was made on the basis of quota method of sampling.

The instrument includes the communication efficacy scale and classrooms environment inventory to assess the psychosocial characteristics of the classrooms environment.

The major findings of the study revealed that (1) regular exposure to ETV programme results in higher post ETV scores both by boys and girls in science and social studies. (2) boys' ratings show low but positive association between the perceptions of communication effectiveness of ETV programme and classrooms environment in science and social studies. (3) girl's ratings show moderate but positive association between the perceptions of communication effectiveness of ETV programme and classrooms environment in science and social studies. (4) the predictability of student's performance in science and social studies by using communication efficacy and classroom environment scores in science and social studies do not reveal positive results.

Besides, the home TV environment contributes directly/ indirectly to the perception of communication effectiveness of ETV programme and classrooms environment in science and social studies. It does not directly relate to student's performance in different academic subject.

The findings show positive association between the perception of communication effectiveness of ETV programme and classrooms environment. This in turn, is expected to contribute to academic performance.

Effectiveness of Jurisprudential Inquiring Model of Teaching in Developing Values

M.Ed., C.I.E., D.U., UMESH KUMAR SHARMA, 1991

The study mainly deals with the kind of effect of intervention strategies, attitude scale and Jurisprudential Inquiring Model based instructional material lays impact on values of sixty students of class IX. The study proceeded by formation of two equivalent groups: control and experimental group based on the results of an attitude scale. The control group was taught by traditional method. After teaching three lessons (one each on pollution, population and drug-addiction) to both the groups, post-test was administered. It was found that Jurisprudential Inquiry Model was more effective as compared to traditional approach in inculcation of desired values in pupils.

❑❑❑

PUPIL CHARACTERISTICS

A Comparative Study of Adjustment of Boys and Girls in Co-educational and Segregated Schools

M.Ed., JMI, I.S. SURI, 1976

The study mainly concerned itself with finding out whether boys and girls of the segregated schools were better adjusted than those of co-educational schools or *vice versa* and whether general mental ability has relationship with adjustment or not. The tools Raven's Standard Progressive Matrices and the Bhagias School Adjustment Inventory were used for the study. The sample was drawn from five schools from zone IX (Boys and Girl). 172 students in the age group 15-16 were selected.

The study showed no difference in the thinking and observation of boys and girls from co-educational and segregated schools. The segregated boys and segregated girls differ significantly in the adjustment with school administration and general environmental facilities and conforms at school.

Attitude Towards School Among Secondary and Senior Secondary School Children in North Delhi

M.Ed., JMI, SHAYAMA RANI BHARDWAJ, 1988

The study was carried out mainly with the objective of examining the attitude of secondary and senior secondary school children towards school programme and teachers, social acceptance and parental attitude towards the school. The sample comprised of 120 school students from two government schools in North Delhi Zone. They were administered Rao's School Attitude Inventory. It was found that there was a favourable attitude of students towards the school programme. But significant difference was found between the classes IX and XI students in their attitude towards teachers. They however did not differ in their attitude towards social acceptance.

A Study of Sex Education at Primary Level

M.Ed., JMI, K.S. BHARDWAJ, 1976

The study was carried out with the objectives of discussing and evaluating various factors largely responsible for growing sex awareness among school going children, discussing the consequences of this growing sex awareness, discussing pros and cons of introducing sex education at primary level, knowing the opinion of teachers and parents regarding this problem, suggesting a suitable curriculum of sex education at primary level and listing various problems and difficulties arising of the introduction of sex education. As sample for study, 200 teachers and parents were selected. The findings revealed that 80% of the parents favour some kind of formal agency to impart sex education. 66% parents were desirous to learn more. A large number of parents were in favour of sex education. School is considered to be the best agency to impart sex education. 91% favoured primary stage as the best stage to start sex education.

A Study of Adjustment and Academic Achievement of Class XI Students Involved in Various Co-curricular Activities

M.Ed., JMI, SEEMA KHAN, 1989-90

Mainly the study concentrated on examining the extent of participation of students in co-curricular activities, identifying the least and most popular co-curricular activities among students and the difference in academic achievement and adjustment of participants and non-participants of co-curricular activities.

The study designed to analyse the relationship (if any) between the academic achievement and adjustment of participants and non-participants in co-curricular activities revealed that there was no general trend of liking of a particular type of activity between those students who participated in maximum activities (80 per cent) as compared to those who took part in fewer activities.

A Comparative Study of Peer-acceptance, Self-perception and Teachers' Perception of the "Save Our Soul" (Sos) Village Children And General Children

M.Ed., JMI, ANURADHA, 1986

The objectives of the study were to study the self-perception of SOS village children and general children of the society, to study the teacher's rating of students' perception of SOS village children and general children and to know the peer-acceptance of SOS village and general children. 25 children from two groups that is, SOS and general children were selected (age group 9 to 11 years) as sample of the study. Children of both groups belonged to five schools namely (1) Vidya Bhavan Mahavidyalaya, Lodi Colony. (2) Bhartiya Vidya Bhavan. (3) M.C.D. School, Lajpat Nagar. (4) Blue Bells School, G.K. (5) M.C.D. School, Laxmi Bai Nagar. The tools used in the study where Harter's Perceive Competence Scale for teachers and students and peer-acceptance attitude was identified with the help of sociometric technique.

The study reported that SOS village children possess the qualities needed for developing balanced personality but their qualities were not realized by their teachers. The sociometric technique also showed peer-acceptance attitude.

A Study of Various Areas of Adjustment Among Test-Anxious and Non Test-Anxious Students

M.Ed., C.I.E., D.U., VEENA VERMA, 1986

The objectives of the present investigation were to study the relationships if any, (1) between the test-anxious and the non-test-anxious public school boys group in various areas of adjustment. (2) in the test-anxious and the non test-anxious government schoolboys group in various areas of adjustment. (3) in test-anxious and non-test-anxious public schoolgirls in various areas of adjustment. (4) in test-anxious and non-text-anxious government schoolgirls in various areas of adjustment. (5) between public school boys and girls on test-anxiety variable. (6) between government school boys and girls on test-anxiety. (7) between low S.E.S. boys and middle S.E.S. boys on test-anxiety. (8) between low S.E.S. and upper middle S.E.S. boys on test-anxiety. (9) between low S.E.S. and high S.E.S. and boys on text-anxiety. (10) between middle S.E.S. and upper middle S.E.S. boys on test-anxiety. (11) between middle S.E.S. and high S.E.S. boys on test-anxiety. (12) between upper middle S.E.S. and high S.E.S. boys on test-anxiety. (13) between low S.E.S. girls and middle S.E.S. girls on test-anxiety. (14) between low S.E.S. and upper middle S.E.S. girls on text-anxiety. (15) between low S.E.S. and high

S.E.S. girls on test anxiety. (16) between middle S.E.S. and upper middle S.E.S. girls on test-anxiety. (17) between middle S.E.S. and high S.E.S. girls on test-anxiety. (18) between upper middle S.E.S. and high S.E.S. girls on test-anxiety.

500 students (boys and girls) from Government and Public schools of Delhi were selected as sample for study. The tools used were Dutt-Gupta Personality Inventory, Test anxiety scale by Malika, Socio-economic status scale by Urmil Nagpal. The major findings of the study were: (1) There is significant difference in test-anxious and non-test-anxious public school boys in various areas of adjustment. (2) There is significant difference in test-anxious and non test-anxious government schoolboys in various areas of adjustment. (3) There is significant difference in test-anxious and non-test-anxious public schoolgirls in various areas of adjustment. (4) There is no significant difference in test-anxious and non test-anxious government schoolgirls in various areas of adjustment. (5) There is significant difference in public schoolboys and girls on test-anxiety. (6) There is no significant difference between govt. school boys and girls on test-anxiety. (7) There is significant difference between low S.E.S. boys and middle S.E.S. boys on test-anxiety. (8) There is significant difference between low S.E.S. boys and upper middle S.E.S. boys on test-anxiety. (9) There is significant difference between low S.E.S. and high S.E.S. boys on test-anxiety. (10) There is significant difference between middle S.E.S. and upper middle S.E.S. boys on test-anxiety. (11) There is no significant difference between middle S.E.S. and high S.E.S. boys on test-anxiety. (12) There is no significant difference between upper middle S.E.S. and high S.E.S. boys on test-anxiety. (13) There is no significant difference between low S.E.S. girls and middle S.E.S. girls on test-anxiety. (14) There is no significant difference between low S.E.S. girls and upper middle S.E.S. girls on test-anxiety. (15) There is no significant difference between low S.E.S. and high S.E.S. girls on test-anxiety. (16) There is no significant difference between middle S.E.S. and upper middle S.E.S. girls on test-anxiety. (17) There is no significant difference between middle S.E.S. and high S.E.S. girls on test-anxiety. (18) There is no significant

difference between upper middle S.E.S. and high S.E.S. girls on test-anxiety.

To Study a Group of Junior Science Talent Scheme Students with Respect to Scientific Creativity and Home Background

M.Ed., C.I.E., D.U., MANISHA ARORA, 1988

The main objectives of the study were to select a few Junior Science Talent Search Examination awardee and those who sat for examination but could not pass it, to find out home background differences of the two groups — selected and non-selected and to prepare case studies of both the groups.

The investigator developed own tool and interview schedule. The purposive sampling technique was adopted. Class X students from Raisina Bengali School were selected for pilot study for pre-testing. And for further study, students from five English-Medium Schools were selected. The case studies of 10 students were also prepared who were selected for Junior Science Talent Scholarship.

The major findings of the study were: (1) All the students selected for JSTS happen to be from public and private schools studying through English Medium. (2) The selected group was more homogenous than the non-selected group. The range of marks in the selected group was 69-90% and the same for non-selected group was 69-89%. This shows that brighter the group (although achievement-wise difference was not significant) less homogenous the group members are in any exercise that calls for convergent type of thinking. (3) The mean score of the scientific creativity test for the awardee group was 62.58 and the same for non-selected was 41.53. This difference of scientific creativity score was found significant. (4) The highly creative children are less interested in convergent thinking and the examinations in school are generally based on convergent thinking only. (5) A child's achievement is more provided by his/her parents who are enthusiastic about their studies and who have higher educational and professional status. (6) The average family educational level of selected students was slightly higher than the non-selected students.

A Study of Test-anxiety on the School Students of Delhi With Reference to Certain Variables

M.Ed., C.I.E., D.U., FATAH SINGH MUKHIJA, 1980

The study was taken up to study the anxiety students experience during their tests from different socio-economic strata. The sample selected comprised of 500 students of IX and X class from six schools that included four government and two public schools. The tools administered on them were Sarason's Test Anxiety Scale and Socio-Economic Scale. The major findings the study arrived at highlighted that high socio-economic group was found to have least anxiety scores and low socio-economic group showed maximum. Public school children showed less anxiety but public schoolgirls showed greater test-anxiety than boys.

A Study of the Contribution of Project Work at the +2 Level in Biology to the Development of Certain Inductive Aspects of Scientific Thinking

M.Ed., C.I.E., D.U., 1983

The objective of the study was to assess the ability of science students of senior secondary classes.

The sample comprising of 94 students were taken from class XII biology group of four public schools in Delhi. All schools selected followed the All India Senior Certificate Examination System. The study is an *ex post facto* study where experimental and controlled groups were formed on the basis of marks obtained in the test of scientific thinking.

The major findings of the study were as follows: (1) Investigatory projects done at the +2 level in biology are not contributing significantly towards the development of scientific thinking in the students of schools under study. (2) The existing methods of conducting and doing project work are not up to the mark. This influences the poor performance of students in the test. (3) The conditions in the school classroom, library, laboratory are not congenial for effective planning and execution of projects. Students and teachers are not satisfied about the conditions under which they have to work and feel strongly that the evaluation is also not proper.

An Investigation of the Reading Interest and its Impact on Creative Writing of Class XI Students in an English Medium School in New Delhi

M.Ed., C.I.E., D.U., GEETA SAHANI, 1987

The objectives of the study were to make a survey of the reading interests of class students perusing different academic streams; to study the factors regarding certain aspects of reading time spent, the type of materials handed, sources of getting reading materials, reasons for choosing the reading material utility and value as they perceive of the reading interest they have; to study whether students belonging to different academic streams differ in their reading interest; and to find out the impact of their reading interest on their creative writing.

The sample was drawn from 3 different academic streams. It consisted of 600 students from class X distributed in 12 sections. Two testing devices were used in the study: (1) Reading interest inventory I and (2) Reading interest inventory II.

The major findings of the study revealed that most of the group spent their leisure time in reading and the materials they handled were of their own choice. They mostly gave home, school, friends and purchase as sources for getting the reading materials. Their reasons for choosing the reading materials included language, theme, interest, style, plot and character. The utility and value as they perceived of the reading interest they had was that reading helped them in their grammar, vocabulary, expression. They did differ in their reading interest in that the arts group preferred reading best sellers and classics; the science group gave top preference to science and general knowledge; the commerce group to adventure in the creative writing. For inter judge reliability, the total scores of the 2 judges were co-related and found to have some inter-judge reliability. All three academic streams agreed that reading interest did have an impact on their writing.

A Comparative Study of the Learning Style of High and Low Ability Students in English Language

M.Ed., C.I.E., D.U., 1982

The objectives of the study were: (1) to find out the learning style adopted by students in studying English. (2) The extent of utilisation of critical reading, creative reading by students on the basis of which they can be categorised as high ability and low ability. (3) The frequency of various cognitive aspects used in reading which add up to the making of learning style adopted by the core and elective English group. (4) The various processes involved in creative reading and creative reading gives an idea to the teacher in English to manipulate her teaching materials according to the needs of study.

II Grade students of Springdales Senior Secondary School were taken up as sample of the study. In order to assess their learning styles, they were administered a tool prepared by the investigator.

The major findings revealed by the study were: (1) The group as a whole showed a bent for creative reading ability as was clear from the scores on items measuring originality, flexibility and fluency. (2) Their score on the items measuring flexibility was the highest originality and fluency following suit respectively. (3) But on the two items measuring elaboration the fourth domain of divergent thinking — the score of the sample was poor. In fact it ranked as the second last score. (4) The score of the group as a whole displayed their proficiency in the use of the first three categories of the Cognitive Domain—Knowledge, Comprehension and Application. The score was highest on items measuring Comprehension, next on knowledge and least on Application. (5) The group's performance on the item measuring Analysis was just average. (6) The performance of the group on items measuring synthesis and Evaluation — The last two were most complex categories and performance was very poor. (7) By means of statistical analysis, fifteen students fell in the high ability range and seventeen in the low ability; only one student came in the average category. (8) At .01 level of confidence, there was a significant difference between the mean performances of the high and low ability groups. The group hence was found to be a heterogeneous one, with two distinct categories adopting two distinct kinds of 'learning styles'. (9) The high ability groups scored more than double on the items measuring creative reading ability than the low ability students. (10) On the various sub-parts constituting creative reading ability - they scored the highest on flexibility, second highest on finality and then on fluency. Relative by the difference was much larger on associational fluency than that on ideational icy. (11) Likewise the six categories of the cognitive domain, the high ability students scored very high as compared to the low ability group. (12) However, in comprehension, the second category of the cognitive domain, the low ability group displayed an edge over the high ability group. (13) The maximum difference in the performances between the two groups was found in the sixth and most complex category of the cognitive domain, was that of elaboration. Although the scores in respect of both the groups were rather low, the ratio of the difference between the two ability groups were 1:8. (14) Both, the high and low ability students, displayed a gradual diminishing performance as the complexity of the six categories increased. (15) Out of fifteen students in the core English group, nine fell in the high ability group and six in the low ability. (16) Out of the eighteen Elective English Students, six fell in the high ability group and eleven in the low ability group. (17) The difference between the mean performances of the two groups belonging to the Core and Elective English groups was found to be non-significant. The difference was due to chance factors and hence may not correspond to a similar difference in the actual population. (18) The Core English group performed relatively better on items measuring creative reading ability, than the Elective English students. (19) Only on associational fluency— a sub-part of creative reading ability, the Elective English group scored higher than the core English group. (20) On knowledge, application and analysis, the Core English group performed better than the Elective English group, although the difference was not significant. (21) On comprehension, synthesis and Evaluation, the Elective English group scored higher than The Core English group. (22) The teacher's teaching style seem to have influenced the students' 'Learning Style'.

An Investigation into the Extent of Deficiency of Class X Students in Hindi Language as Revealed Through CBSE'S Secondary Examinations Answer Books

M.Ed., C.I.E., D.U., RAJNI JOSHI, 1986

The study was conducted by keeping the following objectives in view: (1) to identify and study the errors of class X students in respect of Hindi language. (2) to collect and classify these errors with a view to provide classroom teacher an insight into the nature, magnitude of these errors and (3) to suggest if possible a remedial programme with regard to these errors.

The sample of this study consisted of a set of 100 answer books selected at random from among the answer books of candidates who appeared in Hindi (Core) examination in March 1985.

The major findings show: (1) Ignorance of correct symbol of a particular sound leads to script error. (2) Ignorance about the rules of grammar leads to serious mistakes in writing including syntax. (3) Not all the errors in Hindi writing can be attributed to the filter language influence. (4) Quite a number of script error seem to be more due to the lack of perfect match between the sound, pronunciation and writing of Hindi words. The other causes of scripts errors are: (5) The absence of suitable textbooks and Teacher guides. Lack of specialised guidance to the teachers for teaching Hindi as the second language. Lack of specially qualified or trained teachers. Absence of reference books and specific material. No special work is done by the teachers. Un-interested teachers. Lack of motivation from teachers to students. Lack of suitable methodology of language teaching. Ungraded books. Lack of clarity regarding: Hindi language and literature, and Aim of teaching Hindi (Whether teaching as first language or second language), Influence and interference of teacher, his/her pronunciation, the filter language and linguistics.

A Study of Factors Associated with Problem-solving Ability in Physics

M.Ed, C.I.E., D.U., V.R. SOMAN, 1990

The study centred around intelligence, achievement, achievement in mathematics, physics, reading comprehension and problem-solving strategies. It envisages following objectives: (1) to study the relationship of problem-solving ability in physics to intelligence as measured by scores in Advanced Progressive Matrices. (2) to develop a programme to enhance problem-solving ability. (3) to study the effect of this programme.

The sample comprised of 32 students of class XI (science) of Kerala Education Society Senior Secondary School, New Delhi of average age of 16 years were selected. The study proceeded mainly with administration of a pre-test in physics numericals and progressive matrices to all students. On the basis of obtained scores the students were divided into experimental and control groups. On the basis of posttest after teaching through different methods, their ability to solve problems in physics were explored. A questionnaire was developed by the investigator to study the factors. And on the basis of analysis, following major findings emerged: (1) There is an almost significant positive correlation between Raven's test score and problem-solving ability in physics. (2) There is a low positive correlation between achievement in mathematics and problem-solving ability in physics. (3) There is moderate positive correlation between achievement in physics and problem-solving ability in physics. (4) There is negligible correlation between reading comprehension skill and problem-solving ability in physics. (5) The programme designed by the investigator produced a substantial gain in score in problem-solving in the experimental group. In the number of students scoring more than 50% in problem-solving the experimental group showed an improvement while the control group remained static.

A Comparative Study of Problems Faced by Students of the Academic Stream and the Vocational Stream

M.Ed., C.I.E., D.U., 1983

The study was carried out by keeping following objectives in view: (1) To locate the problem areas which trouble students of the academic stream. (2) To locate the problem areas which trouble students of the vocational stream. (3) To compare the problems of the vocational and the academic streams obtained from (1) and (2). (4) To find out the special problems faced by students of the vocational stream as different from those of the academic stream.

The sample was taken from one Industrial Teachers Institute and three Government Boys Senior Secondary Schools, comprising of 200 boys — 100 from ITI and 100 from the schools. All the boys had passed out class Xth. A problem check list was prepared by the investigator and this was administered on them. The study's main aim was to compare the I.T.I. boys and the schoolboys in the problems faced by them. This was done with the help of statistical analysis of the scores obtained on the problem check list administered to the two groups. The raw scores were also compared both area-wise as well as item-wise. This exercise facilitated in drawing conclusions and listing findings for the study.

The main finding of the study was that the vocational students face considerably more problems in the economic area. They seem to be coming from comparatively economically disadvantaged homes. Also, problems in other areas seem to be affected by this lone factor.

A Study of the Factors Contributing Backwardness in Reading Hindi Among VIth Class Students *M.Ed., C.I.E., D.U.,* 1983

The objectives of the study were: (1) To identify the 6th class backward readers (Hindi) of Shaheed Udham Singh Samarak Secondary School. (2) To find out causes that are responsible for backwardness in reading Hindi for each backward reader selected for the study and (3) To suggest a remedial programme.

It is an intensive study. The case study approach was used. The following tools were administered: (1) Group Intelligence test and Standard Progressive Matrices (2) Questionnaire for students, parents and teachers, (3) Diagnostic tests (4) Observation and (5) Interview.

The major findings highlight the following: (1) Causes responsible for backwardness in reading Hindi were (a) Visual and auditory defects (b) Perceptual defects (c) School factors —Irregular attendance, long leaves and attitude of teachers (d) Home conditions — The child's conception of reading is intimately connected with home attitudes towards pictures and newspapers letter and books, words and speech. (2) Economical and intellectual climate in the house; lack of motivation for reading and completion of homework.

A Study of 'Creative Expression' in Written English in Some Schools of Delhi

M.Ed., C.I.E., D.U., DEVASMITA GUHA, 1983

The objectives of the study were : (1) To prepare a test to evaluate 'creative expression' in written English; (2) To find out the extent of 'creative' ability in language shown by two groups of students. (3) To find the relative distribution and extent of 'creative expression' in two groups of students.

This study is an attempt to find the extent of creative expression in written English two groups of students of class IX selected from two English medium schools of Delhi. This study corporates a comparative analysis of creativity between these two schools. A test had been designed to achieve the objectives. The sample consisted of 33 students of class IX of Modern School and 48 students from Ramjas Public School of the same class.

The major findings of the study were: (1) The extent of 'creative expression' in written English by the two groups of students were found. The lowest score obtained was 8.5 and the highest 20.5 out of a maximum of 25. (2) 7% of the students were found to have a high degree of creative ability in English. (3) There was no significant difference in the 'creative expression' in English, in the two groups of students, despite their varying socio-economic background. (4) The co-efficient of correlation between the teacher scores on creativity and creativity test scores was found to be .68. This denotes a significant relationship between the two. (5) The co-efficient of correlation between the teacher's ratings on creativity and investigator's rating was found to be .89. The high correlation suggests minimal subjectivity in assessment of the creativity tests. (6) Qualitative analysis of creative composition shows that though few possess that rare degree of creative ability required of a potential artist, most of them display surprising depth of understanding and insight into their experience.

A Comparative Study of Syntactical Complexity in Written English of Students Across Different Grades

M.Ed., C.I.E., D.U., 1985

The study kept the following objectives in view : (1) To study the levels of complexity which exist in the writing of students as regards structured, semi-structured and free compositions with an increase of grades. (2) To study the frequency of use of qualifiers, modifiers, phrase structure, clause structure and unusual syntax. (3) To study the difference in mean sentence length in written expression across school grades. (4) To study the difference in performative use of complex syntax across various grades.

The sample of the study comprises of one co-educational English Medium School of Delhi where Hindi is the mother tongue of majority of students from class VIII, X and XII. 75 students were selected from this school. The tools administered on these students consisted of a set of stimuli exercises/ themes to elicit performative knowledge in English syntax through written work. The stimuli were of three types namely, structured, semi-structured and free.

The major findings as reported in the study were : (1) As far as the structured language stimuli are concerned (i) The written expression of students of grade VIII is syntactically more complex than the students of grade IX grade XI. The difference between the level of syntactic complexity of students of grade VIII and IX is significant, while that between the students of grade VIII and XI is not significant, (ii) The written expression of students of grade IX is syntactically less complex than the written expression of the students of grade XI. Though the difference is not highly significant. (2) As far as the semi- structured language stimuli are concerned (i) The written expression of the students of grade VIII is syntactically more complex than the written expression of the students of grade IX and XI. In both the cases the difference between them is highly significant, (ii) The written expression of students of grade IX is syntactically less complex than the written expression of the students of grade XI but the difference is not significant (3) As far as the overall syntactic complexity of the written language is concerned, it was found that (i) The written expression of students of grade VIII is syntactic more complex than that of the students of grade IX. The difference between them is highly significant, (ii) The written expression of students of grade VIII is syntactically more complex than that of students of grade XI. Though the difference is not significant, it is not due only to chance factors, (iii) The written expression of students of grade IX is less complex than the students of grade XI but the difference is not significant and is due to chance factors. (4) The students of grade XI write longer sentences than the students of grade VIII and the students of grade VIII write longer sentences than the students of grade IX. (5) Students of grade XI use maximum number of complex and compound sentences, students of grade VIII use complex and compound sentences less in number than the students of grade XI, students of grade IX use the least number of compound and complex sentences, (i) Grade VIII students use maximum numbers of qualifiers, in their written work whereas, the students of grade IX use them the least as compared to the students of grades VIII, X and XI. (ii) The students of grade VIII use the maximum numbers of modifiers and modifier phrases. Grade XI students use modifiers and modifier phrases lesser in number than do grade VIII students but more in number than grade IX students. Grade IX students use the least number of modifiers and modifier phrases.

An Investigation into the Causes of Lack of Interest in Studies Among Students of Class XI

M.Ed., C.I.E., D.U., KRISHAN KUMAR BHARDWAJ, 1980

The sample for the study consisted of 75 students of class XI from three Senior Secondary Schools of New Delhi Municipal Committee. The *major* findings reported in the *study* were: (1) 50% students reported that they practically had no help in their studies from home. They did not have suitable place for study purposes at home. (2) 40% reported that they did not get *adequate* books, copies and other stationery whenever they asked for. (3) 34% of students did not get sufficient time to *study* at home. (4) In few cases students indulge in bad company and do not like to sit in classrooms. (5) Students often *earned* the feeling that in spite of *hard* work they were unable to get satisfactory marks. They develop *negative* feeling towards studies. (6) A *large* number reported that they get difficulty particularly in English and Science subjects. (7) A large number reported that they want more encouragement from parents and teachers to *study* which is lacking. (8) Level of interest in studies depends on teachers to a *large* extent. They also lose interest if teachers do not *explain* subject *matter* properly, if *adequate attention is* not *paid* to individual student and if teachers ignore the questions raised by students and they display *partiality* with students.

Profiles of Mathematically Talented Boys and Girls

M.Ed., C.I.E., DU, SHIKHA FOTEDAR, 1994

The study intended to *identify mathematically talented* boys and *girls*, to investigate special needs of these children, to *study* their emotional problem, to investigate *social* problems *faced* by mathematically tale boys and girls and to explore their career problem to study the difference in spatial ability, verbal ability, personal factors and attitude towards mathematics.

33 students who scored *about* 85% marks in maths in CBSE examinations of Xlth standard were selected. They were administered Raven's Progressive Test, Space Relation Test and Four schedules for assessing verbal ability of student's perception of self of mathematical talented *boys and* girls the attitude of these students towards maths, personality factors of mathematically talented *boys and* girls developed by the investigator. Scores obtained in maths in CBSE and Xllth standard *terminal* examinations were also *taken* into account.

The major findings of the study were: (1) Mathematically talented boys and girls score highly on intelligence test. They have high verbal and spatial ability. While the girls are better in verbal ability and achievement tests, boys fare better in spatial test. (2) The common personal traits of these students are compassion, independence, non-aggressiveness, non-assertiveness, self-confidence, obedience, punctuality and aspiration. While the girls are high on non-aggressions, obedience, punctuality and compassion, boys are high on assertiveness, independence and confidence. (3) Boys are interested in reading science fiction while girls enjoy reading romantic stories. (4) Challenging jobs are preferred by boys and girls prefer safe and steady jobs. (5) Girls are more examination oriented than boys and hence experience greater frustration than boys if they perform below their expectations. (6) Greater number of boys like to participate in maths quizzes than girls as they feel challenged. (7) Majority of mathematics talented girls prefer to take medicine as a career while boys favour engineering. (8) Most of the Math talented boys and girls do not have a warm relation with their parents and there seem to be a severe lack of communication. They perceive their parents especially fathers as demanding and authoritarian. (9) Most of the boys and girls were self-confidence and mature. They have focused ambitions and are aware of their potential and limitation. (10) Mathematical talented students do not have very close friends. (11) All students feel that their school has not done anything to nurture their talent. They do not consider their teachers as competent enough and think them to be bookish.

A Study of Miscue Analysis in English Language Acquisition among Students with Differential Reading Ability

M.Ed., C.I.E., D.U., ASHWANI KUMAR, 1987

The objectives were framed to study the miscues and their nature as revealed through the study for proficient readers as well as average readers the typology of miscues made by proficient average readers, the significant of difference if any between proficient and average readers in terms of the quantum of miscue, to analyse the miscues qualitatively in terms of semantics and grammatical categories, to study the psycho linguistic processing reflected in various types of miscues made by proficient and average readers and to study the reading comprehension of the proficient and average readers.

The sample consisted of class III students of a English medium school in Delhi. 15 children were selected, 5 above average, 5 average and 5 below average category. The tools used were Sabharwal's Reading Proficiency Scale and Miscue Elicitation-cum-Comprehension Passages.

The major findings showed the following: (1) The above average group tends to make fewer miscues as compared to the average and the average in turn make fewer miscues as compared to below average readers. (2) The below average readers made maximum improvement in their comprehension scores as more clues were provided. Above average made least improvements. (3) The above average could give correct response to almost all questions in the first attempt. Average readers showed decline and almost all below average students failed to give correct response. (4) Above average readers were confident about themselves. They answered in complete sentences. There was qualitative decline in the manner in which the questions were answered by average and below average readers. (5) Below average readers experienced difficulty in understanding meanings of the words in the passage and revealed difficulty in reading content words.

Problem-solving Strategies in Relation to the Identification of Mathematically Talented

M.Ed., C.I.E., D.U., ANITA SHARMA, 1994

The study attempted to analyse critically the tests generally being used in identification of mathematically talented with a view to frame a test to identify mathematically talented and to explore problem-solving strategies used by them.

For the conduct of the study, an Achievement Test constructed by the investigator was administered on 70 students of Government Composite Model School, 40 students of a public school, 25 students from D.P.S. Mathura Road and 135 class XI students from medical, commerce and non-medical group.

The major findings of the study show: (1) Boys are more mathematically talented than girls. (2) Mathematically talented are high achievers. (3) Mathematically talented use Heuristic method sometimes using insight in problem-solving. (4) Mathematically talented are able to find out the missing information in the problem and are able to select the ways to determine the missing information. They seek out for new methods and alternative approaches. They tend to approach a problem in logical manner. They have deep interest in subject and feel fresh and happy after solving a challenging problem.

A Study of the Extent of Divergent Thinking in the Foods and Nutrition Courses as Conceived by Class XI Home Science Students of Delhi

M.Ed, C.I.E., D.U., JYOTI BHANSALI, 1982

The objectives of the study envisaged to prepare a test in divergent thinking in foods and nutrition, to study the distribution and extent of divergent thinking ability in two groups of students in a public and government school, to study the correlation between divergent thinking in foods and nutrition and academic achievement in the same subject.

The sample consisted of 51 home science students of class XI. from the public school and 31 from government girls senior school belonging to the same class. A tool to induce divergent thinking was prepared and administered on the sample.

The results show that the girls of public school were more divergent in their thinking as compared to the girls of government school. Similarly there was positive and high correlation between divergent thinking and academic achievement in case of public schoolgirls.

Development and Validation of Scale to Assess the Attitude Towards Science for Secondary School Students

M.Ed, C.I.E., D.U., A.S. RAUTELA, 1995

The study envisaged to develop a scale to assess the attitude of secondary school students towards science. It was confined to one Senior Secondary School, in which 250 boys and 150 girls studying in class IX and X were selected for developing the scale. The developed scale was administered on these students. Item analysis etc. was done on the basis of response of these students' reliability and validity of the scale was computed. The attitude scale toward science can effectively be used to improve science teaching, learning and instruction, on industrial, educational, health and political organizations.

A Comparative Study of the Factors Affecting Specific Backwardness in Physical Science and Life Sciences among the Students of Class IX of Government Schools of Delhi State

M.Ed., C.I.E., D.U., 1983

The objectives of the study were to study some of the factors related to specific backwardness in physical science and life sciences, to study the common and differentiating factors related to specific backwardness in physical and life sciences. The Sample of the study consisted of 4 government senior secondary schools, two schools for girls and two for boys. The tools used in the study were three achievement tests constructed by the investigator, Intelligence tests, Raven's Progressive Matrices, Study Habits Inventory, Forced Choice Technique and deferential Aptitude Tests. The major finding of the study highlighted that specific backwardness in a subject is related to study habits in a test. Achievement in physics and life sciences depend on the study habits in those subjects.

A Study of the Written use of Second Language with Respect to Social Class

M.Ed., C.I.E., D.U., 1984

The study mainly aimed at studying quantitatively how students performed on reflective, prose, narrative prose, descriptive prose, to verify if there is any differences in quantitative aspects among students belonging to various social strata and, to study qualitatively the differences, if any, in the written expression across various social strata.

The sample was restricted to XIth class boys and girls from one English medium school in Delhi. The socio-economic status questionnaire and Language elicitation tests were administered. The findings highlighted that there is a definite difference in the written expression across various social strata. The social background of students does however influence the written use and expression of second language even if they are in the same English medium school.

A Study of Written English (Prose) Comprehension of Teenagers in Government Model Schools and Other Government Schools

M.Ed., C.I.E., D.U.

The study was carried out with the objectives of studying differences in reading prose comprehension among the sample subject with respect to descriptive narrative and expository prose, to study the overall differences in reading comprehension with respect to summated score on various types of prose passages and to study difference in reading comprehension with respect to

(a) ideational content (b) contextualized meaning of words, phrases or clauses and (c) contextualized levels in terms of synonyms and antonyms.

Development of a unit in Physics for Gifted Students Using Enrichment Triad Model

M.Ed., C.I.E., D.U., VANDANA SAXENA, 1993

The primary objectives of the study were to identify the particular needs of gifted in physics, to consider the implication of those needs for content, teaching methods and learning rate, to develop a programme which can be used in regular classrooms situation, to use "Enrichment Triad Model" for modification of a unit in physics, to provide advanced level understanding of the knowledge (content), methodology (process) and artistic areas of expression that are used within a particular discipline, to involve whole of the school population in the process of learning.

Sample comprised of 50 high achievers of class X and XI, 20 PGTs, 20 TGTs from various schools of Delhi and 50 students of class X and XI, 3 physics teachers from senior Navyug School at Sarojini Nagar, one specialist of gifted education. For the purpose of feedback the sample comprised of 10 students and 5 PGTs from various schools of Delhi, 5 students and 5 PGTs in physics of senior Navyug school, 5 principals from different schools of Delhi and one specialist in gifted education. The tools administered on the sample comprised of a Questionnaire and an Interest Inventory designed by the investigator.

A unit in physics using enrichment triad model was developed for gifted children on the basis of response and feedback received by students, principals and specialists.

An Investigation into the Psychological Abilities Involved in Learning Modern Mathematics at the Secondary Level

M.Ed., C.I.E., D.U., UJJAL SINGH, 1980

The present study tried to achieve the objectives of studying the correlation between abstract reasoning and achievement in Modern Mathematics, to study the correlation between Numerical ability and achievement in Modern Mathematics and to study the correlation between space relations and achievement in Modern Mathematics.

The following findings were arrived at:

1. Abstract Reasoning and achievement in Modern Mathematics are highly correlated to the extent of + .769 which was found significant.
2. Numerical ability correlates significantly with achievement in Modern Mathematics to the extent of .335 which was found significant.
3. Spatial ability was not found significantly correlated with the achievement in Modern Maths.
4. Partial correlation of co-efficient r 12.34 under r 13.24 were found significant while r 14.23 was found not significant.
5. Multiple correlation co-efficient r a(234) = .812 was found highly significant.
6. Reasoning and Numerical ability play significant role in determining success in Modern Mathematics.

Development of Remedial Course in Mathematics or Raising the Standard of Low-achievers of Grade VI.

M.Ed., C.I.E., D.U., AJEET SINGH MALIK, 1995

The objectives of the study were as follows:

(1) To find out the reasons of deficiencies in the achievement of the course content in the grade VI. (2) To develop a remedial course for the low-achievers in mathematics at the level of grade VI. (3) To find out the ways and means of communicating the content of remedial course to low-achievers. (4) To study the effect of the material course communicated to the low-achievers.

The main cause of deficiencies in the achievement of the course-content in the grade VI, is the poor command over computational skills, which are learnt at primary level. The analysis of errors made by the students in Brueckner's diagnostic test, shows that 54% students did wrong operation; they multiplied instead of dividing a fraction by another fraction. 54% students were deficient in computational skills. Majority of students were lacking in comprehension of the process of division. 34% students faced difficulty in reducing fractions to lowest terms. 68% students faced cancellation difficulties.

The remedial course improves the performance of the low-achievers, by remedying the defects. The difference between the means of pre-test and post-test scores, is significant at .01 level, which further shows that the group had made significant improvement in mathematics.

A Study of the Written Vocabulary of the Sixth Class Children in Delhi Schools

C.I.E., P. PASRICHA and S.K. DAS, 1959

The study made preliminary attempts at the analysis of the written vocabulary of the children studying in the sixth grade of Delhi schools. A sample of 527 students from twelve different schools was selected. The conclusion drawn from this study was that the development of language passes through the mere accumulation of words and proceeds on to the mastery of some of them, thus adding to the repertoire of correct vocabulary of the child. With better environment and stimulation the child completes this process sooner than the children with poorer environment can afford to do.

Backwardness in Mathematics and Basic Arithmetic Skills

Ph.D., C.I.E., D.U., R.C. GUPTA, 1972

The purpose was to provide a standardised tool to the teachers and research workers whereby they would be able to diagnose the weak areas in mathematics. 180 boys and 176 girls were selected for the final study. The important findings were: (i) low-achievers in mathematics have poor command, whereas high achievers have good command over basic arithmetic skills; (ii) basic arithmetic skills can be quickly and conveniently mastered by the course of self-help in basic arithmetic skills.

An Investigation into the Interrelationship Between Measures of Selected Guilford's S1 Factors and Set Concept Achievement of Secondary Level Students of Delhi State

Ph.D., JMI, AMBA DUTT TEWARI, 1985

Mainly the study envisaged to identify the reasoning ability structure of IX class students studying in government boy's higher secondary schools of Delhi. The tools used in the study comprised of Reasoning ability test battery by Girishbala and set concept achievement test constructed by the investigator.

The findings of the study revealed that most of the reasoning ability tests had significant positive correlations among themselves.

Influence of Environmental Conditions in Science Learning: A Study of Secondary School Students

M.Phil., JMI, NARIM AHMED, 1986

The main objective of the study was to determine the combined and individual effect of environmental conditions at home, school and classroom in science learning in respect of below average, average and above average students. The sample consisted of 80 below average, 82 average and 80 above average students drawn from three government senior secondary schools. Jalota's Group Test of mental ability were administered on the selected sample.

The study revealed that for below average students, home environment, classroom environment and combined environment do not have any significant relationship with science learning while school environment has significant relationship. For above average, home environment, school environment, classroom environment as well as combined environment variables has very significant relationship with the science learning. For the average students the combined environment variable has significant relationship with science learning, whereas home environment has no significant relationship.

A Comparative Study of Interest in Science Among Government and Public School Students of West Delhi

M.Ed., JMI, A. AALAM KHAN, 1990

The main objective of the study was to compare the girls and boys of the government school and public school in terms of interest in science. The major findings show that the public school students show more interest in science than government boys.

Attitude Towards Science Subject Among Secondary School Children, A Study in East Delhi

M.Ed., JMI, RAJESH KUMAR SHARMA, 1988

The main objective was to study the attitude of school students towards science subject. 100 students from East Delhi school

(50 boys and 50 girls) were selected as sample of the study. Science Attitude Scale by Grewal (1977; was administered on the selected sample. The main finding of the study revealed that 57% of students could not decide upon their attitude towards science subject and 41% had moderate positive attitude toward science subject. They had neutral attitudes about the subject. There was also a significant difference in attitude among public school students and government school students. School environment did play an important role in bringing a positive attitude towards science subject.

A Comparative Study of "Affective" Development of Students Going Through General Science Programme and Pure Science Programme at the end of Middle School Stage (VIII Grade)

M.Ed., JMI, MARY CHACKE, 1970

The study was carried out to know whether there was significant difference in affective development of children going through general science programme and pure science programme, between girls and boys and between students coming from different value orientation strata. The tools used in the study was the Value Orientation Scale.

It was found in the study that there was no significant difference between the means of affective development scores if general science group and pure science group of different schools, of general science group and pure science group of girls and boys, between girls and boys so far their affective development is concerned, between high group of value orientation and the low group of value orientation of both general and pure science group of different schools, between the high group of value orientation of both general science group and pure science group of girls and boys.

An Investigation into the Difficulties Faced by VII Class Students in Solving Problems of Arithmetic

M.Ed., JMI, RAJENDRA SINGH, 1970

The study carried out in five schools indicate defective methods of teaching arithmetic although no significant difference existed between the abilities of boys and girls in working process sums in arithmetic.

An Investigation into the Problems of Urdu Medium Students in Learning English

JMI, ERIC Funded, R.P. SRIVASTAVA, 1995

The study attempted to diagnose the problems encountered by the school stage students from Urdu medium background in learning English as a second language. A sample of six Urdu medium secondary schools was selected from the walled city area of Delhi. The hundred and ten students, (fresh entrance to class X) comprised the sample. Tools used included a diagnostic test, a test of written expression in English and an unstructured interview. The collected data were treated using Mean, SD and 't' test. The major findings of the study were: (1) In English comprehension, learners found answering direct questions easier than those whose answers had to be inferred or generalized from the given text. (2) The decreasing order of difficulty in the three aspects of English language were comprehension, grammar and vocabulary. (3) The learners generally responded more to multiple choice items than to open-ended items where they were required to furnish the whole answer.

An Investigation into the Socio-economic and Educational Background of Students Offering History as an Elective Subject at Senior Secondary Level in the Schools of Delhi

M.Ed., C.I.E., D.U., 1984

The objective of the study was to investigate as to what extent the social economic status of pupils influences to study scientific and other subjects.

The factors taken up for assessing socio-economic status of pupils offering history are: type of occupation, type of houses they live in, area in which situated, income of the family, sources of income, members of the family, education of the family interests and hobbies of students, other facilities and hindrances.

The study was conducted on 240 senior secondary students from 2 public, 2 government boys', 2 government girls' senior secondary schools. A socio-economic scale was constructed to study these schools.

The major findings of the study were: (1) The parents of both Science and Commerce students got better educational background than that of the arts students. It is found that 51.25% arts students and 11.25% commerce students have parents who are illiterate or have studied only up to primary whereas Science group has none in these two categories. As regards to the education of the fathers, it is found that 92.5% fathers of both the Science and Commerce students are graduates and postgraduates. 52.5% Science students and 45.5% Commerce students have fathers specialising in Science and Commerce respectively whereas only 42.5% father of the arts group are graduate and post-graduate. About the education of the mothers, it is found that 71.25% Science students and 58.75% Commerce students have graduate and post-graduate mothers. Science group has got most number of Ph.D's as parents and all the children of M.B.B.S. parents have offered Science subjects. It shows that arts group has the lowest educational background and Science group the highest. Education of the parents is an important factor which influence the students in the choice of subjects at the senior secondary level. (2) As regards the occupation of the parents, it is found that 85% fathers of science group and 50% fathers of Commerce group are engaged in higher service group whereas only 22.5% fathers of the arts students are in the higher service group and 12.5% fathers of the arts group are in the lowest group whereas the other two groups have none in the lowest group of occupation. About the occupation of the mothers, it is found that 70% Science and 40% Commerce students have mothers in the highest group of occupation while only 2% mothers of the arts students are in the highest group of occupation and mothers of arts students are more in the lowest groups of occupation than that of the other 2 groups. (3) As regards to the income of the parents, it is found that 38.75% parents of science group and 33.75% parents of the Commerce group are in higher income group whereas only 16.25% parents of the arts group are in a higher income group. 13.75% parents of the art groups are in the lowest group of income whereas the other two groups have none in this category.

It shows that choice of the subjects is significantly related to the monthly income of the family. (4) Both Science and Commerce students avail more physical amenities than that of the arts group. The difference between the socio-economic and educational background of the 3 groups is significant. The difference between the means of Science and Arts groups and arts and commerce groups is highly significant while the difference between the means of science and commerce groups is not significant. (5) The difference between the 3 groups of both Public and Government Schools is highly significant and the difference between the 3 groups within the school is also highly significant both at .05 and .01 level.

Investigation into the Relationship Between the Interests of the Students in Jamia School in Relation to Certain Variables

M.Ed., C.I.E., D.U., ABUL LAIS, 1990

The study proceeded with the objective of finding out the impact of sex on interests, of religion on the interest, of socio--economic status of the individual on his/her interests, of age and grade on the interests of students.

It was confined to Jamia Secondary and Senior Secondary School. It was conducted on 400 students of class IX and XI. The tools used were socio-economic status scale and Interest Inventory by Dr. K.K. Jain.

The main findings were: (1) There is no difference in the academic interests between boys and girls. Girls have higher aesthetic interests than boys. Boys have higher economic interests than girls. Boys have higher interests in health, sports and games. Boys have higher mechanical interests than girls. Girls have less interests in outdoor activities and adventure.

A Study of Achievement Motivation in Relation to Personality Dimension (Extroversion-Introversion) and Scholastic Achievement Among the High School Pupils

M.Ed., C.I.E., D.U., AMARJEET KAUR, 1986

The main objective of the study was (1) to find out the distribution of achievement motivation items among the students; (2) to find out the distribution of personality traits like extroversion and introversion; (3) to find out the distribution of how variables like extroversion, introversion are related or influence n-achievement and (4) to find out the distribution of the Pearson correlation among the variables like achievement motivation, extroversion-introversion, scholastic achievement.

The study was confined to 392 pupils studying in XI and XII class from six higher secondary schools from urban area of Delhi. They were administered the Mukherjee's Sentence Completion test and Mausley Personality Inventory.

The major findings were: (1) The V-Ach (HS) score in the case of girls is higher than that of boys. (2) The V-Ach (FF) score is higher in the case of boys than in the case of girls. (3) The Extroversion-Introversion score is higher in the case of boys, than that of girls. (4) The Extroversion-Introversion score and V-Ach (HS) score are related to a high degree than Extroversion-Introversion and V-Ach (FF) score. (5) The extreme groups on the Extroversion-Introversion scale differ on n-Ach (HS) and n-Ach (FF) score significantly. (6) Scholastic achievement score is higher for girls than that of boys. (7) The V-Ach (HS) score and scholastic achievement score are positively correlated. (8) The V-Ach (FF) score and scholastic achievement score are negatively correlated.

Some Correlates of Under Achievement in Mathematics

M.Ed., C.I.E., D.U., JYOTI SHARMA, 1995

The objectives of the study were to (1) explore the concept of underachievement in mathematics. (2) identify problem-solving strategies in mathematics. (3) development of a test to identify underachievers in mathematics. (4) explore errors in problem-solving strategies used by underachievers. (5) explore the attitude of underachievers towards mathematics, interest in mathematics among underachievers and academic self-concept of mathematics underachievers and (6) build up a theoretical model depicting underachievement in mathematics.

In order to conduct the pilot study, ten students of class IXth were taken up which was later extended to 36 from one school and 60 from other. Groups of underachievers were formed by grouping students who secured marks ranging from 40% less in mathematics and more than 60% based on the teacher evaluation of their performance in mathematics.

The major findings as reported in the study were: (1) Underachievers have no sound knowledge of basic skills and lack of proper understanding of mathematical concepts. (2) Negative attitude towards Mathematics — Most underachievers score low in mathematics because they had negative attitude. (3) Mathematics concepts need proper logical thinking with a sound knowledge of basic concepts students found difficult to understand. (4) Some students suffer from Attential Sequencial Dyscalculia. Number of such students is very low (only 5 found in this study). These students sometimes skip the steps or something forgot to complete the question — ignored by signs of addition, subtraction etc.

An Investigation into the Leisure time Activities in Relationship to their Vocational Interest *M.Ed., C.I.E., D.U.,* ARCHANA GUPTA, 1985

The study was carried out by keeping with the objective of examining leisure time activities of 120 class XI Government Senior Schoolgirls, their vocational interests and relationship between leisure time activities and vocational interest. They were administered two questionnaires on leisure time activity and vocational interest constructed by the investigator. It was found that the leisure time and vocational activity pursued by commerce, science and arts students mainly ranged between outdoor, literary activities, artistic, scientific, social, commercial, academic, mechanical and clerical. Priorities are different for each category.

Comparative Study of the Self-concept Anxiety and Achievement of Adolescent Girls Studying in Single Sex Schools and Co-Educational Schools *M.Ed., C.I.E., D.U.,* JASJEET GULATI, 1989

As title suggests, the study attempted to analyse the difference between the self-concept anxiety academic achieve of adolescent 115 girls of XIIth class from two schools, one coeducational and other single sex school. They were administered Anxiety Scale by D.N. Srivastava and Govind Tiwari, Self-Concept Inventory Raj Kumar Saraswati and Cumulative of percentage of total marks attained in CBSE examinations of class X. The study showed that the girls in two schools did not differ significantly in their anxiety but qualitative analysis showed that girls in single sex schools had little anxiety level. This difference was due to the rigid involvement and authoritarian attitude of teachers. There also existed a significant negative relation between anxiety and academic achievement. Higher the level of anxiety and poorer was the academic achievement.

A Comparative Study of Some Factors Responsible for High and Low Achievements *M.Ed., C.I.E., D.U.*, SHIVE KUMAR MUNJAL, 1980

The study mainly was carried out to know the effect of anxiety on academic achievement and the difference in the anxiety and extroversion of high and low achievers in chemistry. Dutt's Personality Inventory and Mausley Personnel Inventory were used as tools in the study on 60 low and high achievers (30+30) from four schools. The study reported that high achievers are significantly lower in anxiety as compared to low achievers. High achievers in Chemistry do not differ significantly from low achievers on Extroversion.

A Comparative Study of the Vocational Aspiration of High Achiever and Low Achiever Students of Class XI of Senior Secondary Schools of Delhi Territory

M.Ed., C.I.E., D.U., 1983

The objectives of the study were to provide suitable opportunities, openings and facilities to both high and low achievers (Academic) in view of their aspirations and abilities, to make useful suggestion and provide guidance to the students and parents and even teachers in respect of vocational choice, to provide facilities for their vocational placement and follow up work.

As sample of the study, 147 students were selected through a stratified random sampling to whom two types of questionnaires were administered.

The study revealed significant changes in the vocational aspirations of low achiever students and differences in vocational aspirations between low and high achievers, low achiever boys and low achiever girls, low achiever students belonging to the different income level groups, and high achiever students belonging to different socio-economic groups. Educational factors too exerted influence on both the low and high achiever students to a great extent but there was a difference in the degree of influence. The low achiever students were more influenced by the general standard of education and not much by education of parents and siblings.

A Study of Academic Achievement in Relation to Adjustment and Achievement Motivation

M.Ed., C.I.E., D.U., 1984

The main objectives of the study were to find out the relationship between academic achievement and achievement motivation, between academic achievement and adjustment in its varied context such as home, society, emotional hostility, masculinity and femineity. The sample consisted of 220 Ninth class boys from two government schools. The tools used in the study were marks obtained by the boys in final examinations, Projective tests, Thematic Apperception Test, Bell's Adjustment Inventory and Prayag Mahta's Achievement Inventory. The major findings of the study revealed that students who had good home adjustment were adjusted well in other areas as well like health, social and emotional adjustment. Children with good adjustment got high percentage of marks or good academic achievement led to better adjustment in all areas. Children with good adjustment and high percentage gave more achievement related responses. Students who gave more achievement related responses were found to be better adjusted than children who gave more task related and unrelated response.

An Investigation into the Relationship Between Interests and Personality Traits of Boys and Girls of Class VIII and XI

M.Ed.. C.I.E., D.U., 1985

The study mainly concentrated upon knowing and comparing the interests and personality traits of 137 boys and girls of classes VIII and XI. For this purpose 137 students of Army Public School were selected and Bernreuters Personality Inventory and Interest Inventory developed by Investigator were administered on them. The major findings of the study revealed that the boys of class VIII and class XI had no interest in academic area but more interested in talks, discussions and reading materials etc. Girls did show academic interest but they showed maximum interest in social activities. Boys of class VIII were more interested in scientific and related activities as compared to girls of class VIII. In rest of the areas, girls showed more dominance over boys.

A Study of Measured Creativity and Scholastic Achievement Among High and Low Intelligence Group at the Higher Secondary Stage

M.Ed., JMI, SURESH C. AHUJA, 1973

The study attempted to measure the creativity and scholastic achievement of high and low group of students by selecting a sample of 500 class XI students from 3 non-government higher secondary schools for boys and one government higher secondary school. The tools used were Cattell's Group Test of Mental Ability, designed by R.B. Cattell and A.K.S. Cattell and High School Personality Questionnaire. The findings revealed that those having low intelligence test score may have moderately fair creative output.

Stress in Relation to Academic Achievement: A Study of Secondary and Higher Secondary Class Students of a School in Delhi

M.Phil., JNU, R. DAS, 1989

The present study has attempted to ascertain whether there is a difference in the academic performance of students in terms of different types of school organisational climates, teacher effectiveness and teacher's job satisfaction, as well as whether the interaction of the above three factors in any way influences the academic performance of students.

Four types of schools were taken and 309 students from both classes IV and V from different schools, and 40 teachers were taken as sample for this study. The tools used were: Organisational Climate Description Questionnaire (OCDQ) devised by Sharma (1973) to assess the climate that exists in the school, Teacher Characteristic Description Form (TCDF) devised by Aurora (1973) to measure the effectiveness of teachers, Job Satisfaction Investor (JSI) devised by Indiresan (1973) to measure the job satisfaction of the teachers. The Academic Performance of students was considered in terms of the marks obtained by the students of classes IV and V in their annual examination conducted by the schools from the school record.

The results obtained show that: (1) The Academic Performance of public school students in both classes IV and V were significantly better than those from missionary, government and municipal school (in class IV). (2) The Academic Performance of students varied in terms of the Organisational Climate of the school in both the classes IV and V, that is, students from the open climate schools had shown significantly higher academic performance than those from the closed climate. (3) The academic performance of students differed significantly in terms of the effectiveness of the teacher (in class IV). That is, students taught by Highly effective (HE) teachers showed better academic performance. (4) The academic performance of the students from classes IV and V differed significantly in terms of the job satisfaction of the teachers (in class IV, and in class V). In other words, students taught by the teacher having high job satisfaction (HJS) showed better academic performance than those taught by teachers having low job satisfaction (LJS). (5) The teacher effectiveness combined with the specific type of climate in the school led to differential level of academic performance amongst the students of classes IV and V respectively. In other words, students of open climate school taught by the highly effective (HE) teachers scored high in academic performance than any other combination of school climate and teacher effectiveness. (6) Differential level of job satisfaction of the teacher combined with certain type of school climate led to a differential level of academic performance amongst the students in class IV. That is, students of the open climate school taught by the Highly Job satisfied (HJS) teacher showed better academic performance, than any other combination of school climate and the job satisfaction of teachers. (7) A combination of high level teacher effectiveness and job satisfaction of the teachers and the type of school (public school) in which the pupil studied led to a significantly high academic performance among the classes IV and V students respectively as compared to any other combination of teacher effectiveness, job satisfaction and the type of school. (8) A differential level of organisational climate combined with certain type of effectiveness and job satisfaction of teachers lead to a differential level of academic performance among the students (in class IV and in class V), that is, in an open climate school the students, who were taught by the highly effective teachers and having high job satisfaction also showed significantly better academic performance. (9) A positive correlation was found among the teachers in terms of teacher effectiveness and job satisfaction in the public school and missionary school respectively (r=.41 and .45), whereas a negative correlation was obtained between these two factors in the government and municipal schools respectively (being -.38 and -.39). That is, as the effectiveness of the teacher increased and reached higher level job satisfaction also increased linearly in the case of public school and missionary school, was in the case of government school and municipal school the relationship was in opposite direction. That is, as the effectiveness of teacher increased and reached higher level, the job satisfaction decreased and reached a lower level.

A Study of Some Factors Related to Scholastic Achievement

Ph.D., C.I.E., D.G. RAO, 1965

The study was undertaken to find out the relationship of intelligence, study habits, socio-economic status, and certain attitudes towards the school with the academic achievement of the grade VIII pupils of Delhi. 500 boys of twelve higher secondary schools of Delhi formed the sample. The scholastic achievement of pupils was measured using the Jamia Achievement Test Battery which included three important school subjects, *viz.,* social studies, general science and mathematics. The CIE Group Test of Intelligence was used to measure intelligence. An inventory was developed on the pattern of the Wrenn's Study Habit Inventory to measure the study habits. The Kuppuswamy's Socio-economic status. For measuring attitude towards school, a new tool was developed.

The major finding of the study reported that the three independent variables — intelligence, study habits and school attitude were significantly related to the prediction of scholastic achievement, while socio-economic status was not.

A Study of High Achievers with Respect to their Needs and Interests

M.Ed., C.I.E., D.U., SUMAN DAS, 1988

The objectives of the study were to study the socio-economic status of the high achievers, average and the low achievers, to study and compare the interest pattern of the high achievers, average and the low achievers, to study and compare the needs of high achievers, average and the low achievers.

The sample was drawn from two girls' schools of Hindi medium. 99 and 83 students of class VIIIth were selected consisting of high achievers, average and low achievers. The tools administered on them comprised of socio-economic scale developed by Jain, interest inventory by Jain and needs inventory constructed by the researcher.

The findings show that the high achievers have interests in academic and intellectual areas and high order needs than the average and low average achievers. The socio-economic status of school and family did affect the achievement, interests and needs of students. Similarly the high achievers showed maximum needs for achievement and acquisition. The high achievers of two schools had same interests, same intensity and extent of needs pattern.

A Comparative Study of Reading Attainment Across Various Types of Schools in Delhi

M.Ed., C.I.E., D.U., 1985

The primary objectives of the study were to find out the differences if any between student samples drawn from two schools in terms of overall Reading Attainment and in terms of factual, interpretive and evaluative comprehension and the number of references made to the given passage, to study and assess to what extent the Language Programme in the sample schools is geared towards the development of higher order reading skills.

R.B. Cattell's Scale III, Form A Culture Fair test and a group of three reading comprehension tests were administered on a sample of 10 students of Grade XI that out of these 10 students, 5 were from the privately run English medium public school and the remaining five were from a state-run English medium school.

A Study of the Relationship of Some of the Personality Traits Associated with Academic Achievement of Students at the Higher Secondary Stage

M.Ed., JMI, KAMALA MADHAVA, 1971

The study was carried out with the objectives of finding out the relationship of some of the personality traits associated with academic achievement of students at the higher secondary stage. The sample was drawn from four higher secondary schools. The major findings reveal that personality characteristics are associated with academic achievement. The higher neuroticism, the poorer is performance. The higher emotional stability, better the performance and less tense are better achievers in academic subjects.

A Study of Relationship Between Adjustment and Academic Achievement of Students of Higher Secondary Level

M.Ed., JMI, KHALID MOHD. ABRAR KHAN, 1988

The objectives of the study mainly confined to finding out the adjustment of class XI arts group students, finding out the academic achievement score of class Xth and the relationship between adjustment and academic achievement of class XI/X Arts students.

The sample consisted of 50 Arts students of class XI in Higher Secondary school of Jamia Millia Islamia. The tools employed for data collection comprised of the adjustment inventory for school by N.M. Bhagia, academic achievement of students of class XI on the basis of final result and the measurement of School Adjustment by N.M. Bhagia (1966).

A Study of Vocational Interest Among Secondary School Students in Relation to Sex and Socio-economic Status

M.Ed., C.I.E., D.U., SUSHIL KUMAR SHARMA, 1991

The main objective of the study was to find out the vocational interest of X class students of Government Schools in Delhi in different vocational interest areas.

The sample selected for the study comprised of 200 students belonging to government schools. They were administered SES scale and Vocational interest inventory. It was found that the most popular interest area in boys was Defence and police whereas in girls most preferable jobs were teaching at school level and medicine in academic area. Boys were also interested in outdoor activities in comparison to girls.

A Study of Pupils Perception of Educational Needs and Their Personal Goals

M.Ed., C.I.E., D.U., NEENA VIRMANI, 1983

The objectives of the study were to find out the degree of prevailing classroom climate as perceived by the pupils, to find out the relative order of perception of various sectors of class climates as recorded by the students, to find out the relationship between pupils' perception of educational goals and their achievements, to find out the relationship between achievement and the class climate as perceived by the students and to find out whether the perception of class climate due to longer association with the school is stronger in the older group in comparison to the new group of students.

The sample of the study consisted of 84 class Xth students of all sections from one school. The pupils personal inventory prepared by the investigator was used to study the problem.

The major findings of the study revealed that there exists a better relationship between achievement and class-climate *i.e.* high achievers perceive better class-climate and *vice versa* although not so good relationship existed between self-assessment and achievement. The study also showed that long association with the school effects the attitude of a student.

A Study of Language Proficiency in Terms of its Various Correlates as Perceived by the Teachers

M.Ed., C.I.E., D.U., 1984

Objectives of the study were enumerated as follows: (1) To study the overall general proficiency in first language of the students. (2) To study the general language proficiency in .narrative mode of use. (3) To study the general language proficiency in descriptive mode of use. (4) To study the general language proficiency in reflective mode of use. (5) To study the influence of the three correlates *e.g.* Socio-Vocational Status, Educational level of the family and Economic Status on language proficiency. (6) To study whether students with various levels of Socio-Vocational Status, Educational and Economic status manifest differences in language proficiency.

The sample was drawn from two Government Boys' Senior Secondary Schools. 179 students and 90 teachers from five Government Boys Senior Secondary Schools were selected. Four tools were used for the study namely, Teacher Opinionnaire, Socio-Economic and Parental Education Scale, Cloze Test Questionnaire and Personal Data for students.

The major findings of the study reveal the following: (1) No significant difference among three levels (upper, middle, lower) of economic status. A child coming from upper economic status has the same level of language proficiency as a child who belongs to a lower economic stratum or a child who belongs to middle strata. (2) Educational background of the family has an effect on the child's language proficiency pertaining to descriptive and reflective mode of language use. (3) Socio-Economic status does not effect the child's language proficiency because upper class people may have all the facilities to provide better education but middle and lower class set certain ideas for the children and cultural values for them.

A Study of Relationship Between Socio-metric Status of Pupils and their Performance in Academic and Non-academic Areas

M.Ed., C.I.E., D.U., POONAM CHOPRA

The objectives of the study were to compare group structure of different classes, to find out if there is any difference in sociometric status according to different criterion, to find out the relationship, if any between socio-metric status for each criterion and academic achievement, between socio-metric status for each criterion and non-academic performance, to compare the teachers' ratings on non-academic performance with academic achievement and to compare teachers' ratings on non-academic performance with students' socio-metric choices on various criteria.

Leisure Time Activities of Students of Different Subject Streams

M.Ed., C.I.E., D.U., SATISH KUMAR, 1996

The objectives of the study were to study the leisure time activities of students of different subject streams and to compare the leisure time activities of students belonging to urban and rural areas. The sample comprised of 120 class XI students from Arts, Commerce, Science streams from rural and urban areas of Delhi. A questionnaire was developed for these students. The major findings of the study were (1) Leisure time activities pursued by science students in order of rank participation in academic-like activities, scientific activities, commercial activities, outdoor activities, recreational activities, literacy activities, games, sports and physical activities, social activities, mechanical activities, arts and craftwork activities, clerical and economic activities, indulging in sex and romantic activities. For lower students, the order of preference is Commercial activities, Recreational activities, Social activities, Games, sports, physical activities, Participation academic-like activities, Literary activities, Scientific activities, Outdoor, Mechanical activities, Clerical and Economic activities, Indulging in sex and romantic activities,

Arts and crafts activities. The arts students prefer in order Recreation activities, Commercial activities, Social activities, Games, sport, physical exercise, Literary activities, Portion academic-like activities, Scientific activities, Outdoor activities, Indulging in sex and romantic, Arts and craftwork activities, Mechanical activities, Clerical and Economic activities. (2) There is no significant difference in the preferred of activities between urban and rural areas. (3) Similar activities are preferred and least preferred by commerce students of both urban and rural background. (4) There is slight variation in the preferences of urban and rural science group. The least preferred activities by urban students are clerical and economic arts and craftwork, indulging in sex and romantic activities and mechanical activities. While rural students least prefer indulging in sex and romance, outdoor, mechanical and clerical activities and (5) Commerce and arts students show similarity in their choice of leisure time activity as compared to science and commerce group and science and arts group as correlated values verified.

A Study of Some of the Correlates of Reading Ability Amongst Primary School Children of Delhi

Ph.D., JNU, ZHCES, SSS, JAY ANTI ROY, 1987

The present study was set out with the main objectives of ascertaining the correlates of Reading Ability, ascertaining the relationship between Reading Ability and academic performance, between Reading Ability and personality traits, personal attributes and home background of students, ascertaining whether Reading Ability differs in terms of different types of school and ascertaining whether improvement in Reading Ability will lead to improvement in the academic performance of students.

The whole study was conducted in two phases. In Phase I, the correlates of Reading Ability were delineated and in Phase II an attempt was made to ascertain if improvement in Reading Ability led to improvement in the academic performance of students.

For the 1st Phase of this study, a sample of 360 students were taken from three different classes *(viz.* Class II, III and IV) of four different types of schools *(viz.* Public school, Missionary school, Navyug school and Central school). They were administered the Reading Ability test (devised by Researcher), intelligence test (A.N. Misra, 1971), phonic ability test (J.M. Hughes, 1975), home background instrument (devised by Researcher), and personality traits (devised by Researcher), Students' academic performance (marks) of the previous examination were noted from the school's Report Card. For Phase II, 45 students of class III studying in Navyug school were taken with 15 students each (7 with good Reading Ability and 8 with poor Reading Ability) for Experimental group, Control Group I and Control Group II respectively.

The research design used for the Phase I study was intercorrelation matrix and the Phase II, *ex post facto* experimental design. The statistical method used were inter-correlational matrix, stepwise regression analysis, t-test and trend analysis.

The results obtained were (1) Reading Ability was constituted of a number of factors such as personality traits, intelligence, phonic ability, reading habit of students, reading interest of students, health of students, availability of reading materials at home, parents' education, parents' occupation and reading habit of parents. (2) Reading Ability was positively and significantly correlated with academic performance. (3) Reading Ability was a function of types of school; specifically, Missionary school students had the highest Reading Ability scores, followed by students of Public school, Navyug school and Central school in that order. (4) Reading Ability varied in terms of differential personality traits amongst students. (5) Reading Ability of students differed significantly in terms of their personal attributes. (6) Reading Ability was positively and significantly correlated with home background. (7) Reading Ability did not differ as a function of sex factor, except in the case of class II, Missionary school students wherein girls had significantly higher Reading Ability scores than boys. (8) Improvement in Reading Ability led to better academic performance amongst students.

Children's Perception of Teachers' Attitude Towards them and its Relationship with Self-perception, Home Environment and School Achievement

Ph.D., Edu., JMI, DEBAS, J.K., 1979

(CHECK WITH JMI-PH. D) The objectives of the study were to know:

1. the attitude of teacher (as measured in terms of their perception of the pupil's characteristics) towards students belonging to different cultural backgrounds,
2. how students perceived their teachers' evaluation regarding the same characteristics,

3. the relationship between students' perception of their teachers and self-perception regarding the same characteristics, and
4. the relationship of the attitude of teachers' and students' self-perception to school achievement.

The sample consisted of all male students of class IX studying in government boys' higher secondary schools of Delhi in north district, having Hindi as medium of instruction and belonging to different cultural backgrounds. The tools used for the study were Advanced Progressive Matrices for measuring intelligence. A Cultural Status Scale was developed by the investigator for measuring home environment or cultural status of students as well as the Pupil's Characteristics Rating Scale to assess three kinds of perception, namely, pupils' own perception about themselves regarding some of their personality characteristics, pupils' perception of teachers' evaluation on the same characteristics and teachers' attitude as measured in terms of their perception of pupils' characteristics.

The findings of the study were:

1. Children's perception of teachers' attitude towards them was significantly related with pupils' self-perception, teachers' perception of pupils' characteristics and school achievement (in physical sciences), whereas it was not significantly related with the cultural status of students.
2. Teachers' attitude towards children coming from advantaged homes was more favourable than towards children coming from disadvantaged homes.
3. School achievement (in physical sciences) was not significantly related with the cultural status of students whereas teachers' attitude (as measured in terms of their perception of pupils' characteristics) towards students was likely to affect their school achievement (in physical sciences).

Physical Fitness Norms for Boys and Girls in Grades Nine of Delhi State

Ph.D., Phy. Edit., Jiwaji Univ., SARITA TYAGI

The study mainly attempted to develop physical fitness norms for boys and girls of Grades IX to XII of Delhi State. The sample comprised of 6000 boys and girls drawn from 50 schools. The findings showed no difference in the physical fitness of girls and boys.

A Study of Relationship Between Socio-economic Status and Conservative of Number and Substance in Delhi School Children

Ph.D., JMI, NILIMA KUMARI, 1983

The study was carried out by keeping in view the objectives of finding the relationship between socio-economic status and conservation of substance and the conservation of number. The main study was conducted in second shifted schools of South Delhi.

Three hundred children were selected from twenty schools for the study. Four tools were administered on them, *viz.* Socio-economic status scale, Raven's Coloured Progressive Matrices, a tool to assess the level of development of conservation of substance and a tool to assess the level of development conservation of Number. Each child was administered all the tools.

The major findings of the study revealed that: (1) Socio-Economic Status is highly correlated with conservation of substance and Number. (2) Conservation of substance and conservation of Number are highly correlated. So a good conserver of substance is very likely to be a good conserver of Number. Only a few exception to this general trend will occur as the correlation is pretty high (r = .998). (3) Intelligence is positively related to the level of development of conservation of substance one who is high in intelligence is likely to be a good conserver of substance. (4) Intelligence is positively correlated with conservation of Number. One who is high in intelligence is likely to be a good conserver of Number.

A Study of Scientific Creativity and Mathematical Creativity among IX Class Students in Delhi Schools

M.Ed., JMI, RAJSHREE JOSHI, 1988

The major objectives of the study were to examine the scientific creativity among IX class students of Delhi schools, to study their mathematical creativity and to find the relationship between scientific creativity and mathematical creativity. A sample of 200 students from six 6 different schools was taken up.

The major findings of the study showed that students possess very low scientific creativity. Out of a sample of 200 students, only 3% were able to achieve the threshold value while the rest 97% failed to attain the reference mark. They also possess very low divergent thinking ability in Mathematics.

Correlation of Academic Motivation in High School Students

M.Ed., JMI, H.C. ARORA, 1970

The main objective of the study was to find out how for academic motivation is correlated with academic achievement, whether, socio-economic status plays a vital part in motivation and achievement or whether age and intelligence correlates with academic motivation. The study was conducted on two government (boys) higher secondary school from Shahdara zone and New Delhi public school. They were administered Inventory, Intelligence test, socio-economic status scale. The major finding revealed that academic motivation is significantly correlated with academic achievement in high school students. It is least correlated with intelligence.

A Study of Factors which Students Think have Good or Bad Effect on their Scholastic Attainment Inside the School

M.Ed., JMI, SUNDER DAS CHHOKRA, 1970

The main objective of the study was to identify the factors which the students think have good or bad effect on their scholastic attainment inside the school. The study revealed:

(1) Separate rooms for separate classes and subjects are needed. (2) The school should always be away from the noise of the town. (3) The school equipment such as furniture, separate comfortable seating arrangement for every student, cemented and whitewashed walls decorated with charts, maps and inspiring mottos. (4) An able principal with impressive and dynamic personality. (5) Timely medical check-up helps in maintaining good health. (6) The students think religious education should not be imparted in schools. (7) Importance of

games should not be minimised. (8) Financial help in the form of books, money and clothes, fee-concessions and maintenance of grants etc.

An Investigation of Spelling Error Problems and Higher Secondary Level in South Delhi Schools Among Hindi Students

M.Ed., JMI, VIJAY KUMAR KAUSHIK, 1990

The objectives of the study were to find out the spelling mistakes of XIth class students having Hindi as a main subject, the areas of the errors. A comparative study of spelling errors in Hindi committed by students of class XIth studying in the rural and urban schools of South Delhi. 80 students of XI class were selected as sample for the study. The findings revealed that the students of class XI of government schools commit a variety of errors. Several type of spelling errors of marked frequency were brought to light. Rural area students and urban area students commit almost similar type of mistakes.

The Social Context of Educational Aspirations of Higher Secondary Students

M.Ed., JMI, A.C. DHINGRA, 1973

The main objective of the study was to survey the educational environment in the families of the students, to identify the factors or reference groups which were largely responsible for the determination of their educational aspirations, to examine the academic achievement of students and others, school factors affecting their educability and discover the extent of autonomy in the students with regard to the sharing of their educational aspirations. As sample of the study, 160 students of class XI (132 boys and 28 girls) were selected. The tools to elicit information used were an interview schedule for the students, a questionnaire for the parents and a rating scale for teacher's assessment of students.

The findings of the study revealed: (1) The majority of students were rated as average by teachers. (2) Parents of the majority of students (70%) consider their wards to be obedient and 75% hardworking and 69% of good health. Parents of 65% of students were convinced that their wards were interested in studies while those of 45% students believed that they wished to read but not write. (3) The occupational aspirations of parents in respect of their wards were in this order: Businessmen 17%, Doctors 15%, teachers 13%, Government servants 11% and pilot 5% etc. As many as 28.12% parents were of the view that their wards should follow their own occupation, 40% felt that their wards should not be indulged in their profession and for 31.83% they were not sure as to what they will do in future.

A Study of the Effect of Creativity Enhancement Intervention on The Creative Potential of Class IX Students

M.Phil., ZHCESSS, JNU, G. KOUL, 1990

To ascertain the effects of creativity enhancement intervention on the creative potential of students, a sample of 68 male students, studying of class IX of a Hindi medium Government School of Delhi were assigned randomly to experimental and control groups respectively. A pretest-past test experimental control group design was used.

To achieve the objectives of the study it was hypothesised that there may be no difference in the composite creativity scores, in the verbal creativity scores and in the non-verbal creativity scores before and after the intervention programmes and further there may be no difference in the scores of students on the fluency, flexibility and originality factors of creativity before and after the creativity intervention programmes.

Instructional materials in the form of activities/exercises were specially prepared by the Researcher as a part of the creativity intervention programmes in an effort to enhance the creative thinking abilities of the students.

Four subtests of the Passi's test of creativity were used, three of which were verbal and one was non-verbal. All these tests were administered before the start of the intervention programmes and once again 3 months after the intervention programmes. Results indicated that the intervention programmes was effective in fostering the creative thinking abilities of the students, particularly the verbal creativity of the students. The intervention programme was not significantly effective in fostering the non-verbal creative thinking abilities.

Results also imply that the creativity intervention programmes had a significant positive effect in enhancing the fluency and flexibility factors of creativity, while the originality factor was not as sensitive to fostering effects. Further, the findings show that the treatment had a significant effect on the enhancement of verbal fluency, flexibility and originality components of creativity, and was not as effective in enhancing the non-verbal fluency, flexibility and originality components of creativity.

The results of the study have thus shown that creative thinking particularly verbal creative thinking can be enhanced in children by devising suitable creativity intervention programmes.

A Study of the Behavioural Problems of Backward Children in Schools *M.Ed., C.I.E., D.U.,* SHIVANI DHIR, 1988

The objective of the present investigation was to compare the adjustment of the backward with that of children of average achievement, to compare backward achievement group and average achievement group on observable covert behaviour problems and to compare the intelligence of backward achievement and average achievement groups. The sample was drawn from one English medium co-educational school where Special Education Cell had been created and mentally retarded and educational backward children study in classes VII and VIII. 82 backward students were selected to conduct the study. The tools administered on them comprised of Adjustment Inventory, Teachers Rating scale and Intelligence Tests - Ravens Progressive Matrices.

The major findings of the study revealed that although both the groups live in more or less similar home conditions and have comparable home backgrounds and interpersonal relationships, the backward achievement group show many more behaviour problems than average or above average achievement group. Similarly, the above average achievement group shows greater intellectual functioning than the below average group.

A Study of Merit Scholars in a Public School: The Disadvantage of Being Advantaged

M.Ed., C.I.E., D.U., BEEBA SOBTI, 1990

The main objectives of the study were to appraise academic performance of merit scholars, to assess the interaction of merit scholars in classrooms, to analyse the participation of merit scholars in non-academic activities, to make an in-depth study of four scholars which are representative cases of promise on the one hand and betrayal of it on the other. 18 merit scholars constitute the sample chosen incidentally with the criterion that the duration of their stage in their respective school should range between 1—5 years. The tools used in the study comprised of academic performance of merit scholars, School Records/Report cards, Observation schedule, Sociometry on measurement of interpersonal relationships, Interview, Rating scale, Problem checklist, Sentence completion test and Paragraph writing and Drawing samples.

Certain major findings stand out significantly with respect to: (1) Merit scholars: The academic records of the Merit Scholars indicate overall low performance which is consistent over two years. The lowest and highest percentages recorded as regards aggregates was 11.16% and 65.8% respectively. Only 5 merit scholars out of a total of 18 passed in English. All students possessing passing aggregates passed in English. 60% of the times the merit scholars remained silent during class discussions. 80% of the times the merit scholars were unwilling to volunteer response. The merit scholars were ignored by their teachers 65% of the time. The merit scholars rarely spent time with their friends. Fear of failure and desire to be popular were the major problem areas as perceived by the merit scholars. The merit scholars scored low scores on positive traits like sociability, responsibility and perseverance and were highly rated on negative traits like aggressiveness, stubbornness and carelessness as rated by teachers. In sociometry, as many as 13 merit scholars did not have any popularity rating. The highest sociometric score attained by a merit scholar was 21 and highest sociometric score attained by non-merit scholar was 98. The interview revealed that the majority of the merit scholars felt alienated in the school and hostel environment. (2) Weaknesses in the school programme: There is no allowance made for individual differences in the classroom situation. Alien hostile environment is unsuitable for the natural growing up of the merit scholars. The perception of teachers towards merit scholars is of viewing them as unresponsive. The teachers thus have a poor opinion about them. The school is maintaining the economically deprived as economically deprived, by not recognizing their special needs and effectively blocking their progress and improvement. There is no provision for remedial classes.

Personality Factors Among Handicapped and Non-handicapped Children: A Comparative Study

Disabilities and Impairments, Vol. 9(1), 30-36, R. BHARADWAJ, 1995

The study was carried out on the handicapped and non-handicapped children, mainly who are congenital blind and cerebral palsied with reference to their personality orientations and to open new vistas in the care of cerebral palsied children. Three types of children *viz.,* the non-handicapped, blind and cerebral palsied, constituted the final sample of 90 children between the age of 8–14 years selected at random. Cattell's Children Personality Questionnaire adapted in Hindi by Kapoor and Rao was used for the purpose of data collection. The Duncan's Range Test was used to treat the data. The major findings revealed that both the cerebral palsied and the blind children had lower mental capacity as compared to non-handicapped ones. The blind and the cerebral palsied children were emotionally less stable as compared to non-handicapped ones. Both the blind and the cerebral palsied children were more expedient as compared to non-handicapped ones.

A Comparative Study of Learning Disabilities Between Boys and Girls in Delhi Schools

M.Phil, JMI, HEMANT TAHILIANI, 1990

The study was carried out with the objectives of identifying, and finding out the prevalence rate of learning disabled children and their categorisation according to the severity of the problem. The study was conducted on 217 students of second and third standard. The tools used for the study comprised of teacher made rating scale consisting of five areas of learning and behaviour: personal and social behaviour, classroom and spatial organization, motor coordination and spoken language, Draw-a-man test for Indian children, teacher made composite battery consisting of the variables on reading comprehension, writing difficulties, listening and textual comprehension, mathematical achievement and oral expression (speaking). The major findings reported that out of 217 students taken up for study, a total of 71 students were found as 'At Risk' learning disabled students. A total of 55 students (25%) were learning disabled. Out of total learning disabled population, 36 were boys and 19 were girls. Thus, ratio of prevalence of learning disability amongst boys and girls comes to 5: 4.

A Study of Effectiveness of Self-instruction Training on the Academic Performance of Young Bearing Disabled Children

M.Phil, JMI, P.S.S. SEKHER, 1994

The main objectives of the study were to identify children with learning disabilities, identify problem areas in the academic task, implementation of self-instruction training strategy and evaluate the effectiveness of self-instruction training. The sample of the study consisted of 16 children of 5 to 10 years from various SES families taken from St Columbus School from the primary sections. The tools consisted of the Assessment and Intervention tools.

The major findings revealed: (1) Self-instruction training enhances academic performance of children. (2) Eventhough the change in arithmetic performance of four children were found not to be significant using chi square but there was definite increase in their performance during intervention phases thereby supporting the effectiveness of self-instruction training.

Cognitive and Non-cognitive Factors Leading to Success in Computer Science (A Study in Senior Secondary Schools of Delhi)

Ph.D., JNU, ZHCES, SSS, RENU SAHNI, 1990

The present study was undertaken to examine the role of certain cognitive and non-cognitive variables in predicting success in computer science. Additionally examined were issues emanating from gender differences, parents educational level and income, owning a computer vs. not owning one, the amount of time spent on a computer and the most enjoyable activity for a student on the computer.

The sample consisted of 614 students from 13 senior secondary schools of Delhi. Out of these, ten schools were affiliated to the Central Board of Secondary Education, and three were affiliated to the Council for the Indian School Certificate Examinations. The students were from classes XI and XII. Out of the total sample, 526 students had opted for computer science and 88 had not opted for it.

A correlational design was adopted for the study. Two groups were formed — an experimental group consisting of students who had opted for computer science as an elective subject in class XI or XII, and a control group consisting of students who had not opted for it. Because of the affiliation of the student to two different Boards, the experimental group was further split into two groups. The students from the schools affiliated to the Central Board of Secondary Education formed the first experimental group, while students from the schools affiliated to the Council for Indian School Certificate Examinations formed the second experimental group. The experimental and control groups were controlled on age, class and school.

The following variables were included as possible predictors of performance in computer science: algebra problem-solving skill, arithmetic problem-solving skill, procedure following skill, direction following skill, logical reasoning, spatial ability, verbal reasoning, attitude towards computer science, intellectual commitment to studies, performance in maths, English, physics, chemistry and overall academic performance.

The first four cognitive abilities were identified as specific abilities which could transfer to outer science through the low road mechanism of transfer. The remaining three abilities investigated were general cognitive abilities which could transfer to computer science through the high road mechanism of transfer. Cognitive abilities were measured through seven short tests. Six of these tests were adapted by the researcher for the Indian context out of the tests standardised by Mayer *et al.* (1986) of California State University. The seventh test was an adaptation of the Differential Aptitude Tests, which were originally constructed by Bennett, Seashore and Wesman for the Psychological Corporation, New York. Attitudes towards computer science and intellectual commitment to studies was measured through scales devised by the researcher for this study.

Teachers' feedback was also obtained using a proforma prepared by the researcher for this study. Marks in the school subjects (computer science, maths, physics, chemistry and English) and overall percentage were obtained from the school records with the permission of the Principals. Analyses of data (Basic statistics, t-test analysis, correlation analysis and multiple regression analysis) were carried out using an IBM compatible personal computer.

t-test analysis between male and female students revealed that their performance on all the school subjects including computer science was comparable, and both had equally positive attitudes towards computer science. However, the number of females opting for computer science was very small compared to the number of males.

Results indicated that those students who were using a calculator had not performed significantly better in computer science than those who were not. The advantage of having a computer at home also did not result in better performance in computer science. Those students whose favourite activity on the computer was to run programmes written by themselves had performed significantly better than those who preferred to run package programmes or play games on the computer. Students who were spending more time with the computer performed better than those who were spending less time on it.

Effect of Computer Education on the Reasoning Ability, Mathematics and Languages

M.Phil, ZHCESSS, JNU, 1986

The present study was formulated to study the effect of computer studies, which has been introduced as an applied subject at the secondary school level, on verbal and abstract reasoning of students. It was also proposed to examine the transfer effect, if any, of learning of computer studies on the learning of other related subjects like mathematics and English. The sample consisted of 100 students from St Columbus School, Delhi, who had completed class 8 or class 9 in the 1984-85 sessions.

Pre-post-research design in a matched group framework was adopted for this study. Two groups were formed: (1) experimental groups who had undergone computer studies course for one year either in class 8 or in class 9. (2) Control groups who had not undergone it. The results of this study show that the computer students (students of experimental groups) scored slightly lower scores than their matched control group in English. Further, the difference was more in class 8 than in class 9. Though the difference was not significant, it cannot be ignored.

This study was an evaluative study. The main findings were that a positive transfer effect of learning computer studies was visible on mathematics; and a slightly negative transfer effect was visible on English, reasoning of computer students was slightly superior to their matched control group.

Impact of Schooling on the Development of Scientific Attitude — An Exploratory Study

M.Ed., C.I.E., D.U., SEEMA SRIVASTAVA, 1996

The study is based on the following objectives: (1) to find out how scientific are school going children, to find out how our formal education system influences the scientific attitude of the respondents, to find out if there is any gender difference with regards to the scientific attitude of students.

The study reveals that 12 students have high scientific attitude, 66 students have average scientific attitude and 22 students have low scientific attitude. In Group-II, 8% children have average scientific attitude, 42% have low scientific attitude and 50% have very low scientific attitude. It was also observed that Group-I had performed better in all aspects of scientific attitude. The formal education, that provides long duration socialisation in the traditions of modern science and other areas of education influenced the scientific attitude of respondents. Those who were not socialised in this tradition (Group-II) scored low. A significant difference was observed in means of the school going children and children without schooling. The mean of the scores of scientific attitude of Group-II was found to be lower than the mean of the scores of the Group-I. In general the findings reveal that formal education level of an individual does play an important role in developing scientific attitude. This difference may be accounted for by the factors like the socio-cultural environment of the school, the facilities available in the school, nature of interaction between the students and the teacher etc. There was no significant difference found in the mean scores of the male and female children at the 0.05 level in Group-I and Group-II. As the concept of scientific attitude adopted with a generalised one, it is possible that the differing sex roles have not differentially affected their scientific attitude. Consequently no difference is observed in their means.

A Study of Workload of School Children

M.Ed., C.I.E., D.U., ANIL KUMAR, 1984

The study was mainly carried out with the objective of assessing and comparing the workload of classes 7th, 9th and 11th of Arts, Commerce and Science Streams from Public, Central Government Boys Schools, Government Girls Schools and Government Aided Schools. The study made an attempt to know the opinion and perception of children regarding their workload and desirable amount of work.

The study also envisaged to find out whether or not students get time for other activities useful for proper development of their personalities. Self-constructed tools were administered on 50 students of five schools.

The study revealed the following: (1) Students of class VII seems to be over-burdened. The minimum time to complete their home assignment is 2.36 hours and maximum time is 4.30 hours which is much more than recommended by Review Committee on the curriculum for the ten-year school. The Committee recommended at the most 2 hours supervised study incorporated in the school timetable in preference to home assignment. (2) The bag of the students is also heavy. On an average they have to carry 12 note-books and 10 books in their school bag every day. Periods for other activities provided in the school timetable are also less than recommended by the Review Committee. (3) Students of class IX also seems to be overburdened. The minimum time to complete their homework is 2.51 hours and maximum is 4.58 hours, which is more for them. (4) Most of the students think that self-study is not sufficient to get through the examinations or to complete the course. (5) Most of the students find time for sports, recreation, reading for pleasure, going for movies and social relations, but they want that study work should be reduced. (6) While responding to the question 'how they will spend their spare time if study work is reduced', few students have written that they know they will never find time for such activities. (7) Examination system of Central School is that in each of the three terms there are two unit tests; then half-yearly examinations and annual examinations. Whereas in all other types of schools there are quarterly examinations *i.e.* 1st quarterly, half-yearly, third quarterly and annual therefore more stress is there on the children of Central Schools. (8) No homework timetable exists in the schools in practice. Students sometimes get home work in all subjects on other days they do not get any home assignment. (9) Students of Central School are more sincere in doing homework and bringing note-books to school as they have marks for home assignment. (10) A number of students of XI class in all types of schools except Central Schools can be seen only with one note-book in the school. (11) Students of Central School have to do some project work in such term and they have marks for it, but students of all stages do not like it. They want that it should be deleted. (12) A number of students in all schools except Central school and Government Girls school confessed in informal conversations that they get home assignment but they never complete it.

A Comparative Psychosocial Study of Students Using and Not Using Unfair Means During Annual Examinations in Government Senior Secondary Schools

M.Ed., JMI, ADHIKARI, 1984

The main objectives of the study were to compare school adjustment of students using fair and unfair means and to study the family environment of such students. Two government boys senior secondary schools were taken up as sample for the study. The school adjustment inventory by N.M. Bhagia, the family environment scale by Rudolf H. Moos and Bernice S. Moos were used in the study. The findings of the study revealed that there is average degree of school adjustment among the students involved and not involved in using unfair means. Both groups do not differ in their school adjustment. There is a lower degree of expressiveness of active recreational orientation and conflict with the group using unfair means. There is lower degree of family environment with respect to conflict, active recreational orientation and control within the group not involved in using unfair means. There is lowest degree of conflict within the group not using unfair means.

An Investigation into the Pattern of Relationship between Pupils Space Concept Maturity and their Achievement of Geometrical Concepts

Ph.D., JMI, NAIYER ALAM, 1986

The study was concerned with innovations in the geometry curriculum. It specifically investigated the pattern of relationship between pupil's maturity of space concepts and concept achievement in geometry so that strategies in curriculum development could be worked out to secure harmony between the geometry curriculum with the stage of cognitive maturation of boys from six Hindi-medium government boys' schools in South Delhi. In the results it was reported that both general space concept maturation and maturation of mental imagery emerged as significant determiners of achievement of geometrical concepts. Similarly the results also show that general space concept maturation and maturation of mental imagery are both viable determiners of scholastic achievement in geometry.

To Study the Effect of Goal Setting on the Performance of the Child

M.Ed., C.I.E., D.U., BHARTI SALWAN, 1993

The objectives of the study were to compare the performance of the three groups of students: the ones who have decided about their goal; the ones who have not decided about their goal; and the ones who are confused and need career guidance to see the effect of social class and parental qualification on the performance of students; and

A sample of 180 students comprising 93 boys and 87 girls was taken at random from the Air Force Golden Jubilee Institute, Subroto Park, Cantonment Area, Delhi. A questionnaire containing questions on their decided goal, subjects chosen, hobbies, parental qualification and earnings was constructed by the investigator.

The major findings of the study were: (1) The performance of students who have decided about their goal is much better than students who have not decided about their goal as well as students who are confused and need career guidance. (2) After comparing the performance of students of the lower, middle and upper class, it can be concluded that most of the students who have performed well belong to middle class. (3) After seeing the effect of parental education and qualification on the performance of children it was seen that most of the high achievers have highly/very highly educated parents.

Learning Strategies and Learning Outcomes of Senior Secondary School Students

M.Phil, ZHCESSS, JNU, SANDHYA, 1991

The present study was undertaken to explore the under stream specific differences among learning strategies and learning outcomes, the values, school adjustment and academic performance of the students. Matching variable were gender (Male and Female) and stream (arts, commerce and science). Learning strategies, values, school adjustment and academic performance were taken as explanatory variables. A 2 × 3 factorial design and quota sampling was used. The sample consisted of 180 students (90 Boys and 90 Girls) from Senior Secondary classes of a large government school in Delhi. The students selected were from three streams (arts, commerce and science). The tools used were Ramsden's Approaches to Study Inventory (ASI), modified by Sen, Super and Neville's, the Value Scale (modified by the present researcher) and Saxena's Adjustment Inventory.

The major findings were: (1) Gender differences are significant on deep strategy, in that the female students use deep strategy more frequently and give more importance to values. (2) Stream differences are significant on learning strategies and learning outcomes. Arts students use surface strategy more frequently. Commerce and science students gave more importance to values than arts students. Commerce students showed better school adjustment. Science students achieved better in academic performance. (3) Learning strategies and learning outcomes differ across gender and stream. Surface strategy is used by male students from science more frequently. Female students from commerce and science give more importance to values. (4) For male students, deep strategy is related to high score on values and school adjustment. (5) For female students, deep strategy is related to values and academic performance. Surface strategy is negatively related to academic performance. Strategic strategy led to a high score on school adjustment. (6) For arts students, deep strategy is related to values and school adjustment, to school adjustment for commerce and to values for science students. (7) The factor analysis of items on the value scale yielded 10 factors. After clubbing 5 factors namely peer-group influence, personal competence, creative values, achievement value and being helpful to others were found meaningful and interpreted.

To Study the Effect of Written Feedback given by Teachers on Children Self-concept

M.Ed., C.I.E., D.U., NEERAJ, 1993

The objectives of the study were to study the effect of different types of comments on different aspects (*e.g.* academic and non-academic) of self-concept, to find the effect of academic and non-academic comments on the child's self-concept, to find out the effects of teacher's labelling through their comments as intelligent or slow learner on the students self-concept, to see the effect of comments when directly addressed to the students or parents, to determine whether comments reflect teacher's expectations from the child to show how such expectations effect the child's self-concept and to see if teachers give importance to the individual differences in their comments.

A purposive sample of 90 students of class V were selected from an English medium public school. They were administered an academic self-concept inventory, a perception of teachers' scale, an open-ended questionnaire developed by the researcher and a self-report on perception about themselves. In order to see the effect of teachers written feedback on children's self-concept, the data was collected in the form of comments given by teachers in students' diary, note-books and report cards. A content analysis was done. The outcomes were classified into broad categories of factors affecting self-concept. These factors affected self-concept differently and were important as they correlated to each other *i.e.* one leads to another. These categories were correlated with the scores achieved by students on academic self-concept inventory administered. It was found that students having good parent, teacher and peer relationships achieved high than those whose relationships were not so good with either of these. Students who set high goals and had high aspirations were confident of themselves to achieve these goals. They were found to have high self-concept. Though other students also had high future goals but were not sure to reach their goals and had low self-concept. Students having positive views about their own physique, nature and behaviour showed high self-concept than those who were uncertain about everything. Results when correlated with scores on ASCI concluded that students with high scores had positive view of teachers. They liked teachers on the basis of their teaching. They were also liked by the teachers as they thought themselves to be intelligent, disciplined, answering the questions in the class and completing all the work in time. They always get good remarks and praise helped them to do better. Students having low self-concept liked teachers who were not strict but jolly in nature. Sometimes they were liked by teachers but majority of the teachers did not like them as they did not give answers in the class, did not complete their work in time, performed poorly and disturbed the class. But praise helped them do better to some extent. A child who received largely positive academic comments had high academic achievement than a child getting largely negative academic comments. Students with more positive (encouraging) remarks show high positive self-concept than those who received negative (discouraging) remarks. It was also found that teachers' praise helps the child to develop confidence and feeling of competence in them, in turn affecting the self-concept. Thus, it is reasonable to conclude that encouraging remarks like well done, excellent, etc. helped children develop positive self-concept in comparison to discouraging remarks like poor, very poor, weak etc. which led to negative self-concept.

❑❑❑